YOUR IRISH ANCESTORS

YOUR IRISH ANCESTORS

BY J. ANDERSON BLACK

PADDINGTON
PRESS LTD

THE TWO CONTINENTS
PUBLISHING GROUP

ISBN 0-8467-0028-X
Library of Congress Catalog Card Number 73-20957
© Copyright 1974 Paddington Press Ltd
Printed in the U.S.A.

IN THE UNITED STATES
PADDINGTON PRESS LTD
TWO CONTINENTS PUBLISHING GROUP
30 East 42 Street
New York City, N.Y. 10017

IN THE UNITED KINGDOM
PADDINGTON PRESS LTD
1 Wardour Street
London W1

IN CANADA
distributed by
RANDOM HOUSE OF CANADA LTD
370 Alliance Avenue
Toronto, Ontario

Library of Congress Cataloging in Publication Data

Black, J   Anderson.
   Your Irish ancestors.

   1. Ireland—Genealogy.   2. Ireland—History.
3. Names, Personal—Ireland.   I. Title.
CS483.B55   929'.1'09415   73-20957
ISBN 0-8467-0028-X

CONTENTS

AUTHOR'S NOTE

One of man's most basic instincts is curiousity about his origins, both individually and as part of a larger social group. Nowhere is this awareness of the past and sense of national identity more acute than with the Irish. Throughout its five thousand years of history, Ireland has never had an absolute monarch, save its Union with England. Most of the time it was ruled by scores of petty kingdoms and later by large earldoms, both of which were based on the family unit. For instance, the O'Neill family controlled the greater part of Northern Ireland for more than 700 years, as did the MacCarthys in the South West. This, perhaps, is why the Irish were among the first to introduce hereditary surnames.

Ireland has a population of approximately 4½ million, yet it is estimated that today there are more than 40 million people of direct Irish descent living in America. Most of them left Ireland during the nineteenth century and, more specifically, during the terrible years of the Potato Famine. Because census records were comparatively sophisticated by the nineteenth century, a positive link between an American present and an Irish past can often be established. It is for this vast population of Irish-Americans, Irish-Australians, Irish-Canadians and Irish everywhere that this volume is intended.

This book is divided into three major sections. The first is a popular illustrated history of Ireland from the Bronze Age to 1921. The text concisely covers this vast time span and concentrates on the structure of kingdoms, earldoms, dynastic marriages, immigrations and emigrations. The second section describes individual Irish names and discusses in detail their origin and history. The final section is a do-it-yourself guide to genealogical techniques which gives details and illustrations of records and other sources of genealogical information. Those names which are included were selected on the basis of eminence and numerical strength. Finally, then, most Irishmen, both in Ireland and abroad, should find themselves included.

The author and publishers would like to take this opportunity to thank all those who assisted in the compilation of this volume. At the back of the book there is an extensive bibliography but there are two sources of information which must be mentioned individually. Firstly, Edward MacLysaght whose works on Irish genealogy are unquestionably the finest ever published on the subject and secondly Heraldic Artists in Dublin who both directly and indirectly provided invaluable information.

IRELAND AND ITS PEOPLE

The antiquity of Irish civilization is obvious to the most casual observer. Throughout the magnificent countryside, standing stones and giant megolithic monuments are scattered in their thousands, an impressive reminder of a rich and resourceful people who inhabited the island more than five thousand years ago. Of the engineers and builders responsible for these great stone structures, however, we know little. Irish pre-history does, however, offer some clues.

It is now certain that Ireland was inhabited before 6,000 BC by a race of hunters and fishermen who used weapons and tools of flint. The country was covered with a dense forest of pine, elm and oak and the first Irishmen, not versed in the arts of farming, inhabited only the coastal regions. They were, according to anthropologists, tall, broad-shouldered men with red hair and fair complexions, characteristics which are clearly discernible to this day in various parts of Ireland.

It was in the Mesopotamian Valley that techniques of crop cultivation were first developed during the fourth millenium BC. This essential element of civilization spread rapidly throughout the Middle East and, from there, westwards through Europe. The first farmers are thought to have reached Ireland around 3,500 BC, bringing with them knowledge of crop cultivation, animal husbandry, pottery, spinning and weaving. They built houses of timber and thatch and used tools of polished stone, manufactured by specialist craftsmen. These neolithic farmers were the first of a succession of invaders and immigrants who will be seen to shape the history of Ireland. It was these people who built massive stone monuments, not for the benefit of the living but for the dead, which sometimes weighed thousands of tons and must have required not only technical know-how but also considerable social organization. Many of the stones, notably at Newgrange, were decorated with complex zoomorphic symbols which were superbly executed without the aid of metal tools.

Metalwork, like farming, was first developed in the Middle East and it is thought that sometime around 2,000 BC, the first metal-workers reached Ireland where they found rich deposits of both copper and tin, the elements of bronze. From this alloy, they produced weapons, tools and utensils which they used not only for domestic consumption but also as the backbone of a rich export trade to Britain and other parts of Western Europe. It is for their goldwork, however, that these early Irish metalworkers will be best remembered. In the Dublin National Museum one can see ornaments of exquisite beauty produced in Ireland during the second millenium

BC from gold mined in the Wicklow Hills.

Both the monuments and the goldwork suggest that the Bronze Age Irish lived in comparative peace and prosperity but, once again, there are no written records from the period to confirm or deny this theory. Whatever peace they did enjoy, however, was destined to be destroyed with the coming of the Celts.

THE COMING OF THE CELTS

The Celts originated from South West Germany in a district corresponding with what is now Bavaria. They were a sophisticated, agricultural nation who established themselves as brilliant warriors armed with weapons of tempered iron. It was inevitable, therefore, that they should seek new lands to conquer and develop; by the seventh century BC they were expanding West into France; South to Italy and Spain; and East to Greece and Asia Minor. When they first reached

Britain and Ireland is uncertain, but most experts consider they came in waves of increasing volume between 500 and 150 BC.

With their greater tactical skills and superior stature, it is unlikely that the Celts met much resistance from the bronze-working aboriginal Irish population.

The arrival of the Celts was, perhaps, the most significant event in Irish history for, while initially minority rulers, they brought with them a life-style which was destined to provide the country with its language, religion and customs for many centuries. The Irish, in fact, are the only Celtic nation to have survived to the twentieth century.

Still, our historical researchers are hampered by the lack of written records. Before the fifth century and the arrival of Christianity, the only form of writing known to the Irish was *ogam*

ABOVE: *A decorated stone found at the megalithic tomb at Newgrange in the Boyne Valley.*

which was a simplified version of the Roman alphabet and even this was used solely for funereal inscriptions. Laws and history were passed down verbally by the learned men or *fili*, the most venerated members of early Celtic society. They were the poets, philosophers, religious leaders and lawyers with a rigorous training, but their records must be viewed with caution. Many traditional Irish stories, dating from the time of Christ, were first committed to paper in the sixth and seventh centuries, and by this time fact was obviously intermingled with legend. The most famous of these epic tales was the *Tain Bo Cualgne* which tells of the rivalry between Maeve, Queen of Connacht, and Conchobar, King of Ulster. In it we read of deeds of outrageous daring by the young hero *Cu Chulainn*, and while these must be taken with a pinch of salt, the story does provide us with invaluable information about the

social structure of Ireland during the first four centuries AD.

Celtic Ireland was split into five kingdoms or "fifths" without an absolute ruler. These were Connacht, Leinster, Munster, Ulster and Meath which, with the exception of Meath, survive to this day as the provinces of Ireland. Each of these major kingdoms was further divided into a number of petty kingdoms or *tuaths* which were probably no more than village communities whose king's powers were strictly limited; he was the leader of his people in times of war and their representative in peace but neither made laws nor enforced them.

During the second century AD, we are told, there was a revolt by the pre-Celtic inhabitants of Ireland against the tyrannical regime of the minority rulers. This was effectively suppressed by *Tuathal*, King of Connacht, who emerged as

ABOVE: *A three-faced stone head of a Celtic god found in County Cavan.*
RIGHT: *A gold Gorget from Gleninsheen, County Clare c 700BC. Metalwork of astonishing sophistication was produced by the pre-Celtic Irish. They had their own source of gold in the Wiklow Hills.*

a great military and political leader. It was he who was responsible for combining the kingdoms of Connacht and Meath which he ruled from his castle at Rath Crogan, creating the most powerful province in all Ireland. This was resented and feared by rival kings and the province was under constant attack; the situation was consolidated about 200 AD however by *Conn Ced-Cathach, Tuathal's* grandson, when he made a pact with his main rival *Mogh* who ruled in the South. A

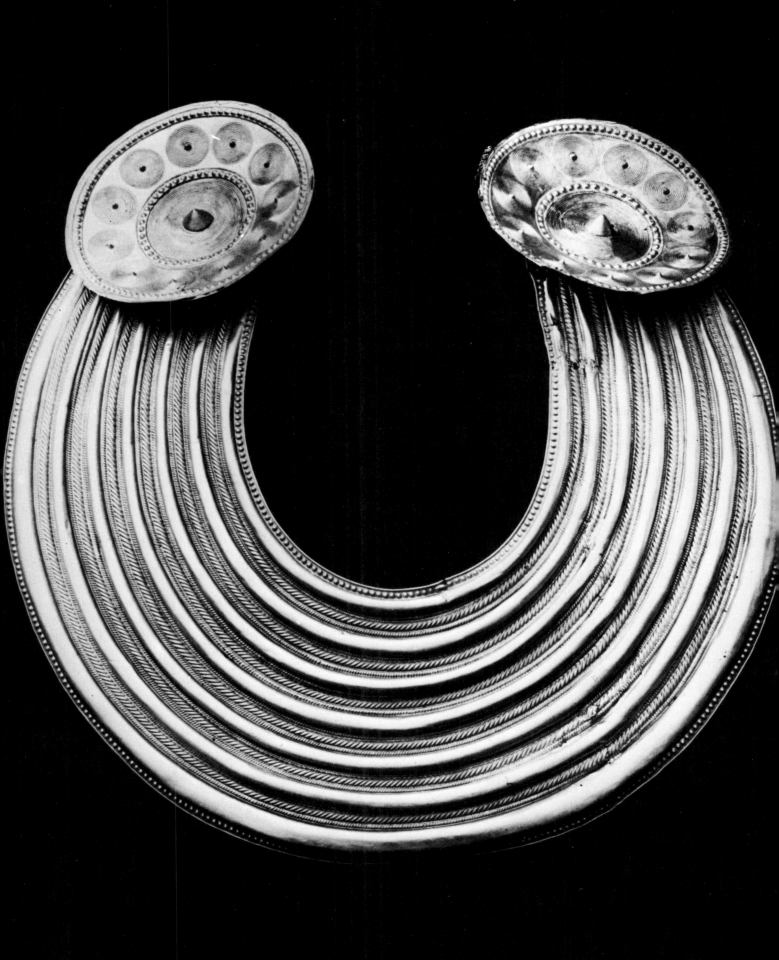

ABOVE: *Early iron-age bronze trumpet found at Loughnashade, County Armagh.*
RIGHT: *The Broighter torc, a highly decorated gold collar made during the first century AD.*
LEFT: *A wooden statue found at Rallaghan, County Cavan.*

boundary was established across Ireland from the Liffey to Galway with the northern sector known as Conn's Half and the south as Mogh's Half. With Mogh's challenge out of the way Conn started to expand his kingdom, pushing the Ulstermen out of the Boyne Valley and the Leinstermen south of the Liffey. The combined kingdom of Connacht and Meath now stretched from the Irish Sea to the Atlantic, cutting Ireland in half. One piece of land captured in this expansion was the Hill of Tara, some twenty-five miles north west of Dublin. This was established as the new capital of the province by Cormac, grandson of Conn. From Tara, Cormac declared himself *Ard Rí* or High King of Ireland. He built great banqueting halls on the hilltop and, every three years, held an assembly of Irish kings where they discussed laws and held festivals of music and poetry, a tradition which was to last for more than seven hundred years.

The title *Ard Rí* was, however, somewhat misleading. It did not mean that the holder was the undisputed leader of the country: the kings of Leinster and Munster, for instance, never sub-

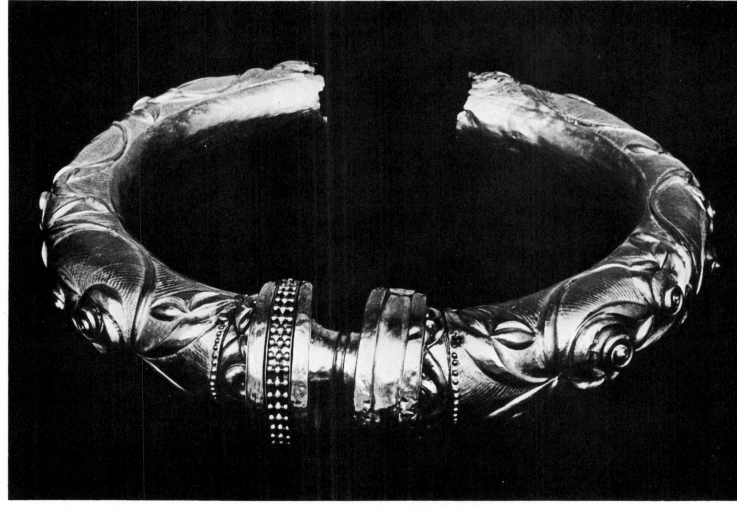

mitted to Cormac. Ulster, in fact, was the only province to be severely eroded after the initial expansions of Conn. There was almost constant warfare between the rulers of the various provinces. The Eogonacht kings, who ruled Munster from their seat at Cashel, were always threatening Connacht and at one stage managed to cross Shannon and capture an area corresponding with what is now County Clare. At the same time, the men of Connacht drove further into Ulster, creating the new kingdom of Oriel, which encompassed the present-day counties of Louth, Armagh and Monaghan.

The High Kingship, nonetheless, was the most

LEFT: *The Turoe stone in County Galway. The ornamentation is typical of the la Tene celtic style.*
BELOW: *A gold boat found at Broighter, County Derry. 1st century AD.*

sought-after position in Ireland and its basic aim remained to rule all Ireland, an ambition which was almost achieved at the end of the fourth century. Niall of the Nine Hostages, *Ard Rí* from 380 to 405, was the greatest of the Connacht rulers. Under his direction the western portion of Ulster was occupied and colonized by his sons Eogan and Conall, who founded the kingdoms of *Tir Eoghain* and *Tir Conaill* and drove the original rulers of the province into the north-east corner of the country. No less than 40 of Niall's descendants succeeded him as *Ard Rí* and were known as the *Ui Neill*, a title which was retained until the eleventh century.

IRELAND GOES CHRISTIAN
Despite their centuries of rule in Britain, the Roman army never set foot in Ireland. This is not to say that the Irish lived in isolation: they traded freely with the Romans, importing glass, pottery

and wine and exporting hides, cattle and the celebrated Irish wolfhounds. The colonization was in the other direction. With the decline of the Roman Empire and the withdrawal of legions from Britain, the Irish, notably under Niall, launched numerous raids on Wales and the West Coast of England and formed colonies. They gained control of the Western Isles of Scotland, founding the kingdom of Dalriada which later spread to the mainland and produced the first kings of Scotland.

Roman persecution had prevented the spread of Christianity in Europe on any considerable scale until, in 313, Constantine issued the Edict of Milan which not only halted persecution but actually gave the Church active support. By the middle of the fourth century both Gaul and Britain were organized into dioceses. Isolated communities of Christians were undoubtedly established in Ireland before the end of the fourth century. These are thought to have reached the country as traders, slaves or as refugees from the barbarian raids which, by this time, were ravaging Western Europe. By 431 their numbers had increased sufficiently to justify Pope Celestine appointing Palladius as the first Bishop of Ireland. We know very little about Palladius except that he worked in the south-east of the country and is thought to have died after only one year in Ireland, too soon to have had any great impact on the pagan population.

The credit for converting the Irish is, of course, traditionally given to Patrick. He was the son of a wealthy Roman Briton, who was captured during an Irish raid and sold into slavery. After working as a shepherd for six years in Ulster, he escaped to Britain from whence he traveled to Gaul and embarked on a clerical training. Throughout his studies, however, Patrick felt a calling to return and convert the Irish from their pagan ways. Legend has it that Patrick landed in County Down in 432 and started on a mission which took him through the length and breadth of Ireland, preaching the gospel and establishing churches. One can understand the relief with which his teaching must have been greeted by an oppressed majority. What is astonishing is that it did not receive more active resistance from the

LEFT: *The Shrine of St Patricks Bell. This jewelled casket, made during the 11th century AD, contains a simple iron hand bell which is generally considered to have belonged to St Patrick.*
RIGHT: *A slab carrying the portrait of St Patrick found at Faughart, County Louth.*

2 cms

kings and *fili* who hitherto had been totally responsible for religious matters. Patrick and his followers were apparently allowed to continue their mission unmolested; certainly there is no record of martyrdom in the early Irish Church. That is not to say, however, that the Christian doctrine was universally accepted. Laeghaire, son of Niall, is reputed to have met Patrick and yet died a pagan and, two centuries later, the *Ard Rí* Diarmaid celebrated the great pagan feasts at Tara. Despite this, the two factions appear to have existed side by side in comparative harmony and in an atmosphere of mutual respect. Sixth century Church laws laid down a code of conduct for Christians towards their pagan neighbors and, for convenience, the borders of dioceses were arranged to correspond with boundaries of petty kingdoms.

The monastic system followed directly after the spread of Christianity and was well established by the beginning of the sixth century. The withdrawal of Roman troops had left Western Europe vulnerable to the barbarians, and the political chaos which ensued, made contact between Ireland and Rome both difficult and hazardous. The Irish monastic system, therefore, evolved in virtual isolation and developed a highly individual character. There were no magnificent stone buildings but timber-built settlements within which the monastic community was completely self-supporting. While their primary function was always religious, the monasteries were the first seats of learning. The great Irish tradition for craftsmanship, in both stone and metal, was also incorporated into the system: masons now produced magnificent high crosses instead of pagan standing stones; goldsmiths made chalices rather than torques and gorgets. A new area of craftsmanship came with Christian scholarship, the copying of religious texts, and during the sixth and seventh centuries Irish monks produced the finest illuminated manuscripts the world has ever seen. Perhaps the most famous of these, the Book of Kells, miraculously survived, and can be seen today in the Library of Trinity College, Dublin.

LEFT: *A 7th century Crucifixion Plaque, thought to be a book cover. Now in St John's, County Roscommon.*
RIGHT: *A 5th century ogham stone from Aglish, Co Kerry. The lines carved into the stone are ogham, the only form of writing known by the pre-Christian Irish.*
PREVIOUS PAGE: *Gallarus Oratory, County Kerry, a beautifully constructed stone church. Local people believe that anyone who can wriggle through the narrow windows will go to heaven.*

RIGHT: *The carved base of an early Irish cross from Moone, County Kildare.*
ABOVE: *A detail of the Braec Maedhoic, an eighth century Irish Shrine.*

Literacy, however, was not restricted to the clergy. The *fili* initially scorned writing as cumbersome and destructive to the memory, but by the end of the sixth century most of them had been forced to realize the advantages of permanent records and many of them were even converted to Christianity. It was during this period that early Irish history, laws and literature were first committed to paper, leaving us a unique combination of Latin and Gaelic manuscripts which combine to provide the richest early mediaeval literary heritage of any country in the world.

Ireland had avoided Roman occupation which, it could be argued, was to her disadvantage. On the other hand she also avoided the barbarian invasions suffered elsewhere in Europe which was certainly to her advantage. By the end of the sixth century the Church was in ruins both in Britain and on the Continent and, despite being comparatively recent converts, the Irish played

a major role in rectifying the situation. They spread both religious and secular learning in two ways – through their monasteries in Ireland which attracted students from abroad, and secondly through missionaries. Many Irish clergy left the country as 'pilgrims for Christ', a voluntary exile considered as the ultimate penance. When abroad they invariably became teachers and thus paved the way for the true missionary movement of the seventh century.

Perhaps the most celebrated Irish missionary was St. Columba or *Columcille*. Columba was born at the beginning of the sixth century, a member of Celtic aristocracy; three of his cousins were *Ui Neill* kings and he himself was entitled to a

33

ABOVE: *Saints'from the abbey at Ballintober, County Mayo.*
RIGHT: *An example of the decorative style of the magnificent Book of Kells.*

kingdom but instead decided to join the Church. During his early years he founded the great monastery at Durrow and in 546 founded another in Derry. For reasons which are lost in the mists of time he decided to leave Ireland in 563 as a 'pilgrim for Christ'. With a handful of other monks, he sailed for Iona, in the Western Isles of Scotland, which was the center of the Celtic kingdom of Dalriada. He remained in Scotland for more than thirty years, during which time he succeeded in converting not only the Celtic population but also the original Pictish inhabitants of the country.

Like St. Columba, St. Columbanus was born into the Irish aristocracy, related to the kings of Leinster. He too turned his back on pagan ways at an early age and entered a monastery. In 591, at the age of fifty, he left Ireland as a 'pilgrim for Christ' and during the last twenty-five years of his life, despite frequent opposition, was responsible for founding monasteries in France, Switzer-land and Northern Italy. His work together with a few others, paved the way for the great monastic revival in Western Europe during the seventh, eighth and ninth centuries.

THE COMING OF THE VIKINGS

During the seventh and eighth centuries, Ireland was free from invasions and enjoyed what has been called her 'Golden Age'. This is not to say that the country was spared from internal conflicts. The four basic provinces subdivided into about 150 petty kingdoms continued with the *Ui Neill* retaining their position as High Kings at Tara. Their rule, however, was still anything but absolute. They had succeeded in controlling the majority of Ulster and had taken a large part

34

RIGHT: *The Tara Brooch, perhaps the most famous and elegant examples of medieval Irish jewellery.*
BELOW: *The Ardagh Chalice, 8th century AD.*

of Northern Leinster, but further advances were stubbornly resisted by the Leinstermen. The main threat to the *Ui Neill* came from the powerful Eoganacht kings of Munster who, in the early eighth century, established temporary supremacy over the *Ui Neill,* when Cathal Mac Finguine forced the *Ard Rí* to submit to him. The Church, however, was not involved in these territorial conflicts and religious, educational and artistic progress continued uninterrupted. The lack of Irish unity, however, left her hideously vulnerable to attack from without. Attack, on this occasion, came in the shape of the Vikings. History has never been particularly kind or fair to the Vikings. They are best remembered as savage and pagan warriors but it should be noted that they were also accomplished farmers, ambitious traders and, above all, they were superb boatbuilders, sailors and navigators. Their elegant craft could voyage safely through the treacherous waters of the North Atlantic yet drew so little water that they could travel up shallow rivers with ease. They were indeed a formidable weapon of assault against an island race.

While the Swedes travelled East into Finland and Russia, the Danes invaded the East Coast of England and Normandy and the Norse sailed west and set up colonies in Iceland and Greenland. From these strongholds the Norse turned their sights towards the Hebrides and Orkney Islands off the Northern coast of Scotland. What started as a series of smash-and-grab raids soon developed into a systematic pattern of conquest and colonization. Ireland first felt the full impact of the Viking raids, not on her own soil, but on Iona which, for four centuries, had been the stepping-stone between the Celtic civilizations of Ireland and Scotland. The Norse raiders first plundered Iona in 795 but it was not until 817 that the Abbot and his monks were forced to abandon their monastery and flee to Ireland. The loss of this tiny island effectively severed communications between Ireland and the kingdom of Dalriada and in 840 the first true Scottish kingdom, independent from Ireland, was established under Kenneth Mac Alpin. Ireland itself was the perfect target for the Norse with its navigable streams, large inland lakes and disunited people. Raids started against the small island communities, mainly monastic, which surrounded the Irish coast. The Vikings already realized that monasteries provided the richest pickings. They colonized the small islands and from there

38

conducted raids against headlands and coastal areas; again these raids were followed by the establishment of permanent settlements, settlements which were destined to become Ireland's first cities. The first of these was Dublin which was founded in 841; later came Cork, Limerick, Wexford, Waterford and Wicklow. From these strongholds the Vikings sailed up the rivers and attacked deep into the heart of Ireland. They plundered the great monasteries, stealing all the great gold and silver work which had not previously been hidden or smuggled abroad. It is fortunate that the raiders were largely illiterate and showed no interest in the magnificent illuminated manuscripts.

The Irish were powerless to resist this ceaseless onslaught: the country was still split into more than 150 petty kingdoms and the rulers were too busy squabbling amongst themselves to organize a united resistance. By the beginning of the ninth century the Vikings were becoming more and more integrated into the Celtic way of life; they were taking Irish wives, which explains the predominance of Norse names in the country today such as Sugrue, Bolan, Sigerson, Elliffe and Tormey.

The first time Viking supremacy was seriously challenged came in 866 when the *Ard Rí*, Aed Finnlaigh, captured all the Norse settlements north of Dublin. Fourteen years later Cervall, King of Leinster, succeeded in capturing the city itself. Just as they appeared to be making some headway in the fight against occupation, the Irish were once again defeated by their own lack of unity. In 908 Flann Sinna, High King of Tara, defeated the great and scholarly Eoganacht King of Munster, Cormac MacCullenan, which left the province weak.

The Vikings invaded and occupied the province from their cities of Cork, Limerick and Waterford and, while they never captured the capital at Cashel, they effectively ruled throughout Munster. The following year Cervall died and the Vikings under the leadership of Sitric recaptured Dublin. This was a considerable blow to Celtic pride and the *Ard Rí*, Niall Glundubh, raised a large army and marched against Sitric but he was slain and his army defeated at the Battle of Kilmohavoc just west of Dublin.

From this time on the Vikings expanded their kingdoms virtually unchallenged and, by the middle of the tenth century, they controlled all

39

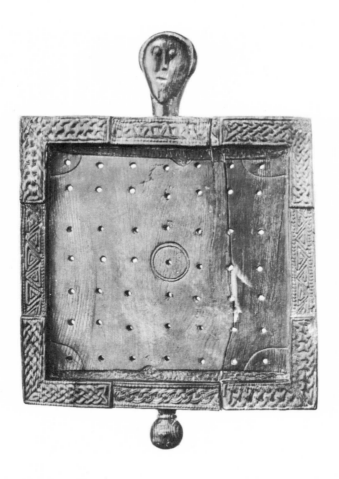

mid and south Ireland. Their supremacy was so complete that the title of *Ard Rí* was abandoned for eighty years. The Irish kings were apparently reluctant to reduce the title, always an empty boast, to a palpable lie. Better things were to come, however. During those eighty years, two great leaders emerged who were destined to return the rule of Ireland to the Irish.

THE RISE OF BRIAN BORU

The once great Eoganacht kings of Munster were now kings in name only. They still sat at Cashel but their province was totally dominated by the Norsemen but even this did not prevent the Irish kings from fighting amongst them for the title of king. The most powerful contenders came not from Cashel but from Dal Cais, a comparatively obscure *tuath* in North Munster which was ruled independently by distant relatives of the Eoganacht kings. During the Norse tyranny the Dalcassians had been driven back until they occupied only a small area of East Clare. In 964 Mathgamain, King of Dal Cais, led an army south, together with his younger brother Brian and, together they succeeded in capturing Cashel and driving out the remaining Eoganacht claimants to the title of King of Munster. From here the

brothers moved against Limerick and succeeded in taking the city from the Vikings led by Ivar together with his allies Donovan and Maelmud, two deposed Eoganacht princes. Ivar and the princes were forced to flee abroad and Mathgamain became the effective ruler of all Munster. In 976, however, Ivar returned and paid a hired assassin to murder Mathgamian, which left Brian to rule in his place. A man of considerable intellect and a great soldier, Brian started a campaign to rid not only his kingdom but also the remainder of Ireland of the Viking occupation. He disposed of Ivar and his Eoganacht allies in battle during 978 and spent the next two years fortifying Munster and making plans for further expansion. While Brian was consolidating the position in the South, another great leader, Malachy, was establishing his supremacy in the North. Unlike Brian, who was considered a usurper by the Irish, Malachy was an *Ui Neill* with a strong claim to the High Kingship and, if the title had not fallen into disuse, he would probably have claimed it. In 981 he defeated a large Norse army at Tara and the following year captured Dublin. He exiled Olaf, the Dublin's Viking ruler, but instead of ruling the city himself and making it the capital of his kingdom,

ABOVE LEFT: *A 10th century wooden gaming board from Ballinderry Crannog.*
ABOVE RIGHT: *A silver penny minted by Sitric, ruler of Dublin, in 1050 AD.*

Malachy declared it a vassel state and put it under the command of Olaf's son, Sitric 'Silkbeard'. This was a decision which was destined to have catastrophic consequences.

In 983, Brian started his program of expansion in the South. His first move was to take hostages from both Ossory and Leinster and force his only two Celtic rivals in the South to submit to him. This left him with two major problems: how to keep his subjects in order, and Malachy, with whom a confrontation was rapidly becoming inevitable. Brian was always the greater of the two men; he had learned Viking tactics and used their boats to conduct raids into Connacht. He eventually resolved the situation with Malachy by negotiation rather than battle. The two men agreed that Brian should rule the South and take over control of Dublin while Malachy should continue to rule the Northern kingdoms.

This situation was never entirely satisfactory; Brian was still determined to become king of a united Ireland, seeing himself as an Irish Charlamagne. He challenged Malachy to a battle at Tara to establish one of them as *Ard Rí*. The challenge was accepted but Malachy's self confidence was not shared by the other northern kings and they refused to back him. Once again the confrontation was settled without loss of blood, Malachy conceded and Brian proclaimed himself 'Emperor of the Irish'.

His supremacy was accepted but widely resented particularly by the Leinstermen who still viewed him as a usurper. He was, however, generally considered to be the greatest of all Irish kings. As a devout Christian he set about repairing the damage inflicted on churches and monasteries by the pagan Vikings. He rebuilt old monasteries and established new ones; manuscripts and other Church artifacts were traced down and restored to their rightful owners. In all these efforts he was backed by Malachy who appears to have accepted defeat most graciously. The Leinstermen, however, were not prepared to accept Brian's rule without a struggle and in 1013 Mael Morda, King of Leinster, made an ally of Sitric, the Viking ruler of Dublin. Brian joined forces with Malachy and prepared to meet the challenge. Faced with the combined army, Mael

Morda realized that his forces were both out-numbered and outclassed and he persuaded Sitric to seek help from Sigurd, King of the Orkneys. In return for his assistance, the Dublin/Leinster alliance offered Sigurd the High Kingship of Ireland and other Viking mercenaries, enlisted from Iceland and Normandy, were promised land if they succeeded in defeating Brian and Malachy.

The forces met at Clontarf on Good Friday, 1014, and Brian struck the greatest blow ever for Irish freedom. Despite the quantity and quality of the opposition, his forces routed the Leinster/Dublin alliance. Brian himself, too old to fight by this time, inexplicably was left unguarded in a tent behind the lines and was slain by a fleeing Norseman. His death was mourned throughout Ireland and he was buried with great ceremony beside the high cross of Armagh Monastery. Even the Vikings pay tribute to Brian Boru's greatness in their sagas: 'Brian fell' they wrote, 'but saved his kingdom. This Brian was the best of kings'.

After the Battle of Clontarf, Ireland was finally freed from the threat of Norse conquest and there was a general move towards the old order.

LEFT: *Brian Boru, High King of Ireland who saved Ireland from the Viking conquest with his victory at the Battle of Clontarf. Brian was also responsible for the large scale introduction of surnames in Ireland.*
ABOVE: *The 11th century Lismore Crozier.*

Those Vikings that remained became Christian and were completely absorbed into the Irish way of life. The two centuries of Viking domination in Ireland had not been without their good points. The most significant benefit to future generations of Irishmen was the building of major cities such as Dublin, Limerick and Cork, which were all established as flourishing ports by the Norsemen and helped put Ireland on the map as a serious international trading nation. Towards the end of their occupation, many of the Vikings had been converted to Christianity and helped rebuild the monasteries that their ancestors had destroyed. Their great contribution in this field was to build monasteries of stone in place of timber. Other benefits included the introduction of a currency and advanced techniques of boat-building and seamanship.

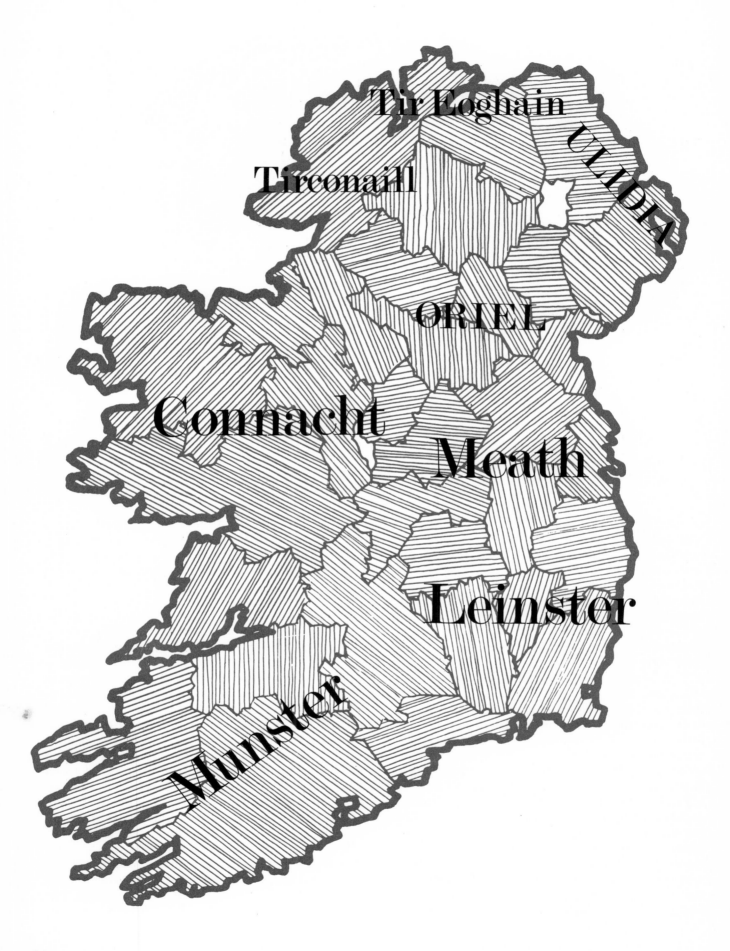

Tír Eoghain

Tirconaíll

ULIDIA

ORIEL

Connacht

Meath

Leinster

Munster

KINGS WITH OPPOSITION

Brian's reign had been of unique importance. He demonstrated to the Irish that a divided country is vulnerable both from without and within. This, sadly, was a lesson which was all too soon forgotten. As far as the student of genealogy is concerned, however, Brian's most important contribution was neither military nor political but the establishment of hereditary surnames. Surnames had been used in Ireland before this time but on a random basis; Brian made them compulsory. He is also credited with having introduced patronymics, i.e. *Mac,* meaning son of, and *O',* meaning descendent of. From now on lines of descent became increasingly easy to trace, and the great Irish names of today O'Brien, O'Connor, O'Rourke, MacCarthy and scores of others, were established for the first time.

After the death of Brian Boru at the Battle of Clontarf, his old rival turned colleague, Malachy, took over the High Kingship, a position which he retained, in name at least, until his death in 1022. Then the sadly familiar struggle for supremacy in the four provinces started all over again, struggles which were to invite the Normans as they had the Vikings. In Munster the O'Brians, descendants of Brian Boru, ruled from their castle at Kincora with periodic challenges for supremacy from the MacCarthys, descendants of the old Eoganacht Kings of Cashel. The O'Connors ruled Connacht

from their capital at Rathcrogan with the exception of the north-eastern sector, known as Brefne, which was controlled by the O'Rourkes. Ulster was divided into three powerful sub-kingdoms, *Tir Eogain* in the North West which was ruled from Tullahoge by the MacLochlainns; to the west of Tir Eogain was the Kingdom of *Tir Conaill* which was ruled by the O'Donnells. To the east and south lay the ancient kingdoms of Oriel and Ulidia which were disputed between the O'Carrols and the kings of *Tir Eogain*. The ancient kingdom of Meath became weak after the death of Malachy and was a constant source of dispute between neighboring kings, passing from the control of one to another depending on their strength of the moment. The fifth province, Leinster, was ruled by the MacMurrough family, after 1042, when Dermot MacMurrough established himself as king. It must be obvious by now that this situation was inflammatory. These 'kings with opposition' were never content to sit back and rule their own province: they all aimed at absolute rule and the balance of power swayed from one family to another during the next century and a half.

Tulough O'Brien became king of Munster in

ABOVE: *A ship carved on a wooden plank. Late 11th century Viking.*
OVERLEAF: *The marriage of Strongbow to Eva by Daniel Maclice.*

1063 and attempted to emulate his distinguished father by becoming *Ard Rí*. In the first ten years of his rule he succeeded in forcing the kings of Meath, Connacht and Leinster to submit to him but his advances were always resisted by the kings of Ulster and his habit of calling himself 'King of all Ireland' was no more than an empty boast. In 1086 he was succeeded by his son Murtough O'Brian who came nearer the position of absolute rule. He controlled Leinster and Connacht and in 1101 he defeated MacLochlainn of Tir Eogain, and forced all the kingdoms of the north to submit to him. He was accepted as High King, but only two years later he was defeated by MacLochlainn and the country was fragmented once again. The supremacy of Munster was not, however, taken over by the victorious MacLochlainns as might be expected. It was the O'Connor kings of Connacht who were to emerge as the dominant force in Ireland during the early decades of the twelfth century. Tulough O'

Connor became King of Connacht in 1106 at the age of eighteen and, despite his youth, quickly proved himself an able and intelligent ruler. He realized that it was important to make his own territory secure before attempting to take on new challenges. He fortified the province, established a substantial fleet of boats on the Shannon and built bridges across the river which gave him quick and easy access to Munster, Brefne and Meath. These preparations took him more than ten years but in 1118 he embarked on a systematic campaign of occupation of his neighboring provinces. His policy was a classic 'divide and rule'. The first step was to lead a large army into Munster in 1118 and divide the province between the O'Brians and the MacCarthys. In 1126 he

expelled Murchad O'Melaghlin from his kingdom of Meath and made his son Connor king in his place; the young prince, however, was soon slain in a local revolt. He also tried to place one of his sons as ruler of Leinster; this too was unsuccessful, but, in 1127, he managed to divide the province into two parts. By 1130 he ruled all Ireland, except Ulster, as had Tulough O'Brian fifty years earlier. In 1131, however, there was a general revolt against his regime and O'Connor spent the next ten years trying to reestablish discipline which thwarted forever his plans to dominate the remainder of the country. While Tulough concentrated on this problem a real rival was emerging in the North, Murtough MacLochlainn, King of Tir Eogain, who had made good his family's boast to be kings of all Ulster. He had forced Ulidia and Oriel to submit to him and thus united the northern province for the first time for centuries. In 1156 Tulough O'Connor died and was succeeded by his son Rory O'

Connor. This was just the opportunity that MacLochlainn had been waiting for; in 1157 he marched south, captured Limerick and divided Munster once again. Two years later he defeated Rory O'Connor, took hostages in all the other important kingdoms and made an ally of King Dermot MacMurrough of Leinster. In 1160 he became High King. But history repeated itself; just as he appeared to have gained control of the whole nation there was a general revolt. Rory O'Connor seized the opportunity, made an ally of Tiernan O'Rourke, King of Brefne, and challenged MacLochlainn for the High Kingship. He achieved this with comparative ease since his rival had a rebellion on his hands and most of his previous supporters deserted and joined O'Connor. MacLochlainn was eventually killed in a battle in 1166.

This left Dermot MacMurrough without an ally and his Leinster kingdom in rebellion. O'Rourke, with whom he had long fought over

49

the kingdom of Meath, invaded Leinster and expelled MacMurrough. This was an action which was destined to lose Ireland its independence for centuries, an independence which has never been totally recovered. With MacMurrough in exile and O'Rourke an ally, Rory O'Connor became High King and for the first time there appeared to be a ruler in Ireland who was universally accepted. He followed his father's example and divided the provinces into smaller units. He divided Munster between Dermot MacCarthy and Donal Mor O'Brien; Meath between O'Rourke and Dermot Melaghlin; Leinster between Donal Gillapatric and his brother Murchad; and Ulster between Murcertach Mac-Lochlainn's son Niall and Aedh O'Neill; Connacht he continued to rule himself. Ireland apparently had stability and unity at last. They had forgotten one man, the exiled King of Leinster Dermot MacMurrough, who was already in Wales gathering support for his cause from the Normans.

THE NORMAN INVASION

It was barely one hundred and fifty years since Brian Boru had finally put an end to the threat of Viking dominance in Ireland and once again the country was in danger, ironically from men of the same stock. The Normans were Vikings who had settled in France and been granted their own territory. Their occupation of France had followed much the same pattern as that of their relatives who had invaded Ireland; they had intermarried with the French, adopted the Christian religion, French manners and French customs. The Normans were natural soldiers who had proved their worth by conquering England, Southern Italy, the Lowlands of Scotland and Wales. It was from Wales that Norman monarchs had looked longingly across the Irish sea and sworn that one day they would make Ireland their own and it was to Wales that Dermot MacMurrough had gone to find allies. The initiative for an invasion of Ireland came from an Irishman.

Dermot arrived in Bristol in 1166, exactly one hundred years after England had fallen to the Normans. He was received by Robert Fitzharding, a friend of King Henry II, who advised him to travel to France and discuss the situation with the Monarch. Dermot eventually tracked Henry down in Aquitaine and submitted to him and, in return for his dubious privilege, Henry gave him permission to enlist help from Norman barons. With promises of territory he attracted a number of the more Welsh/Norman barons including Maurice Fitzgerald, and Robert Fitzstephen. The most powerful and influential, however, was Richard, Earl of Pembroke, nicknamed 'Strongbow', whom MacMurrough lured with promises of his daughter's hand and the Kingdom of Leinster on his death. The whole deal took a considerable time to set up and, impatient for revenge, he set sail for Leinster in 1167 with a tiny Norman force and awaited the arrival of more substantial help. On his arrival, part of his old Kingdom was restored to him by Rory O'Connor who was still firmly established as *Ard Rí*. In exchange for this consideration, O'Connor demanded two of Dermot's sons as hostages, a customary security. It is a measure of Dermot's determination that he blithely continued with his plans, knowing full well that, when his Norman allies arrived, both his sons would be executed, which indeed they were, leaving him only one heir, Donal Kavanagh.

It was almost two years before this happened. In May 1169, Robert Fitzstephen and Maurice de Predergast landed at Bannow Bay in County Wexford with a force of six hundred men. This might sound a puny army but one must remember that these were highly trained professional soldiers equipped with the finest weaponry and armor. The Irish were brave but they scorned armor as ungentlemanly and fought in a very stylized manner with axes and short swords, no match for Norman archers, even when they had superiority of numbers. Dermot, however, was leaving nothing to chance; he decided to wait for more reinforcements.

In the spring of the following year, Maurice Fitzgerald and Raymond le Gros landed with a rather larger force and, in May of the same year, came the man they had all been waiting for, Strongbow, Richard, Earl of Pembroke. Strongbow arrived at Waterford with more than a thousand men at arms to claim his bride Eva, and await his kingdom. The combined forces attacked and captured Waterford and, after killing the city's ruler Sitric, Strongbow and his bride were married in Waterford Cathedral.

Having established a firm foothold in the country, the Normans' main objective was Dublin, which was the most prosperous city in the country. Rory O'Connor realized this and raised an army in an attempt to help Earl Assgal, the city's ruler. The Normans attacked from the south, and in so doing not only established Dublin as the capital of Norman Ireland but also recaptured Leinster for Dermot MacMurrough, who now saw his dream of High Kingship as a reality. This was not to be, however, for the next

RIGHT: *McCarthy's Round Tower at Clonmacnois, County Offaly.*

spring, 1171, he died suddenly, destined to be remembered by the Irish not as a great high king but as a great traitor. Strongbow established himself as King of Leinster, which had been the price of his allegiance to Dermot. He was, however, faced with a number of immediate problems. At home, Henry II was becoming uneasy; thinking that his barons were carving out monarchies for themselves, he ordered them home and it was only after some careful negotiations that Strongbow was allowed to stay without forfeiting his lands in Wales. Even more worrying was the military challenge which was brewing. Asgall, the deposed ruler of Dublin, had fled abroad to find Norse allies in the Hebrides and the Isle of Man. At the same time, Rory O'Connor was building up a substantial army in Ireland itself. By September 1171, Strongbow was faced with attack from both sides. A Norse fleet with more than one thousand men sailed up the Liffey and an even larger force under Rory O'Connor

was approaching Dublin from the west. Unfortunately, for the Irish/Norse alliance, their timing was faulty; the Norsemen attacked before O'Connor's forces were in position and were slaughtered by the Normans under Milo de Cogan. Strongbow's troubles were not over; to the west the O'Connors' army was threatening the city and set up a blockade which was to last two months. O'Connor offered Strongbow the Kingdom of Leinster if he would agree to send his forces back to Wales but this offer was refused and the Normans, short of supplies, decided to attack. They took the Irish by surprise and cut their forces to ribbons at Phoenix Park. Thus after eighteen short months, supremacy in Ireland was theirs.

THE ARRIVAL OF HENRY II

Henry's fears that the Norman barons might establish their own kingdom in Ireland were increased by their spectacular and rapid success in subduing the Irish. He arrived in Waterford in October 1171, only a month after Strongbow's victory; with him sailed a considerable army in a fleet of more than 250 ships. Henry was not intent on further military conflict but wanted to provide a show of military strength in case either

LEFT: *A late medieval illustration showing one of the Burkes of Connacht.*

BELOW: *13th century whalebone book cover.*

PREVIOUS PAGE: *The Rock of Cashel.*

the Irish or the Normans might have ideas of challenging his sovereignty. In addition to his army, Henry carried a Papal Bull, *Laudabiliter,* which had been issued by Pope Adrian and gave the Vatican's blessing to the mission. Many have since claimed that this document was a forgery, for Henry was not in favor in Rome after the murder of Thomas à Becket, but it appears to have served its purpose at the time. Strongbow, spokesman for the barons, submitted to Henry at Waterford and in return was given the kingdom of Leinster with the exception of the cities of Dublin, Wexford and Waterford which he decided to adminster for himself. Meath he granted to Hugh de Lacy who he nominated as Viceroy. One by one, the Irish kings submitted to Henry and they in turn were recognized by Henry as legitimate rulers of their own provinces under his ultimate sovereignty. First to come was MacCarthy, King of Desmond, then came Donal Mor O'Brien, King of Thormand, O'Rourke of Brefne, O'Carrol of Oriel, O'Dunleavy of Ulidia. Only the High King himself, Rory O'Connor, refused to submit and even he, faced with the vastly superior forces of the Normans, offered no active resistance. One might wonder why all these great and proud leaders were so ready to submit without a struggle. True, Henry's forces were impressive, but that had never deterred the Irish before. Firstly it was the old problem, a lack of unity; but even more than that they saw it as swapping one overlord for another. They felt no particular loyalty to O'Connor and they may well have thought that they would have suffered less interference from an overlord based abroad with vast territories to administer in England and France. They were wrong. Without realizing it they had been conquered, really conquered, for the first time. The other function of the Papal Edict was to insure that the Church recognized Henry's right to govern and, in April 1172, after less than six months, Henry sailed for England universally accepted as ruler of Ireland by both Clergy and Laiety without a single drop of blood spilled.

Henry's promise to respect Irish territories beyond the boundary of Meath and Leinster was probably sincere but he had no real way of controlling the power-hungry barons when he was abroad. Raymond de Gros attacked Munster and defeated MacCarthy of Desmond and this fostered Irish unity against the Normans. Donal Mor O'Brien and Rory O'Connor joined forces and drove the Norman forces back from Munster. Strongbow, believing the best method of defense

LEFT: Ireland during the early 15th century.

was attack, led a second force into Munster in 1174 but was routed by the O'Brien/O'Connor alliance which then went on to drive the Normans out of Meath. These two victories started a true war of resistance. The peace initiative came neither from the Barons nor the Irish kings but from Laurence O'Toole, Archbishop of Dublin who naturally feared that, in times of civil war, the Church was likely to be the worst victim. Rory O'Connor and Henry II agreed, under the Treaty of Windsor in 1175, that the country should be divided into two portions and established Rory O'Connor as ruler of Connacht with the responsibility for keeping peace among the other smaller Irish kingdoms. In return for this, O'Connor agreed to submit to Henry as overlord of Ireland and pay him an annual tribute. It was clearly an unsatisfactory arrangement. There was no central government and O'Connor had no way of enforcing his rights other than by force. The barons showed little respect for the Treaty and Henry showed less. He embarked on a program of granting away the very territories which he had guaranteed as secure. A mere two years later, having nominated his son John as successor as Lord of Ireland, he gave the Kingdom of Desmond to Robert Fitzstephen and Milo de Cogan; and Thormond to Philip de Broase. These grants, however, left it up to the beneficiary to enforce his rule in the province. De Broase was repelled by the O'Brien army in Thormond but the Fitzstephen/de Cogan partnership succeeded in capturing both the City and County of Cork, allowing Dermot MacCarthy to retain the remainder of the province, provided he payed a tribute to them. Later the same year John de Courcy, claiming a similar grant from Henry, attacked Lidia and defeated the army of King MacDunleavy. Eight years after he had been made Lord of Ireland, Prince John made his first visit to the country.

IRELAND UNDER JOHN

John was still only seventeen when he landed in Ireland with his army in 1185, and, by all accounts, he was an oafish youth who did little to ingratiate himself with either the Irish kings or the Norman barons. By this time all the leaders of the Norman invasion, Strongbow, Fitzstephen, Fitzgerald and de Cogan, were all dead and many of the lands which had been granted to them were left without heirs. This left the way open for John to bestow earldoms onto his own personal favorites. Like his father, John happily set about granting away land which was supposedly guaranteed to the Irish Kings. It is from these grants that some of the great Anglo-Irish families emerged. To his butler, Theobald Walter, he

granted the larger part of Munster which rightfully belonged to the O'Briens. Walter adopted the name Butler and was the founder of the great Earldom of Ormond. To William de Burgo, the founder of the Burke family, John granted a large area south of Tipperary which de Burgo made secure by marrying Dona Mor O'Brien's daughter. De Burgo also received a grant to invade Connacht but his attempts at conquest were unsuccessful. The western section of Limmerick was granted to the Fitzgeralds along with a large part of Kerry; this family were the ancestors of the Earls of Desmond. After the death of Donal MacCarthy in 1206, the Normans mopped up what little land in Munster remained outside their control.

De Courcy was already well established in the north with absolute control over the old kingdom of Ulidia. The other great province in the north, Oriel, was still in the hands of the O'Carrols but, after the death of Murrough O'Carroll, in 1189, John granted his lands to Bertram de Berdon. This left only the two smaller kingdoms of Tir Conaill and Tir Eogain in the hands of the Gaelic rulers. Tir Eogain was granted to Gilbert de Angulo, later Costello, but it was successfully defended by Aodh O'Neill until his death in 1230. The Fitzgeralds were, at the same time, granted the kingdom of Tir Conaill but successive attempts at enforcing control there ended in defeat. William de Burgo's grant of Connacht, which he too had been unable to enforce, was taken on by his son Richard and in 1224 King Aodh relinquished his claim on all Connacht except for the area around Athlone. Finally, all resistance from the O'Connors failed and a large Norman army invaded Connacht and secured it for de Burgo, leaving Felim O'Connor with Rosscommon for a yearly tribute of £300. The Burkes, the descendants of de Burgo, were now firmly established as rulers of the west.

By 1250, therefore, the Normans controlled all Ireland except for a few small areas which either they did not consider worth contesting or they were allowing Irish kings to rule under close supervision and high taxation. When this had been achieved, a central government was introduced for the first time which was organized by the Viceroy, the king's deputy in Ireland. This post was filled by a Norman lord of the monarch's choice who was responsible for administering a legal system and the exchequer; he also had the right to summon a parliament to discuss matters of policy. The first of these parliaments was held in 1254 and was made up from the great lords and members of the clergy; later a separate parliament composed of commoners was introduced in which they could voice their grievances.

This all sounds as if a satisfactory colonization had been achieved and a government established but the whole situation was riddled with weakness. The Norman Conquest had been achieved not only by the English sovereign but also by independent barons who put self-interest far ahead of loyalty to the English throne. They understandably looked on the lands they had captured as their right. The Viceroy's real power was limited and, frequently, challenged by the Norman lords who, by this time, had adopted the Irish language and Irish customs and naturally started to feel more in common with the old Irish kings than they did with an English ruler appointed from London by an English King. There was also considerable resentment of the attitude of the English court towards Ireland which was looked upon as a source of men, supplies and finance for their wars in Scotland. This exploitation continued on an increasing scale until, by the end of the thirteenth century, they were bleeding the Irish exchequer so much that the Viceroy no longer had sufficient funds to defend his position satisfactorily.

The Norman lords learned something else from their Irish neighbors, the love of fighting among themselves; and it is ironic that the lack of Norman unity was to give the Irish kings the opportunity to reassert themselves when they themselves had been defeated by that very weakness. Irish revolts started on a comparatively small scale, and were generally unsuccessful. In 1260, for instance, Brian O'Neill, King of Tir Eogain, one of the few areas not under Norman control, was recognized by the O'Connors and the O'Briens as High King. Their combined forces confronted the Normans but were routed at the Battle of Down later in the same year. The following year, however, the MacCarthys rose against John Fitzthomas, Earl of Desmond and, despite reinforcements sent to Fitzthomas by the Viceroy in Dublin, his forces were defeated at the Battle of Callan and the MacCarthys regained effective power throughout Munster.

The main weakness of the Irish revolts had always been a backward attitude to military tactics and inadequate weaponry and armor. This situation was rectified by the arrival of mercenaries from Scotland, the gallowglasses, who were highly trained, well equipped and were destined to form the backbone of the Celtic

emouura il ce fu trop grant folie
au il ce fu fellourst le monurie
z confonde du corps z de la vie
au en monstra
amour qui ot au vog qui tant l'ama
au tout son oft de chaptier comanda
urges z nefs z denwur qui pouura
unes portez

uh passa le vor victaur l'amez
en pou de temps car lour fu bel z clez
t le vent bon qui le fist cuourier
uant deuy sourie
mille forde la ne fist pas fiourie
car le mefchief les plautes z les flours
car pouree rgene z les mortels anlours
ne chun ot.

resistance. They first arrived in Ireland with Donal O'Donnell who inherited the kingship of Tir Conaill and, with their help, established himself as ruler of Brenfe, before his death in 1281.

Elsewhere in Ireland the Irish revolt was gathering momentum. In Connacht Aodh O' Connor attacked and defeated Walter de Burgo and the Viceroy in 1270 and, two years later, with the help of the O'Donnells, gained control of a large portion of Meath. The same year the O'Tooles and the O'Byrnes were in revolt in Wicklow and, by 1281, we are told that 'There was great and general warfare between the foreigners and the Gael.'

By the end of the century, the Viceroy's government, without sufficient funds or the undivided support of the Norman lords was unable to keep control. The colony was faced with complete destruction when the final blow came from Scotland.

THE SCOTTISH INVASION

The wars between England and Scotland had been raging for decades when Robert the Bruce eventually defeated the English decisively at Bannockburn in 1314. Bruce then decided to attack Ireland. There were a number of very good reasons for this decision: the English had relied strongly on Irish resources to supply their army and Bruce saw an Irish invasion as an opportunity to cut off these supplies; he also reckoned that the trouble caused by a rebellion in Ireland would divert the English attention from Scotland; and, thirdly, he thought that the Viceroy in Ireland would supply a kingdom for his brother Edward, who, in fact, had a distant claim to some lands in the North. To be successful, Bruce realized that he needed the co-operation of the Irish kings and he managed to persuade them that the invasion was for their benefit, to restore their liberty from the Norman overlords. This rather crude piece of confidence trickery worked and, when Edward Bruce landed at Larne in 1315, with an army of 6,000 men, he was joined by several of the Irish kings from the northern provinces. His campaign was successful from the start. He defeated the forces of Richard 'Red Earl of Ulster' in 1316 and on May Day, the following year, was crowned king of Ireland. This was, however, an empty boast, as it had been with so many previous holders of the title. Some Irish joined Bruce and accepted him as overlord but most just took advantage of the general disorder to grab back land from the Normans. In 1317, realizing that his brother's position was vulnerable and fearing that the primary object of the invasion, to cut off English supplies, was threatened, Robert Bruce

LEFT: *Richard II crossing to Ireland.*

landed in Ireland with reinforcements.

Together the brothers marched south from Ulster, burning, killing and looting, and what support they had enjoyed from the Irish kings vanished. In the autumn of 1317 a new Viceroy, Roger Mortimer, arrived in Ireland with a powerful army and drove Bruce's army back into Ulster and negotiated peace with the rebel Irish kings in Connacht and Meath. The fight against Bruce was further reinforced by a dictum from the Pope which automatically excommunicated all Bruce supporters. Robert Bruce returned to Scotland, which was once again threatened with invasion, and left Edward to defend Ulster. The Normans made no attempt to invade this territory but Edward, determined to reestablish his command in the other four provinces, marched south in the autumn of 1318. He met the Norman army, led by John de Bermingham, at Faughart, not far from the scene of his coronation two years earlier. Bruce's forces were defeated, Bruce himself was killed and his head was sent to Edward II in England. Edward Bruce had arrived in Ireland with a promise to restore Irish liberty but it is not as a champion but as a usurper that he is remembered by contemporary Irish historians. 'Edward Bruce', they wrote bitterly, 'the destroyer of all Ireland in general, both foreigner and Gael, was slain by the foreigners of Ireland, through the power of battle and bravery, at Dundalk . . . and no better deed for the men of all Ireland was performed since the beginning of the world'.

The Scots had failed in their attempt to colonize Ireland but their mark was left on the country. Financial disaster was the main feature of the years after his death. Towns burned to the ground and plundering had drained the country's resources, a situation which was further aggravated by the failure of the harvest. This weakened the Dublin government which could not reasonably be expected to provide the punitive taxes upon which the English had previously relied. The Irish kings, always quick to spot weakness, were planning revolt once again. At last they had learned their lesson; it was no use fighting an armored force in linen costumes and armed with axes. They had been converted and educated in the methods of modern warfare by the gallowglasses. From the Normans they had learned of the advantages of building castles and fortifications. Their traditional enthusiasm and bravery was now backed with science and they were a force to be reckoned with.

PREVIOUS PAGE: *Art MacMurrough Kavanagh meeting the Earl of Gloucester.*
RIGHT: *Richard II and his army in Ireland.*

IRELAND UNDER THE LORDS

In an attempt to strengthen the position of the Anglo-Irish, new earldoms were created. Kildare was granted to John Fitzgerald; Desmond to Maurice – , head of the Munster Fitzgeralds, and Ormond to James Butler. Titles and grants were not enough, however: only a direct invasion from England could have stopped the continual revolt of the Irish kings. The young King Edward III was busy in Scotland and, rather than going to the assistance of the Viceroy, he worsened the situation by drawing forces for his own battles. The earls resented being used in this way, a feeling which is reflected in a statement from the Anglo-Irish parliament at Kilkenny, where the Earl of Desmond spoke against "the English by birth who mis-governed Ireland and complained of the decay of revenue and the loss of a third of the land to the Irish."

The English were rapidly losing their grip. In

ABOVE: *Henry of Monmouth is knighted in Ireland.*

1333, William the young Earl of Ulster was murdered by his own tenants at Mandevilles and the whole of the North was once again controlled by the O'Neills. In Connacht Ulick and Edmund de Burgh, cousins of the murdered Earl, seized control and split the province between them. They changed their name to MacWilliam Burke and ruled the province in the manner of Irish kings. This might appear to have been re-establishment of Norman rule but it was of little consolation to the Viceroy in Dublin for the MacWilliam Burkes were, by this time, Irish in every sense. They spoke Irish, married Irish wives, dressed in Irish clothes, used Irish laws and payed no more than lip service to the Dublin Government. In Leinster too, the Anglo-Irish faced stiff opposition from Donal Kavanagh who proclaimed himself King of Leinster. By 1350 it can be said that only Munster and districts around Dublin were under the Viceroy's control.

Desperate attempts were made by the Viceroy to reestablish his power both over the Irish and rebel Normans; laws were passed forbidding a lord to quarter a private army and the Viceroy appointed regional officials to insure that this condition was observed. The punishment was supposed to be forfeiture of lands and money but the Viceroy soon found he was powerless to enforce any of his measures. In desperation, seeing the colony slipping away from the Crown completely he sent a plea for help to Edward III. The King answered the appeal by replacing the Viceroy with his own son Lionel, Duke of Clarence. Lionel, who arrived in Dublin in 1361, was a realistic man and he soon realized that the situation was so far out of hand that any attempt to reconquer the entire country was useless. Instead, he decided to secure as much of the good land for the Anglo-Irish as was possible and to grant the remainder to the Gaelic kings. While it was never officially proclaimed that the English Crown relinquished the right to govern any part of Ireland, they did distinguish between the land that they effectively ruled, known as English lands, and that which they did not.

The situation was consolidated by Lionel at the Kilkenny Parliament held in 1366 where the famous statutes of Kilkenny were introduced. The basic aim of the statutes was to prevent the Anglo-Irish from losing their 'English' identity which was happening by intermarriage, the use of the Irish language, use of Irish laws and fraternizing generally. It was, in fact, to stop them from becoming completely Irish which we have seen happen to the Burkes in Connacht. It was the first time that the Irish were officially proclaimed second class citizens. The most severe deprivation was their exclusion from Cathedrals and Abbeys and the insistence that any Irishman living within the English colony should speak English. More trivial but offensive conditions prevented colonists from entertaining Irish poets and minstrels, playing Irish games or selling them horses or armor. The English land was now defined as including Louth, Meath, Trim, Dublin, Kildare, Kilkenny, Tipperary, Wexford and Waterford. After proclaiming the statutes, Lionel left Dublin for good and, as one might expect, they were largely ignored but were officially in force for more than two centuries. It is an illustration of this failure that the next Viceroy of Ireland, Gerald Earl of Desmond, was an eminent Gaelic scholar and poet. The Normans continued to marry Irish wives and even the area of Ireland claimed as English land was constantly disrupted by rebellious Irish kings, notably the O'Briens in Thormond and the MacMurroughs in Leinster.

The decline of the colony continued, and by the time Richard II acceded to the English throne in 1377 the situation was really desperate. England was at war with France and Scotland and this, together with threatened civil war at home, was as much as the new King could manage. He was unable to come to the rescue of the Dublin Government which was now at the point of bribing Gaelic kings not to invade what little territory remained in their possession. In 1394, however, there was a truce with France and for the first time Richard took a serious look at the Irish problem. Unlike Edward III, he decided to visit the country for himself rather than sending a Viceroy. He arrived in Dublin with an army of more than ten thousand men, the largest force ever to land in Ireland up to that time, but despite this, decided on a policy of negotiation rather than military conquest. On the whole his attitude was rather more reasonable than any of his predecessors but still he seemed to misunderstand the Irish mentality completely. The Irish had no tradition in written agreements and about as much respect for them. Richard's aim was to allocate land on acceptable terms both to the Irish and the Anglo-Irish. One by one the Irish kings came and swore homage to Richard as their ancestors had done to Henry II. He should have been suspicious when he obtained promises with such apparent ease, particularly from the Mac Murroughs who agreed to leave Leinster forever and win new lands for themselves elsewhere. It is hard to believe that this rebellious king ever had the remotest intention of honoring the promise. With the Gaelic rulers confined to their lands in the West, Richard naively believed he had solved the Irish problem and returned with his army to England leaving behind Roger Mortimer, the heir to the English throne, as Viceroy. The King was hardly over the horizon when the trouble started again. The MacMurroughs refused to abandon their lands in Leinster and soon Mortimer was involved in full scale warfare. In July 1398, Mortimer was killed in a Battle at Kellistown, when, as an act of bravado, he went out into battle wearing only a linen dress. Richard received the news and left for Ireland in dismay and fury, swearing to avenge his heir's death. He arrived at Waterford in June 1399 and promised to defeat MacMurrough who he held responsible for young Mortimer's death, but, despite his superior strength, his campaign was a total failure. MacMurrough, since he was being pursued, could dictate the terms on which the

ABOVE: *An Irish banquet in the middle of the sixteenth century. Even at this time, the Irish chiefs were semi-nomadic and considered it quite proper to eat outdoors.*

battle was fought and he chose the woods which suited the Irish style of warfare. Despite putting a price on MacMurrough's head, Richard was never to get his revenge and, more tragic for him, his absence from England was to cost him his throne and his life. After a short stay in Ireland he received news that his rival, Henry of Lancaster, had landed in England to claim the throne. He returned immediately but had already lost the initiative and left behind him an Ireland with the smallest English power since the invasion of Strongbow. Only Dublin and a few of the surrounding counties remained faithful to the crown, an area which was subsequently called the Pale. The Lancastrians had enough problems

70

in France and at home to keep them fully occupied and they were glad to forget Ireland which showed no signs of yielding financial rewards or manpower without a great investment of both.

ARISTOCRATIC HOME RULE

We now enter a period of rule in Ireland by the Great Earls, independent from England which they were destined to remain until the Tudors gained the English throne.

The north and western parts of Ireland remained under the control of the great Gaelic families, notably the O'Neills, O'Donnells and O'Connors with smaller provinces dominated by the O'Rourkes, O'Reillys, the MacDonnells, Magennis, MacSweeny, O'Doherty and O'Kellys. But, as the fifteenth century got under way, Ireland was more and more dominated by the great Anglo-Irish earldoms; the Butlers of Ormond, the Fitzgeralds of Kildare and the Fitzgeralds of Desmond.

For the first half of the century, the Butlers were unquestionably the most powerful of the three, ruling over Kilkenny and Tipperary. They were feudal lords over several other great Anglo-Irish families, including the Graces and the Purcells and, in addition to these, claimed rents from many of the old Gaelic rulers such as the O'Carrolls and the O'Kennedys. James Earl of Ormond (1408-52), nicknamed the White Earl, was the most powerful man of his day and commanded considerable loyalty from Gaelic and Anglo-Irish alike. Both races feared and resented interference in their internal administration from England and Dublin. They supported the White Earl who, by appointing himself Viceroy, had enormous power over the Dublin government, dividing offices amongst his followers and creating a regime designed primarily to suit Irish interests. Unlike many great Anglo-Irish families, the Butlers had not adopted the Gaelic ways of life and, when the White Earl died, his heir married an English girl and seldom visited his Irish estates.

The power now changed into the hands of the Earls of Desmond who ruled Kerry, Cork, Limerick and western Waterford from their seat at Tralee. Like the Butlers, the Desmonds held sway over lesser rulers both Anglo-Irish and Gaelic. These families included the great MacCarthys, traditional rulers of Munster, and the O'Sullivans together with the English families of Barry, Roche and Barrymore. In the midlands the earldom of Kildare, destined to become virtually absolute rulers of Ireland, was still comparatively weak at this time but their lands were extensive and strategically placed on the edge of the Pale. Kildare's influence also spread far beyond the actual boundaries of the Earldom with both English and Gaelic families paying rents to him from the counties Kildare, Carlow, Offaly, Leix and Wicklow.

This was the political situation which greeted Richard, Duke of York, when he first visited the country in 1449. After the murder of the Duke of Gloucester, Richard was the most likely heir to the English throne. He was a clever man with an excellent war record in France, he held vast estates in England and was heir to several others in Ireland. It is natural, therefore, that he should be considered the most suitable candidate for the post of Viceroy in Ireland. His appointment killed two birds with one stone; firstly, the king saw it as a method of reestablishing English rule in the wayward colony but, perhaps more important, he saw it as a way to get the ambitious duke out of the way for a while. Richard managed to gather great support in Ireland. Both the Anglo-Irish

RIGHT: *Processional cross made for Cornelius O'Connor of Kerry in 1479, found at Ballymacasey.*
OVERLEAF: *The English army on the march in Ireland during 1581.*

and Gaelic rulers were flattered by the appointment of a prince of royal blood, a prince who they firmly believed to be destined to become the next King of England. One by one rulers submitted to him and did homage. Not even the most rebellious families such as the MacMurroughs appeared able to resist his influence. Later in 1449 Richard's wife gave birth to a son, Edward, and the ties between the English throne and the earldoms was further strengthened when the Earls of Ormond and Desmond stood sponsor for the infant Prince. Richard's stay in Ireland was short-lived, however; disorder was rife in England and opinion appeared to be supporting his claim to the throne. Ireland seemed to be safely under his control and in 1450 he left for England, leaving the Duke of Ormond as his deputy.

In 1459, Richard was back in Ireland again, a refugee after his army had been routed by the Lancastrian forces at Ludford Bridge. He was greeted with all the pomp and ceremony more befitting the victor than the vanquished. Despite an absence of almost ten years, Irish loyalty had remained firm. This was not to say that the Irish leaders did not make as much capital as they could out of the political situation on the other side of the water. A parliament was held at Drogheda the year after Richard's return which brought sweeping changes to the Irish constitution. Richard granted Ireland the most basic element of self-government: parliamentary independence. In return for this privilege, he demanded absolute loyalty to himself and his son Edward, making it high treason to plot against either of their persons. In addition to this, Richard used the new parliament as a means of recruiting forces for his battle in England. York's nephew, the Earl of Warwick, set the example by sailing to England with a substantial force in 1460 and succeeded in defeating the Lancastrians and capturing the King. When he received this news, Richard sailed for England leaving the Earl of Kildare to govern in his place. Richard was killed in battle but his son acceded to the throne during the following year, 1461. With this the Irish lords seemed to have got it all their own way. They had a king in England who suited their purposes with his close links to the earldoms and legislative independence, a system which they themselves could administer to their own advantage. Once again, however, internal strife was to

And marching on in warlicke wise, set out in battayle ray,
He doth pronounce by hearty doome: the enemies pryde to lay,
And all the rable of the foes, by bloudy blade to quell
That rising shall assiste the sorte, which trayterously rebell.
Deliuering them to open spoyle, from most vnto the least,
And byd them welcome hartely, vnto that golden feast.

For what is he of all the Karne, that may withstand her power,
Or yet resist so great a Prince, one minute of an houre,
If he or they both tagge and ragge, for mayntenaunce of their cause,
Durst venture to approche the fielde, to try it by marshall lawes.
Not one of this rebelling sort, that thinkes himselfe most sure
Is able to abide the Knight, or presence his endure.

dog any chances of peaceful unity within Ireland. The Butlers of Ormond had unwisely supported the Lancastrian cause in the Wars of the Roses and, immediately after he became King, Edward IV had James, Earl of Ormond, beheaded for treason. His house was attained and, while his brothers both took the title of Earl, they spent little time in Ireland. This left the way open for the earls of Desmond to establish their supremacy once again. Thomas, seventh Earl of Desmond, took the title in 1462 and emerged as a natural leader. He was a cultured and scholarly man who found great favor with the Gaelic rulers, and was trusted and respected by Edward IV who appointed him Viceroy in 1463. As his power increased, however, he became resented and feared, particularly by the Anglo-Irish who thought him too fond of Gaelic customs and suspected that he had ambitions to become absolute monarch. They conspired to get him dismissed from the post of Viceroy and, in his place, appointed John Tiptoft, Earl of Worcester, who, under the guise of Yorkist loyalty, had the Earls of Desmond and Kildare arrested on charges of 'Trasons alliances and fosterages with Irish enemies'. Desmond was convicted and beheaded but Kildare managed to escape to England where he was pardoned and reinstated by the King, who was shocked by the brutality of his Viceroy. This did little to console the Desmonds who wanted vengeance for the murder of their leader. Garret, the Earl's brother, raised a large army of mercenaries and wrought havoc throughout the province. James, the Earl's son and heir, also rebelled; he married an O'Brien and established strong ties with the Gaelic rulers of the province, swearing that neither he nor his successors would ever attend an English Parliament except of their own free will. The loyalty of the great Earldom of Desmond was thus lost to the English. Edward realized that he was powerless to control the Irish situation without a vast expenditure in money and resources, expenditure which he was both unable and unwilling to undertake. The decline of Desmond left the way open for the earls of Kildare to become virtual rulers of Ireland.

THE KILDARE ASCENDANCY

After the departure of John Tiptoft, the post of Viceroy fell to Thomas Fitzgerald, Earl of Kildare. His power was not seriously challenged since the Desmonds, the only family strong enough to do this, had sworn against any parliamentary involvement. Thomas used this position to considerable advantage, passing laws which expanded and strengthened the authority of Kildare. On his death in 1477, the Earldom passed

to his son Garret More (Great Gerald) and with the title came the post of Viceroy. Garret More continued much in the ways of his father, expanding and reinforcing his territory and authority. The fiction of the King's power in the country was given a certain credibility by appointing an absentee lieutenant to whom the Earl of Kildare was nominally answerable. What territory Garret More Fitzgerald was unable to grab by military assault or legislation, he married into. His sister married the eldest son of Henry O'Neill, Lord of Tyrone; his five daughters married into the O'Neills, O'Carrolls, Butlers, Burkes and the MacCarthys. In this way, the great Anglo-Irish and Gaelic families were united by marriage. This formidable alliance ensured Garret More absolute power; he was, in fact, King of Ireland in all but name.

When Richard III was killed on Bosworth field in 1485, Garret More looked vulnerable for the first time. Like his father he was an avowed Yorkist and the last Yorkist king was dead, but Henry VII overlooked this fault and allowed him to continue as Viceroy. Even after Garret More and his Irish allies had backed Lambert Simnel's abortive attempt to regain the English throne for the Yorkist cause, Henry found it politic to forgive. He merely sent over an envoy through whom the Irish lords pledged their allegiance to the English throne but this gesture did not affect Garret More's absolute power. When a second pretender to the English throne, in the person of Perkin Warbeck, received active support, however, Henry's patience was finally exhausted. Garret More had never actually been a party to the conspiracy but it was becoming obvious that Ireland was a convenient springboard for rebellion and Henry relieved Kildare of his office. In his place he appointed Sir Edward Poynings as his Viceroy, who arrived in Dublin in 1494 with a substantial army with a brief to restore Ireland to 'Whole and perfect obedience.'

Poynings was a professional soldier but his new post demanded of him the qualities of politician and legislator. His immediate solution was military supremacy but this was to prove far more difficult than he had anticipated. The only Irish support he received was from the Butlers and, while he managed to drive many of the King's enemies from the Pale, his advances into the North were stubbornly resisted. By the end of his first year Poynings realized, as had so many of his predecessors, that there was no military solution to the Irish problem and, in

77

December 1494, he called parliament at Drogheda where he passed the Statutes of Drogheda or 'Poynings' Law'. This effectively removed from the Irish parliament the right of autonomous legislation. From now on any law passed in the Irish Parliament was subject to ratification by the English Parliament. This removed the most powerful element of self-government granted to the Irish by Richard, Duke of York. The main object, of course, was to prevent the Irish Government from supporting claimants to the English throne such as Simnel and Warbeck. Other recommendations included that the post of Viceroy should cease to be life-long and/or hereditary; the statutes of Kilkenny were re-introduced and measures were taken to protect the Pale. Henry, however, did not see any immediate benefits of Poynings' Law. Their introduction would have required a substantial subsidy from the English Exchequer and, in 1496,

ABOVE: *Revolt followed by submission was the pattern of Irish life. Here Thurlough O'Neill submits to Sir Henry Sidney after the uprising in Ulster.*

he recalled his Viceroy. He realized that the only man in Ireland equipped to govern the country was Garret More Fitzgerald, Earl of Kildare, whom he previously arrested and locked in the Tower of London. Garret More was reinstated with a few conditions. He married Henry's cousin Elizabeth St John and signed an undertaking to observe the laws introduced by Poynings. In fact, Garret More continued on a policy of absolute monarchy paying no more than lip service to the conditions which he had undertaken. On his death in 1513, the position of Viceroy passed to his son, Garret Og (young Gerald), who continued very much in his father's ways. The monarchy in England, however, was

Tyrones falfe Submifsion afterwards rebelling.

no longer so weak and the days of Kildare supremacy were numbered. News reached Henry VIII that the Earl of Desmond was in league with Emperor Charles V and, convinced that Kildare was no longer in control of the Irish situation, decided upon a new Viceregal policy. He recalled Garret Og to London in 1534 and, a delay in the Viceroy's return to Ireland fostered rumors that he had been executed at the tower. This precipitated a rebellion under the leadership of his son Lord Thomas Fitzgerald 'Silken Thomas'. Thomas had committed the unforgivable crime of mentioning Henry's breach with Rome and in 1537 he was executed along with five of his uncles. This left the great house of Kildare with only one claimant, a twelve-year-old boy who was in exile in France, which left the way open for the Butlers of Ormond to regain control. They had long been enemies of the Kildares and had habitually sided with the Lancastrians. They supported Henry VIII and were actively involved in the enactment of royal supremacy in the Dublin Government of 1537.

The confiscation of monastic property, together with that of rebel rulers provided the Dublin Government with the means to buy loyalty. This brought about the most corrupt administrations ever suffered by the Irish. It was common practice for officials to stir up trouble in the hope that rebellion would ensue and that they would be beneficiaries of the confiscated lands. The main effect of this punitive regime was to drive the Anglo-Irish closer to the Gaelic Irish, both of whom saw themselves as victims of usurpers. The Church too, hitherto bound by the Papal Bull, no longer viewed the English right to rule as legitimate.

Henry decided that the situation should be rectified by negotiation. His policy was 'surrender and re-grant' by which he hoped to ensure the Irish lords' dependence on his sovereignty. To implement the necessary measures, he appointed Sir Anthony St Leger as his deputy in Dublin. St Leger was an admirable choice; he was a soldier, diplomat and administrator with an extensive knowledge of Ireland and its people. He set about making agreements with individual rulers both Anglo-Irish and Gaelic. The idea was that each ruler should surrender his lands to the king and these would be restored to him automatically under knight-service, with certain provisos. These included an agreement to use English Law, observe English customs and disband private armies which had not received the official sanction of the King's Deputy. The demarkation between the Gaelic rulers and the

Anglo-Irish was diminished by bestowing English style titles on both. Thus Conn O'Neill became the Earl of Tyrone; Murrouch O'Brien, Earl of Thormond; Donough O'Brien became Baron of Ibrackin. The same procedure was applied to the degenerate English rulers such as MacWilliam Burke who surrendered his lands and had them restored with the title Earl of Clanrickard. In 1541 a special parliament was held to formalize all these agreements and officially bestow the title of King of Ireland upon Henry VIII. Considerable tact and diplomacy had been shown throughout the proceedings to the point that the parliament was conducted in two languages for the benefit of the Gaelic rulers present. Henry's policy appeared to have worked; he was universally accepted as rightful ruler of Ireland by the Irish and the Anglo-Irish alike who renounced 'usurped authority of the Bishop of Rome.'

As we have seen so many times before, the solution to the Irish problem was never destined to come easily. The basic weakness in the 'Surrender and Re-grant' policy was that it took no account of traditional Irish laws of land tenure. While the great Irish leaders were quite happy to accept the grants made by the monarch, lesser Irish gentry found themselves severely deprived by their own leaders and it was not long before civil war was rife with Irish leaders challenging the King's grants on the basis of ancient Irish law. We see, in fact, a classical conflict between two legal systems observed in an arbitrary fashion according to personal interests. Henry's policy to establish himself as head of the Irish Church appears to have been rather more successful, however. In 1542, a mission of Jesuits visited O'Neill in Tyrone armed with letters from the Pope but they were met with a very cool reception and were soon forced to flee to Scotland. Despite considerable popular opposition to royal supremacy, it suited the lot of the rulers to accept the situation. It is doubtful, in fact, whether many of them cared one way or the other and observed the supremacy as a means of political advantage.

By the time Edward VI came to the English throne in 1547, Ireland was once again a political shambles with the main preoccupation of the Viceroy being to protect the Pale. Attempts to introduce further changes in the Irish Ecclesiastical system were unsuccessful. An edition of the Book of Common Prayer was printed in Dublin but it enjoyed slight interest except by English officials. George Dowdall, Archbishop of Armagh, previously in favor of royal supremacy, drew the line at its adoption and voted to go into exile rather than to abandon the Mass. On the

im Starckes dauerhafftigs Volck behilfft sich mit geringer speiß
zeln, Wans auch die Notturfft erfordert Können sie des Tages
weges lauffen, haben neben Mußqueden Ihre Bogen vnd Köch

accession of Mary I in 1553 Papal authority was formally restored in Ireland. Reformed clergy were then denounced but there was no action taken against them for heresy as was experienced on the other side of the Irish Sea.

A mere seven years later, the Irish were confronted with another complete about-face. Circumstances had forced Elizabeth to adopt the Protestant religion in England and it was obvious for her to extend this policy to her colonies. She appointed the Earl of Sussex as her deputy and he called a parliament in Dublin to pass the acts of 'Supremacy and Uniformity'. These were passed with the minimum delay which has led to the theory that some duplicity was employed in their presentation. Whatever the truth of the matter, the Viceroy realized that these laws would have to be enforced with the utmost leniency and tact if the Anglo-Irish inhabitants of the Pale were not to be driven into an alliance with Catholic sympathizers elsewhere in Ireland who were now completely outside the control of the Dublin Government. The whole new Protestant Church was, in fact, no more than a face-saver and was totally unequipped to withstand the Counter-Reformation which was shortly to be launched against it. Ireland, with its history of comparative religious tolerance, was about to be dogged by the sectarian bitterness which haunts her to this day.

GAELIC REVIVAL AND RELIGIOUS DISSENT
Sussex realized that he was sitting on a powder keg. He warned the Queen that Ireland would bring 'such ruin to England that I am a'feared to think on.' The great center of unrest was Ulster where the Earldom of Tyrone had completely broken down. Con Bacach O'Neill had accepted the title after submitting to Henry VIII in 1541 but, on his death in 1559, the earldom came under dispute. The Dublin government recognized the claim of Con's illegitimate son Mathew, but popular support went in favor of Shane O'Neill, a younger son. He flouted English supremacy by abandoning the English title of Earl, reverting to the traditional Irish of 'the O'Neill'. His attempts to get his title recognized by the Dublin government were unsuccessful as were the government's attempts to defeat Shane in battle. Elizabeth was faced with an intolerable situation where her elected representative was openly defied and decided to ask O'Neill to London to negotiate. O'Neill returned to Ulster in 1562 with the title of 'Captain of Tyrone' and armed with instructions to conquer the MacDonnells, migrants from the Western Isles of Scotland who had established themselves in Antrim, and, less understandably,

es nicht brodt so Essen sie

r die 20 Teütscher

d Lange Messer.

Sr Phillom O Neale of all Ireland
Cheife Traytor

84

the O'Donnells who dominated the old kingdom of Tir Connaill in North West Ulster. In 1567, however, the O'Donnells had their revenge; the defeated Shane O'Neill who was forced to flee to Scotland, where he was found and murdered by the MacDonnells. An act of attainder was passed in 1569 by the Dublin government which declared all the O'Neill lands forfeit. There followed a wave of colonization, not only in Ulster, but also in Leinster and Munster by a number of English Court favorites such as St Leger, Carew, Devereux and Smith who were permitted to attempt plantions. This was too much for both the Anglo-Irish and the Irish rulers who presented a united front in repelling these attempts and the Queen was eventually forced to abandon them and pardon the rebels. This worked in Leinster where the Butlers accepted the pardon in good grace and settled down, but in Munster, James Fitz Maurice Fitzgerald, cousin of the Earl of Desmond, had assumed control and was determined to change a territorial war into a religious one. He was a fanatical opponent to the Protestant faith and was determined to start a Catholic Crusade in Ireland. He gathered support from other Anglo-Irish lords who backed him more because they feared forfeiture of their lands than from real religious convictions. He soon realized that his attempts were unlikely to be successful against a stronger army, and in 1575 he left for the Continent on a recruiting campaign. He returned to Ireland in 1579 with the approval of Pope Gregory XIII but backed by a force of only 300 Italians and Spaniards. He had been relying upon the support of both Desmond and Kildare but this was not forthcoming and FitzMaurice was killed in a skirmish a few weeks after his landing. After his cousin's death, Desmond had a change of heart and adopted the Catholic Cause as his own. In autumn 1580 another Italian/Spanish force of six hundred men arrived at Smerwick on the Dingle penninsula. This time the Queen's Deputy Lord Grey of Wilton decided to treat it as a full scale invasion; he mustered every man possible and marched against the puny army and, when they had conceded defeat, put every man to the sword claiming that, as Papal soldiers, they had no international status. With this one barbaric act the Desmond rebellion was over.

The Dublin government decided against the policy of moderation and confiscated more than three thousand acres of Desmond territory. The policy of plantation was again attempted. The territory was split into lots of between four thousand and twelve thousand acres which were allocated to 'undertakers' who were to plant them with English-born families. The scheme was, once again, a failure. A census taken ten years later showed that only thirteen of the forty eight undertakers were in residence and that less than two hundred and fifty English families had settled there.

Elizabeth's policy in Connaught, where she also faced considerable administrative problems, was considerably better planned and executed. In 1585, Sir John Perrot, the Queen's Deputy, ordered a report on the rights and holdings of both Irish and Anglo-Irish rulers in the province. This was used as a basis for settlement. All lords who were prepared to accept English titles and pay rent to the crown were confirmed in their estates. Plantation was not attempted and life was allowed to continue much as it had previously but with better communication between the individual rulers and the Crown. In Leinster, the Butlers remained faithful to the monarchy but in Ulster trouble was brewing once again.

THE TYRONE WARS

The main challenge to the authority of Dublin centered round Hugh O'Neill, nephew of Shane. This was an unlikely turn of events for Hugh was neither the recognized heir to the O'Neill title — that had gone to his cousin Tulough — nor was he an apparent rebel against English supremacy. He had, in fact, supported the Loyalist cause against the Desmond rebellion and attended the parliament of 1585. For these acts of loyalty he had been granted considerable states in Ulster and, by 1583, he was so strong that he managed to persuade his cousin to relinquish his title as head of the O'Neills and took it on himself. He was a much shrewder politician than Shane had been. Instead of establishing military supremacy over his O'Donnell neighbors, he made an alliance with their leader, Hugh Roe O'Donnell. This was a formidable partnership which, quite naturally, worried the Dublin government but they hoped the partnership would break up of its own accord and attempted to negotiate with Hugh. They were shaken out of their complacency when the Queen's Deputy, Sir Henry Bagnall, was defeated and slain at the Battle of Yellow Ford in August 1598. This victory for the O'Neills sparked off a wave of Gaelic resistance elsewhere in Ireland. In Connaught, the Burks rose and in Leinster the O'Mores and O'Byrnes prepared for battle. O'Neill's position was not, however, as strong as it might first appear. Without heavy artillery and seige weapons, he was powerless to take the walled cities which he knew he must

RIGHT: *Queen Elizabeth and her parliament. Ireland was one of their biggest headaches.*

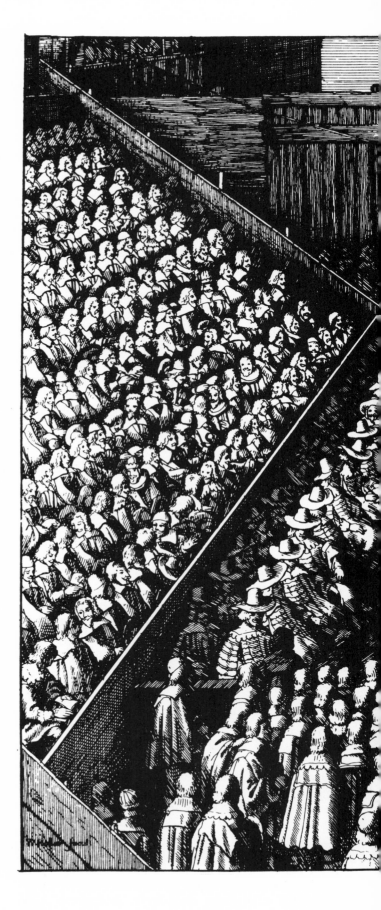

control if his supremacy was to be confirmed. Also there were large areas of Ireland which remained loyal to the English throne. He, naturally, found sympathy in Munster where the lords had suffered great injustices during the plantation. In Connaught, however, where settlement had been fairly executed, he found much less interest in revolution. He decided, as Desmond had done, to turn what was basically a war for territorial gain into a religious war and sought help from Catholic monarchs abroad. Philip of Spain died in 1598 and the throne passed to his son, Philip III, who was sympathetic to the Irish cause and promised to send help. This was what the Queen feared most, an independent alliance between Ireland and Spain which could threaten the English throne. Policies of negotiation were immediately abandoned and the Queen prepared to launch a great army against 'the arch traitor', Hugh O'Neill.

ESSEX AND MOUNTJOY

Sir Robert Devereux was entrusted with the task of quelling the Irish rebellion and he arrived in Dublin on April 15th 1599 with an army of almost twenty thousand men. Essex was a good soldier but was not experienced in the type of warfare conducted by the Irish. Instead of leading his entire force against O'Neill at once, he allowed the Irish rebels to conduct the war on their own terms, as a series of skirmishes, which suited their tactics so well. The result of this policy was that, by July of the same year, Essex's army had been reduced to four thousand men and, when he did eventually reach Ulster, he achieved no more than unofficial negotiations with O'Neill – a far cry from the crushing defeat demanded by his Queen. Elizabeth was furious and recalled Essex in September 1599 and his failure in Ireland was rewarded with the axe in February of the following year. Elizabeth appointed Sir Charles Blount, Lord Mountjoy, as her new Deputy. He was a tactician of a high order and planned a systematic campaign against O'Neill, using garrisons rather than being lured into skirmishes which had destroyed the army of his predecessor. As O'Neill's success started to diminish, so did the support he received from the other Irish leaders. His only hope lay in the foreign aid promised to him by the King of Spain. When the force of four thousand Spaniards did arrive in September 1601, it landed not in Ulster, where it could have been put to some considerable use, but in Kinsale, County Cork, where the rebellion had been effectively subdued and could rely on little or no local support. O'Neill and O'Donnell were left to

BELOW: *The trial and execution of Thomas Earl of Stafford in 1641. Stafford had been Lord Lieutenant of Ireland.*

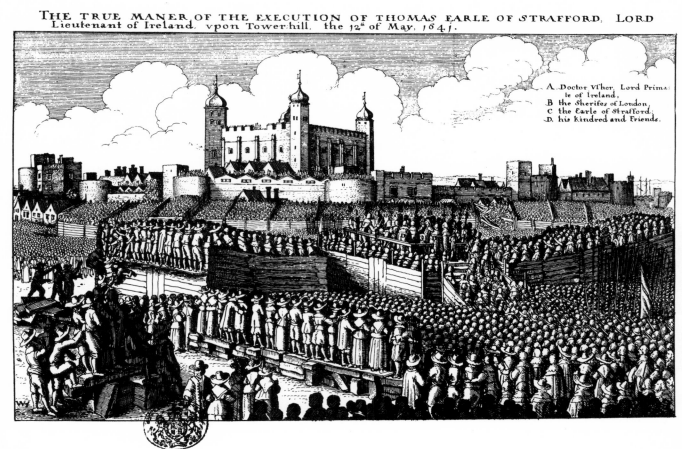

THE TRUE MANER OF THE EXECUTION OF THOMAS EARLE OF STRAFFORD, LORD Lieutenant of Ireland, vpon Tower-hill, the 12ᵗ of May, 1641.

A. Doctor Vsher, Lord Primate of Ireland.
B the Sherifes of London.
C the Earle of Strafford.
D. his Kindred and Friends.

march the length of Ireland to join their allies and camped near Kinsale planning their tactics. They attempted to take the English army by surprise but were routed on December 24th 1601. O'Donnell fled to exile in Spain and died the following year and O'Neill returned to Ulster where he was forced to live the life of a fugitive, leaving the O'Neill seat of Dungannon to Mountjoy who added insult to injury by having the famous inauguration stone destroyed as a symbol of the end of Gaelic resistance. One by one O'Neill's allies deserted him and he was finally forced to submit. It is ironic that this act of homage should have taken place a few days after the Queen's death and, had he known, he could probably have negotiated an honorable settlement with her successor James I, who he had met and with whom had had a considerable amount in common.

IRELAND IN THE SEVENTEENTH CENTURY
Had there not been a change from the Tudors to the Stuarts, just at the end of the Gaelic rebellion, it is doubtful whether settlement with the Irish rulers would have been nearly so humane. Both O'Neill and Rory O'Donnell, younger brother of Hugh O'Donnell, visited King James in London

BELOW: *James II supervises the execution of protestants in Ireland.*

accompanied by Mountjoy who had been appointed Lord Lieutenant. They were received courteously and both restored to their former earldoms without any severe stipulations, either religious or political. Many of the rulers who had remained loyal to the Tudor monarchy complained bitterly that O'Neill had benefited more from rebellion than they themselves had done by loyalty. James knew, however, that O'Neill was a beaten man and that he would probably experience less trouble by restoring his dignity than by his public humiliation. One thing he did not need in Ireland was a martyr to rekindle the flames of Gaelic resistance.

The Stuart reign in Ireland showed every sign of better things to come. King James's attitude at the outset was one of cautious tolerance to every shade of opinion. In 1604 the 'Act of Oblivion' was passed which negated all offenses committed before that date and the King's protection now extended throughout Ireland. With Scotland, Wales, England and Ireland under a single monarch and peace established with Spain, peaceful co-existence appeared to be a reality for the first time. James was believed to be a Catholic; the Southerners re-opened their old churches and started celebrating Mass openly, but this was soon stopped by Mountjoy, who believed that tolerance should be taken just so far. His

successor, Sir Arthur Chichester, was a man of a totally different ilk and made no pretense at moderation whatsoever. The King, who had been responsible for avoiding punitive measures, had had his hand weakened by the Gunpowder Plot. This had strengthened the cause of the anti-Papists and this was just the opportunity that both the English and Dublin Governments had been waiting for.

Chichester introduced what he himself described as 'strong measures' against the Catholic majority, their churches and priests. Jesuits and other priests ordained in Rome were ordered to leave the country, although most of them merely went into hiding. The most damaging move against the Irish, however, came with the plantation of Ulster, a policy which is responsible for the religious bitterness which survives to this day in that sad province. In 1603 Tyrconnell and Tyrone had been restored to O'Donnell and O'Neill respectively but they both resented their new roles under English rule. They were no longer kings but mere landlords, resented by the Dublin government and resisted by officials in their own estates. On September 14th O'Neill's son, Henry, sent a ship to Rathmullen and both O'Neill and O'Donnell left the country forever, accompanied by ninety-eight other Gaelic aristocrats. This 'Flight of the Earls' was not only a blow to Gaelic pride but also paved the way for the plantation. The earls were fully indicted and found guilty of treason and their lands were attained by the Crown. With this successfully achieved, the government went on to confiscate all the land within the boundaries of the six counties – Tyrone, Donegal, Derry, Armagh, Cavan and Fermanagh – justifying the deed on the basis that the Irish lords had taken part in the insurrections of 1601, an offense for which they had received official pardon two years later. In 1609 the six counties were divided amongst undertakers, servitors and natives. The undertakers were mainly English and were allowed to lease land to Protestant Scots and English, the servitors were Scots who were allowed to let to Protestant Irish but at double the rent to the Crown. Native Irish grantees were exempt from the Oath of Supremacy but in return for this consideration were expected to pay triple rent to the Crown. The most appalling transaction was the granting of Derry to a consortium of London companies, from which it gets its present title of Londonderry. To say that the Irish were driven into the hills and the bogs would be an exaggeration but it is certainly true that the richest lands were granted to the colonists.

Unlike the attempted plantation of Munster,

91

this operation was in every sense a practical success and, for the first time, vast areas of Ireland were not only controlled by foreigners but even farmed by them. The success of the Ulster scheme led to plantation schemes in Wexford, Leitrim and other parts of Ireland. It would be true to say that in these areas the native Irish population got a rather better deal.

In 1613, a government was called by Chichester to ratify the plantation. To obtain the majority he required, Chichester undertook one of the earliest and most elaborate exercises in boundary-rigging that any election has witnessed. The opposition, furious at being cheated out of their legitimate representation, petitioned the Crown. They were greeted with a jocular King who insisted that they were the Pope's spiritual subjects and his temporal and, as such, were only half citizens and therefore only entitled to half privileges.

IRELAND UNDER CHARLES I

With the accession of Charles I to the English throne, there appeared once again the prospect of settlement of the religious problems in Ireland. Charles himself was distinctly High Church and was married to a Catholic wife. It seemed logical, therefore, that he should err towards religious tolerance, if not outright support for the Catholics. Charles, however, saw it as an admirable opportunity to extract additional funds from the Irish to bolster his sadly depleted Exchequer. In 1627, he instructed his Deputy, Lord Falkland, to offer the Catholic peers and bishops what he called the 'Graces'. In these, Catholics could obtain permission to practice at the bar and that their land titles were to be made secure against any claims of the Crown. In exchange for these privileges, the recusants were to pay a capital sum of one hundred and twenty thousand pounds. When Charles' agents returned to London, however, they were faced with a strong anti-Papist lobby and the plan was abandoned. Needless to say, the Crown kept what money it had already extracted, yet another grievance to add to the long list accummulated by the Catholic Irish. In 1632, Charles appointed a new Deputy in Ireland, Sir Thomas Wentworth, who was perhaps the greatest man ever to occupy the post. He was, at least, the first to be motivated by ambitions other than self-interest or royal favor. His main aim was to make Ireland a prosperous nation so that she could yield additional revenue and resources for the Crown. He started by purging the Dublin government of its more corrupt elements and then turned his sights on the great landowners and the London companies, whom he saw as a greater threat to the monarchy than the native Irish. In 1634 and 1635, he held a new parliament in which he acquired new and sweeping powers to review land grants. Many of these had been disposed of at pitifully low rents and even these had been systematically avoided. The sums of money he gathered were impressive indeed. The London companies alone were fined a total of seventy thousand pounds for non-fullfillment of conditions. Wentworth was fearless but his measures, needless to say, upset the Protestant capitalists who were eventually to bring about his downfall.

He then embarked on a policy of industrialization and trade development which was severely criticized, particularly by those with vested interests in the English woollen trade. He was insistent, however, that his policies were the right ones and indeed they did produce results. By 1636 he could claim a surplus on the accounts for fifty thousand pounds and raised a considerable army to maintain peace in the country.

He was, however, the most devout loyalist, and, in 1638 when the Scots rebelled against Charles he imposed an oath upon their colonist countrymen in Ulster that they should not join the resistance. He then gathered his army of ten thousand men at Carrickfergus to await the King's instructions. This 'Black Oath' was widely resented by the Scots, many of whom refused to take it but rather forfeit their tenures and went into hiding. Thus, Wentworth increased his own enemies and the King's in Scotland and drove a wedge through the community of Ulster, already discontented with reduced profits.

THE INSURRECTION

By the time the insurrection happened in Ulster in 1641, its occasion was virtually a foregone conclusion. Every faction in the province had an axe to grind. The native Irish had had most of their land attained; the Catholics were paying punitive rents and the Protestants were dissatisfied both with the organization of the Church and the new system of levies imposed by Wentworth. The Irish still had some of their old leaders at home; in the North there was Sir Phelim O'Neill and in the South Rory O'More was organizing a union of the native Irish and the Anglo-Irish. Abroad, many of the Irish who had left with the 'Flight of the Earls' were in constant contact with their kinsmen and were awaiting news anxiously.

The rising at home began with an ambitious plot to capture Dublin Castle by Rory O'More and his ally Conor Maguire, Baron of Enniskillen. The plan was betrayed at the eleventh hour and failed but it marked the start of a general insurrection throughout Ulster under the leadership of Sir Phelim O'Neill. Thousands of colonists were massacred in the process and, while they managed to retain control of Londonderry, Carrickfergus and a few other Protestant strongholds, the O'Neill and his forces effectively controlled the province once again.

The English Parliament immediately voted for an army to deal with Ireland and, faced with severe financial problems, dreamed up yet another odious scheme to deprive the Irish of their land. The English Parliament declared that all lands belonging to the rebels would be forfeited when the rebellion was quashed and sold off 2,500,000 acres of land to freelance subscribers or 'Adventurers' for a total of one million pounds. The fear of confiscation and domination by Puritans drove even moderates to arms and, in 1642, a Catholic confederacy was formed at Kilkenny whose aims were 'to defend religion and the King against sectaries and establish the Catholic religion as full as at any time since Henry VII.' Their forces were soon joined from abroad by the confederate armies of Richard Preston, Earl of Desmond, and Owen Roe O'Neill.

The political situation which followed was one of quite incredible complexity. There were so many factions each trying to achieve different ends that any hope of unity was virtually nil. The native Irish were united to the Anglo-Irish as far as religion was concerned but felt no particular loyalty to an English monarch. In the South the issue was further confused by the presence of James, Marquess of Ormond and his army of Protestant Royalists, and the other Protestant factions in Ulster. The confederation, however unstable its foundations, received some attention abroad. In 1645 Jean Baptiste Rinuccini arrived in Ireland as Papal Nuncis and negotiations started between Ormond's army and the confederates. They failed to agree, however, on the right terms to negotiate or indeed who they should be negotiating with. They were still toiling over these differences in 1649, the fatal year for the Irish. Rinuccini left Ireland defeated, Owen Roe O'Neill, their champion, died and Cromwell's Protestant army of more than twenty thousand men arrived in Dublin. Cromwell's army was superbly fit, well equipped and zealous; Cromwell himself was a brilliant soldier and a shrewd politician. To this sort of combination, the Irish in their disunity had absolutely no answer. In addition to his unquestioned ability, Cromwell was fired with the passion to avenge the massacre of the colonists in Ulster during the 1641 insurrection. This deed he blamed on all Catholics regardless of race, nationality or political persuasion, a judgement which was patently unfair. He conducted his campaign in Ireland with a ruthless efficiency which is now part of Irish

OVERLEAF: *A scene from the legendery battle of the Boyne.*

93

legend. Perhaps his most notorious deed was the siege of Drogheda where, after securing victory, he put more than two thousand men to the sword. This action he justified thus: 'I am persuaded that this is a righteous judgment of God upon those barbarous wretches, who have imbrued their hands in so much innocent blood.'

Cromwell left Ireland after only nine months with the task of controlling Ireland unfinished, but with her spirit broken. He left behind his son-in-law Ireton. Ireland still had no united front against the Cromwellian forces and Ireton was faced with the task of quelling several different armies, fighting under different flags, in different parts of the country. It was not until 1652 that the Irish forces eventually admitted defeat and surrendered en masse. Despite attempts by Protestant extremists, the soldiers were not massacred but sent into exile either to Spain, France or the West Indies where they were sold

into slavery. Reprisals were in fact minimal by mid-seventeenth century standards: fifty-two people were executed by the orders of the Dublin court, including one of the great Irish leaders, Sir Phelim O'Neill. Cromwellian vengeance was not to be wasted on a few executions; the whole population of Ireland was destined to suffer for the dual sins of being Papists and Royalists.

In 1652 the 'Act of Settlement' was passed by the English Parliament which graded Papists by degree of guilt. Common people or holders of less than ten pounds in property, were given a pardon. Others were forced to forfeit their lands and property. The outcome was that only Connaught and Clare were left to the Irish gentry and the remainder was granted to the 'Adventurers' who had financed the war and members of the army who had served in Ireland. In this policy of confiscation, towns were also included and systematically planted with Protestant Eng-

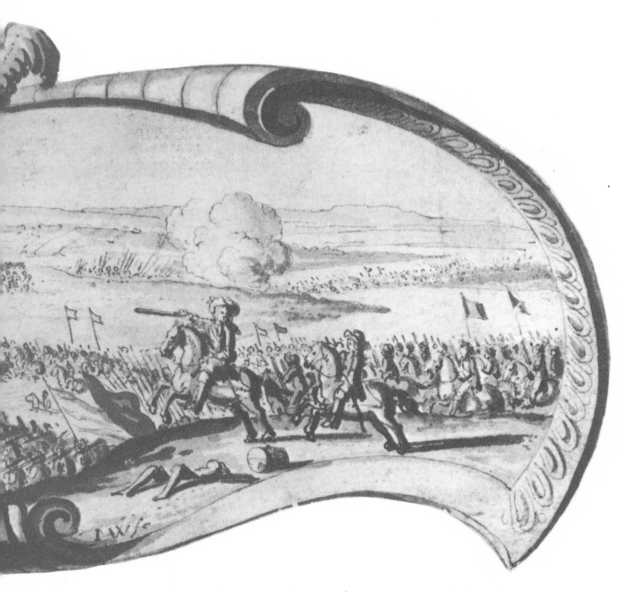

ABOVE: *An artists impression of the Battle of the Boyne.*
OVERLEAF: *The 1st Ulster Regiment of Irish Volunteers.*

lish. In all, it is estimated that approximately 11,000,000 acres of Ireland out of a total of 20,000,000 were confiscated and that these were the richest acres in all Ireland. The basic idea of this scheme was of course to make Ireland an extension of England which Cromwell now ruled as Lord Protector, but it was destined to failure. The Irish common people were needed for farm work and were, therefore, never forced to leave their homelands and many soldiers, after a quick profit, sold their grants to the highest bidder regardless of their nationality. With Cromwell's death in 1658, the real strength of the military government was removed. He had no logical successor and a return to monarchy became inevitable. It was not, however, the Royalist Irish who were responsible for restoring the monarchy in Dublin, but Cromwell's own generals. Charles II was proclaimed King of Ireland on May 14th 1660.

THE RESTORATION

After the Restoration the Earl of Ormond, who had gone into exile with Charles, was raised to dukedom and returned to Ireland as Lord Lieutenant. Charles found himself in a difficult position. He was in fact indebted to everyone in one way or another. He had had support from the Protestant Royalists like Ormond, he had also been backed by the Anglo-Irish and native Irish Catholics, and in the last event he had even been helped by the Cromwellians. He was faced with a situation in Ireland where the Cromwellians felt entitled to retain the lands which they had been granted; the Catholics felt that they should have back what had been confiscated from them. No solution was going to suit everyone. The task was left in the hands of Ormond who, in 1662, passed

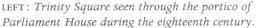

a second 'Act of Settlement' which embodied a claims court where individual cases could be heard and judged on their merits. This of course did not cure the situation since there was one lot of land with two claimants to it. In 1665 a compromise was reached through the 'Act of Explanation' which removed one third of all Cromwellian-held land and redistributed amongst the agrieved Catholics. This settlement met with bitter complaints by both sides. Despite this apparently insoluble problem, Charles II's reign was a prosperous time in Ireland. Catholics, excluded from public life and largely robbed of their lands, flourished in the field of commerce. In fact, religious tolerance was the general policy until 1678 when a Papist plot was uncovered and the English Puritan mania spread to Ireland. Oliver Plunkett, Archbishop of Dublin, and the leading light of Irish Catholicism, was then sent to London, tried and executed in a most barbarous manner.

On February 6th 1685 Charles died, and the Catholic King James II came to the throne. The reactions in Ireland were totally predictable: delight from the Catholic Irish and dismay from the Cromwellians and other Protestant settlers. This feeling was further intensified when the Duke of Ormond was removed from his post of Lord Lieutenant and replaced by a Catholic, Richard Talbot, Earl of Tyrconnel. Talbot raised a large and almost entirely Catholic army which he put at James's disposal. It was the arrival of this army and the mass emigration of Protestants from Ireland to England that became major factors in the King's unpopularity. The revolution in England drove James from his throne and he fled to Dublin and joined Tyrconnel and his army. To the Catholic Irish he was the rightful King and the internal problems of Ireland were much simpler than before. It was the Irish and Anglo-Irish versus the Protestant settlers. James brought with him military advisers from France and French troops were soon to follow. The Catholic army was in control of all Ireland except Londonderry and Enniskillen, who like Scotland and the majority of England recognized the Protestant William of Orange as King.

Parliament passed laws which effectively transferred all lands from the Protestants back into the hands of the Catholics. These measures could not be implemented, however, without a total Jacobite victory. James had to defeat the Ulster strongholds. The siege of Londonderry lasted for one hundred and five days but, despite

minimal supplies, the Protestants held out long enough for English reinforcements to arrive and force the Irish army to retreat. This gave William the breathing space he required to assemble an army. He arrived in Ireland in June 1690. In the meantime, James had received a reinforcement of seven thousand men from France. The two armies met on July 1st on the River Boyne and the Jacobite army was badly beaten. It was not, however, a conclusive military victory; the Jacobite army was dispersed rather than destroyed. On the other hand, it was politically decisive. James fled back to France and left William in control of Dublin and much of the rest of Ireland. The Irish Catholics continued to fight, not now for victory but for better terms of settlement. They found a new leader in Patrick Sarsfield who fought gallantly while there was still some hope of help from abroad. He defended Limerick doggedly but was eventually forced to negotiate a peace with the Protestants after the Catholics had been badly defeated at the Battle of Aughrim in 1691.

Perhaps the most significant feature of the Treaty of Limerick, both from a genealogical and historical point of view, was the clause which made provision to transport to the Continent those soldiers who wished to leave Ireland. This was the beginning of the 'Flight of the Wild Geese' which robbed Ireland of the cream of her Gaelic and Anglo-Irish population. It was these soldiers and their descendants who so dis-

tinguished themselves in the forces and aristocracy of Europe during the eighteenth and nineteenth centuries.

THE PROTESTANT ASCENDENCY
The end of the revolutionary wars left the Protestant Irish dominant economically, religiously and politically. They still did not feel secure, however, from the threat of a Jacobite revival. They decided to secure their position by the introduction of the infamous 'penal laws' which imposed crippling conditions on the Catholic population which were to foster a deep and bitter hatred. Worship itself was not banned but Catholics were excluded from all forms of public life including Parliament, the Army, the legal profession and the Civil Service. A Catholic could not send his children abroad to be educated; he was forbidden to acquire land from a Protestant either by purchase or inheritance. The few remaining Catholic landowners were not allowed to will their land freely: it had to be split equally between all of his children unless the eldest son became a Protestant, when he was entitled to the lot. If a Protestant landowning woman married a Catholic, she automatically forfeited her property to her Protestant next of kin. And so the laws went on, each designed to reduce systematically the Catholic land-holding and power. Of course, these laws were widely evaded but they had the desired effect for the Protestants, a fact which is illustrated by Ireland's failure to rise in sympathy with the 1715 and 1745 Jacobite rebellions. In fact, the only trace that these had any effect on the Irish at all remains in early eighteenth century Gaelic poetry which is dominated by nostalgia for the Stuart cause.

The Irish Parliament was controlled by the Church of Ireland, since both Protestant dissenters and the Catholics were prevented from taking public office. Both factions were also excluded from military service, and for the first time they had a common grievance which helped foster a sense of Irish unity. It was, however, a move without leaders. Between 1680 and 1730 more than 120,000 Irishmen enlisted in foreign armies and these were the very people who were needed by the Irish if they were to offer any serious challenge on either a political or military platform. Ireland was now governed by a despotic government held in Dublin but controlled from Westminster, aimed entirely at

NEILSON. JOHN SHEARES. WILLIAM CORBET. A. H. ROWAN. WILLIAM JACKSON MATTHEW TEELING. ROBERT EMMET. T. WOLFE TONE. T. A. EMMET. THOS. RUSSELL. LORD EDWARD FITZGERALD
MICHAEL DWYER. ARTHUR O'CONNOR. W. J. MAC NEVIN. HENRY SHEARES. J. NAPER TANDY. JAMES HOPE.
H. J. MAC CRACKEN.

THE UNITED IRISH PATRIOTS OF 1798.

promoting Conformist Irish and English interests. During the eighteenth century Ireland enjoyed her longest period of internal peace ever. They at last looked like a defeated race, a race who had given up hope. Living conditions were appalling. Dean Swift, writing in 1827, describes Ireland of the day thus "the miserable dress and diet of the people . . . The families of farmers who pay great rents living in filth and nastiness upon buttermilk and potatoes, not a shoe or stocking to their feet, or a house so convenient as an English hog-sty to receive them." It was, however, these very people who were to provide the backbone of Irish revolutionary thinking.

By 1760 a true parliamentary opposition was emerging, first under the leadership of Henry Flood and later Henry Gratton. They professed loyalty to the Hanoverians but demanded more autonomy for Ireland. This powerful minority group enjoyed the support of the Protestant

ABOVE: *An assembly of the United Irish Patriots in 1798.*
RIGHT: *Theobald Wolfe Tone.*

middle class of the North and Catholics alike. It was an uneasy alliance because many of the Protestants resenting the party's practice of putting forward Catholic policies. Gratton himself was only marginally more liberal. 'I love the Roman Catholic' he said in Dublin; 'I am a friend to his liberty, but it is only inasmuch as his liberty is entirely consistent with your ascendancy, and an addition to the strength and freedom of the Protestant community.' The 'Patriots' as they became known, steadily gathered power but their opportunity for a major breakthrough came with the accession of George III. The British Parliament decided to break the independent power of the undertakers, and to implement the necessary steps they appointed a permanent residential Lord Lieutenant to Ireland. The first of these,

Lord Townsend, arrived in Dublin in 1767. One of his first measures was to limit the life of the Irish Parliament, previously for a reign, to a maximum of eight years. This made popular representation in the Commons more fair. A second and rather less obvious benefit was derived by the 'Patriots', however, a benefit which the British probably considered. The Lord Lieutenant was a representative not only of the King but also of the British Government and his constant presence highlighted the country's lack of independence. This was one of the greatest grievances of the 'Patriots' and gained them a considerable amount of support.

By the early 1770's things were really going in the opposition's favor. The dislocation of trade, caused by British wars overseas, was causing bankruptcies and losses to many middle class moderates. The opposition also used the British troubles abroad to justify the establishment of a standing army in Ireland. The first regular company of the Irish volunteers was formed in Belfast in 1778 and, by the end of the year, units had been formed throughout the country which together far outnumbered the Government forces. While this force was ostensibly to defend Ireland's shores, it was in fact much more a political lever for the 'Patriots'. In this role it was remarkably successful. In 1780 Ireland was granted free trade conditions, and two years later the subordination of the Irish Parliament to the Westminster Privy Council was declared at an end.

The period in Irish history between 1782 and 1800 is generally called 'Grattan's Parliament'. This term is somewhat misleading because the actual administration remained in the hands of a Lord Lieutenant appointed by an English Government. Grattan had indeed brought greatly increased liberty to the Irish Parliament and, with these reforms, the question of the Roman Catholic Parliamentary representation was raised again. While the 'Patriots' had always enjoyed a minority support from the Catholics, both it and the Volunteer army were staffed exclusively by Protestants. It was still a Protestant nation. Concessions were made; the penal laws which had been less severely applied were now repealed almost entirely. This was not enough for the increasing Catholic middle class who, naturally, wanted full emancipation. This, together with their refusal to introduce all the Volunteers' parliamentary reforms, was perhaps the major weakness of 'Grattan's Parliament'. It was, however, a period of considerable prosperity in Ireland, for the middle class at least. Increased parliamentary revenues were used to encourage

trade and industry and establishment of public utilities and buildings. It was during this period that many of Dublin's finest Georgian buildings such as the Custom House and the Four Courts were constructed.

The next overseas event to effect the Irish political situation was the French Revolution which was the inspiration of the 'United Irishmen', a movement which sought to establish Ireland as a republic. They found their leader in Theobald Wolfe Tone, a young Protestant lawyer whose mother was a Catholic. The movement had its headquarters in Belfast and, while predominantly Protestant, it enjoyed considerable support from the Catholic middle class. Parliament had many members who secretly sympathized with Tone's aims, notably Lord Edward Fitzgerald who became the underground leader of the military division of the movement. At one time he boasted to have 280,000 men

George Cruikshank

ready to rise to his command.

The United Irishmen soon despaired of obtaining reform by constitutional means and concentrated on their military potential, aiming at power by armed insurrection. Wolfe Tone left for France where he was appointed Adjutant-General in the French army. From this position he argued the case for a French-led invasion of Ireland. After lengthy negotiations the French leaders agreed to let him have 15,000 men under General Hoche. This force sailed in a fleet of forty-three ships from Brest to Bantry Bay in December 1796, but a storm blew up and prevented them from landing. Discouraged, the French troops returned to France. England, now fully forewarned, passed the Insurrection Act and placed the country under martial law. The United Irishmen decided to rely upon their own strength and, while Wolfe Tone was back in France for further negotiations, there was a general insurrection. Two days before that happened in May 1798, however, Edward Fitzgerald was betrayed and died from his wounds while resisting arrest. The hard core of the uprising was demolished in a matter of three days but sporadic fighting took place, notably in Ulster and Wexford, for a period of some months. The rebels never stood a chance, armed with pikes against guns, manned by untrained troops, and led by untested leaders. In August a small force of French reinforcements arrived with Wolfe Tone but it was too late. A massive army of 30,000 men faced the Franco-Irish; they were defeated; Wolfe Tone was captured and died in prison.

The two years of martial law had been unspeakable in Ireland. Both sides had been involved in non-stop floggings, burnings and hangings. The English Government had had enough. If Irish parliament was a recipe for insurrection, they would abolish it. Pitt decided that Ireland should be governed from Westminster by a Parliament containing a block of elected Irish Members and Peers.

IRELAND UNDER THE UNION

Resistance to the 'Union' was so strong that Pitt had to resort to the most devious methods to ensure that it got through the Commons. He literally bought votes with gifts of cash or the bestowal of honors. To get popular support from the Catholics, he promised full emancipation, a promise which he failed to fulfill. In Ireland moves to repeal the 'Union' both by constitutional and unconstitutional methods were only to be expected.

The Society of United Irishmen, it must be

George Cruikshank

remembered, was a secret society and, as such, it remained after the insurrection of 1798. Their leader was now Robert Emmet, a twenty-three year old doctor's son. He followed Tone's example by visiting France to gain military strength and returned with a promise of men and arms from the War Office. He planned his insurrection for December and set about obtaining arms and gathering funds. His plans could have worked but they ended in total disaster. Thinking he had been betrayed, he put his plans forward to July and so the 1803 uprising ended as a series of drunken skirmishes. Emmet was tried, convicted and hanged at the age of 25. His attempt at revolution had been chaotic but he became a symbol of patriotism to all young Ireland.

This was a time of apalling contrasts in the social standards in Ireland. As Dublin prospered, the country people continued to live in one-roomed mud shacks, living on a potato diet. Even better-off farmers were living in complete squalor. A street ballad of the day expresses the resentment felt by these tenants against the landlords who extorted exorbitant rents from them:
Our absentee landlords have left us,
In London they cut a great dash,
While their tenants at home in poor Ireland
Must pay them the rent in hard cash.

ABOVE AND LEFT: *Two scenes from the uprising of 1798.*
OVERLEAF: *The capture of Wolfe Tone.*

The three and a half million Catholics in Ireland, out of a total population of four and a half million, were almost all living below subsistance level. There were, however, still a few middle class Catholics who were well educated and influential; one such man was Daniel O'Connell. He had studied in France until the outbreak of the French Revolution, finished his legal training in London and was called to the Bar in 1798. He returned to Dublin where, apart from establishing a formidable practice, he became the champion of the Catholic cause. In 1923, with the help of another barrister, Richard Lalor Sheil, he formed the 'Catholic Association'. The aims of the movement were two-fold, to obtain a complete repeal of the penal laws promised under the act of Union, and to protect Irish tenant farmers from the harshness of absentee landlords. The movement won immediate support from all sectors of Catholic society, from merchant to farmer and from priest to peasant. The scheme was financed by a membership fee of one penny a month, which at one stage amounted to several hundred pounds a week. O'Connell had seen two disastrous attempts to change the course of Irish history by

ABOVE: *The execution of Robert Emmet.*

RIGHT: *Robert Emmet whose unsuccessful insurrection was the inspiration of the Young Irelanders.*

insurrection and was intent on using mass public opinion in a way that could neither be ignored nor punished. Their first real opportunity to test the effectiveness of O'Connell's policies came with the Waterford Election of 1926. The Catholic Association put up Mr. Villers Stuart, a Protestant, as a candidate. His opponent was George Beresford who owned huge estates in the district and whose family had sat in parliament for several decades. Beresford was decisively beaten and the 'Association' had struck their first blow.

An even more resounding victory came two years later when O'Connell himself stood as a candidate in the by-election for County Clare. This time the opposition was much stiffer. Mr. Vesey Fitzgerald was seeking re-election after being appointed as President of the Board of Trade. O'Connell won the seat by 2054 votes to 1075. He appeared in Parliament but, on being offered the oath of allegiance, had to withdraw as a Catholic. The rejoicing throughout Ireland must have been something to experience.

The Duke of Wellington, Prime Minister of the day, realized the threat of an armed insurrection and recommended Parliament to pass the 'Catholic Relief Bill', which gave Catholics the right to sit in Parliament and to hold other public offices. This was duly pushed through both the House of Commons and the House of Lords in April 1929. But there was a catch. Another bill was passed at the same time which raised the voting qualifications for Ireland from 40 shillings to ten pounds, which meant many of O'Connell's most staunch supporters no longer had the vote. It was, however, the turning-point in the Catholic fight against oppression.

When the Whigs obtained power in 1830, O'Connell started campaigning in earnest for the repeal of the Union. But he was consistently defeated and had to content himself with promises of enlightened reform. Yet the English government failed to understand the gravity of the situation in Ireland. In 1840, O'Connell returned to Dublin and formed the 'National Repeal Association' in which he proposed to employ the same tactics that had brought him success in his fight for Catholic emancipation. Initially, the movement failed to attract the

111

Merrion Square
20th Nov – 1834

30

My dear Sir

You may imagine _how_ I am surrounded
but I am most desirous to see you – It however
must (for reasons) be _here_ – I want to thank
you most heartily for all the Good – the
unmixed good you have done for Ireland and
the still greater good your visit and your
Knowledge of the state of this country must
produce – I will (be) at home all the evening
and all the morning tomorrow – and all
the time – Anglicé – any time you chuse

Accept my warmest thanks in the name
and on behalf of Ireland – and believe me
always – with sincere regard
                    very faithfully Yours
                         Daniel O'Connell

Wm Cobbett Esq
      M. L.

REJOICINGS AT THE LIBERATION OF DANIEL O'CONNELL: NIGHT SCENE IN A DUBLIN STREET.
From I.L.N. Sept. 14, 1844.

massive support which O'Connell expected. This was probably because the masses were less aware of the need for repeal than they had been for emancipation.

In 1842, the 'Repeal Association' was joined by the three 'Young Irelanders': Thomas Osborne Davis, Charles Gavan Duffy and John Blake Dillon. These three young Irish patriots had recently founded their weekly newspaper, *The Nation,* which was to prove a vital and powerful mouthpiece for future republican politics. O'Connell was now approaching seventy and his hopes for success soared with the recruitment of these three young intellectuals. None of them was yet thirty and they had boundless energy and enthusiasm to lend to the cause. Apart from journalistic campaigning, they organized what they called 'Monster Meetings'. It was at one of these that the first serious defeat in the campaign was encountered. A mass rally had been organized at Clontarf in October 1843 but Robert Peel, the Prime Minister, banned it and mobilized troops. O'Connell cancelled the meeting, fearing bloodshed, but was arrested shortly afterwards

LEFT: *A letter from Daniel O'Connell to William Cobbett MP thanking him for his support for Catholic emmancipation.*
ABOVE: *Rejoicing when Daniel O'Connor was released from prison in September 1844.*

and convicted of seditious conspiracy and imprisoned. He was released the following September but, by that time his health was failing and attention was being drawn away from him by the 'Young Irelanders', who were campaigning for more militant tactics. Their ranks were swelling and they favored the philosophy of Wolfe Tone and Emmet. They did, in fact, organize an insurrection in 1848 but it was a miserable failure. The event was even less memorable because, at that time, Ireland was in the midst of the most dreadful castastrophe of her catastrophic history – the Great Famine.

THE POTATO FAMINE

Since the turn of the nineteenth century Ireland had undergone a population explosion. Most experts believe that it more than doubled in the years between 1800 and 1840. The potato had been the staple diet of the masses since it was

PREVIOUS PAGE: *Conditions in the average Irish country home during the eighteenth century. Punitive rents and absentee landlords made survival difficult.*
ABOVE: *Distress and famine in Western Ireland.*
RIGHT: *A satirical look at the Young Irelanders.*

introduced to Ireland at the end of the sixteenth century and the potato blight hit Ireland in the autumn of 1845. Government action to stem the disease was to no avail and more than half the crop was destroyed. In 1845 and 1847 the blight was even more virulent and the devastation of the crops even more extensive. It is impossible to imagine the total misery and desperation of the Irish in this terrible time. The government was faced with an impossible task of famine relief, and control of typhus and cholera. It is thought that starvation and disease were responsible for more than 1,000,000 deaths in the period of the famine.

The winter of 1846-47 was one of the worst ever recorded and even those who had found shelter in soup kitchens or workhouses were ridden with disease. The only hope of survival was emigration to America and it is estimated that a further 1,000,000 left Ireland, but what proportion ever reached their destination can only be guessed at. Profiteers were using all types of craft entirely unsuited to the Atlantic and many of them foundered. Thousands of others were so diseased or hungry that they were unable to stand the rigors of the journey. It is little wonder that these were known as the 'Coffin Ships'. A monument on Grosse Isle, Quebec carries this horrific inscription
In this secluded spot lie the mortal remains of 5,294 persons, who, flying from pestilence and famine in Ireland in the year 1847, found in America but a grave.
It was in these tragic and appalling circumstances that the great Irish-American population has its roots.

THE RISE OF THE FENIANS
After the failure of the 1848 uprising, James Stephens and John O'Mahony, two of the 'Young Ireland' leaders, escaped via Paris to

YOUNG IRELAND IN BUSINESS FOR HIMSELF.

America where they formed a political society called the *Emmet Monument Association*. They were joined by other expatriate 'Young Irelanders' and republican sympathizers and changed the name of their movement to the *Fenian Brotherhood*. Their aims were simple. They wanted to take power in Ireland by force and without compromise. Through their own publications they spread anti-British propaganda which was readily accepted by the majority of the Irish-American population, particularly those who had been forced to flee from the horrors of the potato famine.

In 1858 Stephens left America to whip up support in Ireland and was soon in contact with a movement called the Phoenix Society. Their policies were similar and they merged to form the Irish Republican Brotherhood. Thousands of

young Irishmen flocked to join the Irish-based 'Fenians' and they started to plan their insurrection. It was basically a working-class movement with an intellectual leadership, which had neither resources nor experience to challenge the government. They looked to their more prosperous brothers in America for these resources.

All the indications are that these would have been supplied if the American Civil War had not broken out in 1861. Thousands of Fenians fought on both sides in the War, some for patriotic reasons and others to gain military experience. Whatever the reason, many of them died in the fighting, others were discouraged and the whole operation was certainly delayed until the war was over in 1865. When the Fenian leaders did arrive in Ireland in that year, they did not receive the open-armed welcome they expected. They of

ABOVE: *Emigration was the only escape from the potato famine. Whole communities were destroyed.*

course expected opposition from all government circles but they had not allowed for the outright condemnation of many Church leaders and the resentment of other Irish-based nationalist groups. While they prepared their rising, they were constantly dogged by betrayals and arrests, but eventually plans were made for February 1867 under the leadership of John Stephens. Much of the support expected from America was not forthcoming because of a split in the party. Bad communications also dogged the plans. A last minute postponement did not reach two units in time and they went ahead and attacked and, by the time the real date came for the Dublin uprising, the government was well prepared.

That is certainly more than could be said for the Fenian forces under Colonel Kelly; their attempts were about as chaotic as the two previous insurrections. The Fenians were not disbanded, however, they continued to operate and to be an important influence on Irish Republican thinking. The uprising also kept Irish discontent in the public eye both in Ireland and England, where, after a few years of stability, they must have started to think that they had solved the Irish question.

The next champion of the cause of Irish independence was Isaac Butt, a man of more moderate views. He was a Protestant barrister who had been a Unionist member of Parliament; he had been so horrified by the famine that he had become convinced that Ireland should have control over all domestic affairs. He certainly did not approve of Fenian methods but he had sufficient sympathy with their aims to defend several prisoners arrested during the 1865–67 plot. He founded the Home Rule Party in 1870 and four years later managed to win more than half the Irish seats at Westminster. Even this powerful lobby was not able to persuade the House and, once again, a moderate was ousted by those impatient for quicker and more effective tactics. His place as head of the Home Rule Party was taken by Charles Stewart Parnell. He and Joseph Biggar MP adopted a disruptive policy by which they brought parliamentary procedure at Westminster to a standstill. The struggle produced another great leader of Irish freedom, Michael Davitt. Davitt was a Fenian who had been arrested in the arms raid on Chester Castle and spent seven years in prison. He was released in 1877 and went to America where he became one of the leading lights of the Fenian movement. He was undecided on his policy for Ireland and when he returned was open to persuasion between armed insurrection and constitutional methods. He reached Ireland in 1879 to find a situation of near famine; bad crops and falling export prices were crippling the farmers. He decided the first priority was to sort out the land situation. He formed the Land League,

whose aims were to assure fixed rents, fair rents, and the freedom to sell. He started his campaign with a series of mass demonstrations but soon realized that these were not enough and made an alliance with Parnell, and together they formed the New Departure.

The Land League was not purely a political movement: it also organized practical help for the distressed. Parnell went to America the following year and raised almost 200,000 dollars for the scheme. Unlike the Fenians, the Land League had the active support of the Church, who threw all their weight behind fund raising and administration. Despite all their efforts, however, evictions continued. The League's techniques to discourage unfairness brought a new word into the English language: 'boycotting'. Captain Charles Boycott, a land owner from County Mayo, defied the Land League and he and his family were soon ostracized by their neighbors. This was in effect a continuation of the disruption techniques applied earlier to parliamentary procedure. Under existing law, the Government was powerless to act against the Land League. Despite the turmoil

RIGHT: Punch *examines the Fenian movement in 1866.*
BELOW: *Attack on the Prison van in Manchester and the rescue of the Fenian leaders.*

THE FENIAN-PEST.

HIBERNIA. "O MY DEAR SISTER, WHAT *ARE* WE TO DO WITH THESE TROUBLESOME PEOPLE?"
BRITANNIA. "TRY ISOLATION FIRST, MY DEAR, AND THEN————"

LEFT: *Charles Stuart Parnell.*
ABOVE: *The rent war in Ireland. A priest has chained himself to the entrance to prevent eviction.*

it was causing, it was in fact a lawful organization and so Gladstone applied for special powers to cover the emergency. Devitt and Parnell were arrested and imprisoned. This had the predictable result of escalating the situation. In 1881, Gladstone was forced to pass another Land Act which, though undoubtedly well meaning, was full of holes. It made no provision for those tenants who were already in arrears and no guidance as to what a tenant could consider a fair rent. The trouble continued; Gladstone was forced to seek an alliance with Parnell and Davitt. This was achieved and some of the coercion ceased. Successive provisions were made to make loans available to tenant farmers who wished to purchase their holdings outright. Davitt's land and rent reforms were now achieved but the policy which obsessed both him and Parnell was Home Rule and that was still anything but a reality. Neither of them would be happy with anything short of complete severance with Westminster. Parnell, with more than eighty members of parliament behind him, decided that this too might be achieved by constitutional means and, when Gladstone was returned to power in 1886, their negotiations began. To-

gether they drew up the first Home Rule Bill and presented it to Parliament in 1886. It was defeated by a mere thirty votes with the Liberal Party split and heavy opposition from both the Unionists, mainly from Ulster, and a section of the Tory party. The support for the bill was, however, getting increasing support in England, Ireland and the United States. By this stage Parnell and Gladstone were working closely together with what they both believed to be a fair solution.

Then tragedy struck. Parnell was named as the co-respondent in a divorce case with Kitty, the legendary wife of Captain O'Shea. There was a predictable moral outrage. Some of Parnell's own party stood behind him but Gladstone declared that, should Parnell continue, he would be forced to resign as the leader of the party and the Catholic bishops were also universally critical of Parnell's misconduct. Even in his own party there were suggestions that he should resign, at least until the air was clear. This Parnell refused to do and there was a resultant division in his own Home Rule Party. Parnell was determined to regain his leadership but the struggle was too great and, on October 7 1891, he died in Brighton worn out at the age of forty-five. Yet another great Irish leader had died on what appeared to be the eve of victory.

Success, however, was not to come that easily to the Home Rule Party nor indeed to Gladstone who continued the fight for the cause after Parnell's death. In 1892, he introduced the second Home Rule Bill; this was carried in the Commons but the House of Lords rejected it by a massive majority. There appeared to be no way that the Lords, who felt they had already abandoned the Irish landlords, would ever concede to this policy. Gladstone himself retired in 1894 and died four years later. Like Parnell, he was never to see an independent Ireland, and his policies had been disastrous for his party. With the exception of three brief years, they put the Tories into power from 1896 to 1906, which dashed all hopes of a Home Rule Bill being introduced.

THE RE-BIRTH OF NATIONALISM

The most important move towards revitalizing nationalism came, ironically, not through the groups formed for strictly political reasons. One evening in 1893, seven men met in a small room in Dublin. They were all Gaelic scholars with a mutual concern to preserve the language. To this end they decided to form a cultural society which was to be called the Gaelic League. The two leading lights of the society, Eoin MacNeill and Douglas Hyde, could not have foreseen the enormous implications of the movement which, as well as preserving Ireland's cultural heritage, was destined to become the most important source of inspiration in the Irish fight for independence.

Initially, their persuits were strictly cultural. They had their own paper, the *Gaelic Journal*, which was edited by Father Eugene O'Growney and carried stories in both English and modern Irish. It also published lessons in basic Irish and, despite a slow start, it became the 'in' thing to speak Irish. The league had branches throughout Ireland, England and the United States and what is surprising is that it attracted every social group and every religious persuasion. Perhaps, for the first time, they felt that being *IRISH* was something of real importance and this made other barriers irrelevant. The Gaelic League was giving the country an identity, a difference which justified her becoming independent.

A few years earlier another establishment was launched which also aimed to promote a sense of Irish identity. In November 1884, Michael Cusack and Maurice Davin formed the Gaelic Athletic Association. Its purpose was to protect and promote traditional Irish games which were being threatened by the wholesale introduction of

RIGHT: *Parnells tactics of 'Obstruction' in the house of commons is defeated when he is ordered out of the house by the Speaker.*

English sports. The Association immediately received the wholehearted patronage of the Archbishop of Cashel and this support was in no small way responsible for its rapid expansion. They established the rules for hurling and Gaelic football and, while not initially basically political, their ranks were soon infiltrated with straight political thinkers. By 1887 they had attracted the attention of the Fenians, who were still a powerful influence on republican thinking. They realized the potential of this large band of able-bodied young men committed to an Irish identity. So, by the end of the nineteenth century, there were two powerful groups, one intellectual, the other athletic, with a highly developed awareness of being Irish. Meanwhile in Parliament they were pursuing a policy of 'Killing Home Rule by Kindness', by introducing liberal reforms in Ireland. The Congested Districts Board was established to improve conditions on the uneconomic smallholdings in the west of Ireland. Another Act replaced grand juries by elected councils. Perhaps the most dramatic change came in 1903 when the Irish Secretary, George Wyndham, passed the Land Purchase Act. This offered generous inducements to landowners to sell their estates to the Land Commission which, in turn, sold them to the tenant farmers on easy terms.

The Nationalist party, split under Parnell, was united once again under the leadership of John Redmond, but hope of Home Rule was remote while the Lords' veto continued. When the Liberals returned to power in 1906 things looked better but the Irish Councils Bill, which offered some reform, was rejected by the Irish Lobby. The Liberals did, however, offer several concessions which were accepted including the National University Act of 1907. The best chance of getting a Home Rule Bill through came when the government was waging a campaign against the Lords and offered independence as a reward for Irish support in the House. In the election of 1910, Redmond had achieved the balance of power and both Liberal and Labor parties were committed to giving Independence. The Home Rule Bill was eventually passed in 1912 and was to be implemented in 1914 if it passed a second reading by the same Parliament.

The Unionists in the North, who wanted Ireland to remain as part of the British Isles, were determined to stop the Act from being introduced. Andrew Bonar Law had replaced A. J. Balfour as leader of the Unionist party in 1911 and he supported threats of armed resistance to the Act. They soon realized that there was no hope for defeating the Home Rule Bill in its

entirety and so they had fallen back on the suggestion that Ulster should be excluded from the independence settlement. Even this claim had its problems because there were 17 Nationalist Members of Parliament and only 16 Unionists in the province of Ulster. Parliament, therefore, ignored Ulster's demands as undemocratic.

The Ulster Volunteer Force was then formed with George Richardson as its Commander in Chief. Arms were imported illegally and, despite this, the force received open support from Bonar Law and other Unionist MPs. Not only were the Volunteers openly organized in defiance of Westminster but they boasted the support of the official army. This claim was proved true by the Curragh Mutiny in March 1914 when all the officers of a cavalry brigade threatened to resign if they were ordered into Ulster. It was perhaps

to prevent a severe loss of face that the order was not given, because by this time regular raids were being operated against Ulster arms depots. The worst moment came for Westminster when a shipment of more than 24,000 German rifles and five million rounds of ammunition was landed at Larne. The British War Minister was forced to resign and Asquith took charge of the situation himself.

While the Irish Volunteers gained strength in the North, there were counter measures in the South with the foundation of the Irish Volunteers. The Nationalists were naturally warned that the presence of an army in the North would delay or even prevent the enforcement of the Home Rule Bill. They formed units of Irish Volunteers throughout Ireland but the heaviest concentration was in the North. By summer 1914, civil war

ABOVE: *The 2nd Royal Sussex Regiment in reserve at the Belfast docks in August 1907.*

looked an inevitability. In July, a conference was held at Buckingham Palace where the leaders of the two sides discussed terms. At first the Unionists insisted on a complete abandonment of the Home Rule Bill but later they were forced to accept an agreement which excluded the six Ulster counties from the Home Rule Bill — Antrim, Down, Derry, Armagh, Fermanagh and Tyrone. In principle there was an agreement but on August 4 1914, England declared war on Germany. The conference was adjourned and the enforcement of the Bill in any form was postponed. Redmond promised full Irish sympathy for the British cause. He renamed the two volunteer forces as the National Volunteers who,

he guaranteed, would fight for the British cause both as coastal defence and for campaigns overseas. In addition to this he embarked on a highly successful recruiting campaign for Irish regiments in the British Army. Redmond's promises that Unionists and Nationalists would serve side by side was an empty boast. Lord Kitchener's mistrust of Irish regiments generally hardened barriers within them. The original Irish Volunteers had been largely recruited from the old Fenian, Irish Republican Brotherhood and they saw the situation as an opportunity to press for full Republican status. Ulster's successful bid to gain Union status and the delay in enforcing the Home Rule Bill had brought the Anti-English feeling in the South to the boil once again. Steps were taken to gain help from Germany and the plans for the Easter Rising of 1916 were well

formed before the end of 1914. Recruiting and training of the Irish Volunteers was started once again but most of the army, including its Commander, Eoin MacNeill, were kept in the dark about plans for an insurrection.

The actual day of the uprising was planned for Easter Sunday. A coded order was placed in the Volunteers own paper and this should have brought some 10,000 men into action. In fact only a fifth of that number were actually involved in the fighting. MacNeill himself was not let into the insurrection plans until the Thursday before Easter. He then realized that his force was too small to effect a coup and gave orders to cancel. The next day, however, news came through of the German ship *Aud* loaded with additional arms and ammunition and this gave new hope, but the *Aud* was captured off the Irish Coast and Sir Roger Casement, the Irish Missionary to Germany, was arrested and MacNeill once again gave the order to cancel.

Patrick Pearse and James Connolly, leaders of

LEFT: *Ulsters opponents, the Irish Nationalist Volunteers parading in Dublin during 1914.*
ABOVE LEFT: *Countess Markievicz.*
ABOVE RIGHT: *Roger Casement.*

the Irish Republican Brotherhood, were determined to go ahead and countermanded MacNeill's orders and the Irish Volunteers marched into Dublin. They failed to capture their primary target, Dublin Castle, but James Connolly took the General Post Office and adorned it with a large banner proclaiming THE IRISH REPUBLIC, and hoisted a Republican tricolor. Patrick Pearse then read the proclamation of the Provisional Government of the Irish Republic:

> "Irishmen and Irishwomen: In the name of God and of a dead generation from which she received her old tradition of nationhood, Ireland, through us summons her children to the flag and strikes for her freedom".

This proclamation was signed by Thomas J.

Clarke, Sean MacDiarmada, Thomas MacDonagh, P. H. Pearse, Eamonn Ceannt, James Connolly and Joseph Plunkett.

The Volunteers also established positions in other parts of Dublin. Michael Mallin and Countess Markievicz took St Stephen's Green; Edward Daly occupied the four Courts; Eamon de Valera captured Bolands Mills. The Volunteers failure to capture the Castle and to break communications with the outside were to prove their downfall. There followed a week of street fighting and looting but on Saturday 29th April it was all over. Pearse was forced to admit defeat and surrendered to General Maxwell. All the leaders were executed with the exception of de Valera and Countess Markievicz, who were both given life sentences. The followers suffered also. More than three thousand men were arrested and sent to prison camps in England. It was in these camps that the Republicans planned their next campaign.

THE TROUBLES

Most of the internees were released from their camps just before Christmas 1916 and returned to a heroes' welcome. Those who had been shot were already martyrs. The atmosphere was ripe for Republicanism by popular consent.

The Sinn Fein Party, which had been formed back in 1905 by Arthur Griffith, editor of the Republican paper, *The Nation,* gathered momentum and, despite a government decree supressing the movement, had a membership of more than 100,000 by 1918.

The General Election was held in December of 1918 and Sinn Fein won 73 seats, the Unionists 26 and the Irish Parliamentary Party only got six. Many of the Sinn Fein candidates were those who had been interned in England during the War. Others, including de Valera, were still inside. All of them refused to take their seats at Westminster and instead declared an independent parliament, Dail Eireann, in Dublin. De Valera, despite being in prison, was elected leader of the Dail with Arthur Griffith as his Deputy. On January 1st the Dail sat for the first time and on that same day the shooting started in the streets of Dublin. There was to be two years of bloodshed before the Irish could achieve their aims, a free state recognized throughout the world. Even then it was an Ireland without Ulster; and when the shooting will end in the streets of that sad province is a question for a prophet, not an historian.

LEFT: *A Sinn Fein sentry on the roof of Liberty Hall.*
TOP RIGHT: *A declaration of intent by Sinn Fein.*
BELOW RIGHT: *Street fighting during the 1916 uprising.*
OVERLEAF: *The legendary declaration of Independence.*

POBLACHT NA H EIREANN.

THE PROVISIONAL GOVERNMENT
OF THE

IRISH REPUBLIC

TO THE PEOPLE OF IRELAND.

IRISHMEN AND IRISHWOMEN : In the name of God and of the dead generations from which she receives her old tradition of nationhood, Ireland, through us, summons her children to her flag and strikes for her freedom.

Having organised and trained her manhood through her secret revolutionary organisation, the Irish Republican Brotherhood, and through her open military organisations, the Irish Volunteers and the Irish Citizen Army, having patiently perfected her discipline, having resolutely waited for the right moment to reveal itself, she now seizes that moment, and, supported by her exiled children in America and by gallant allies in Europe, but relying in the first on her own strength, she strikes in full confidence of victory.

We declare the right of the people of Ireland to the ownership of Ireland, and to the unfettered control of Irish destinies, to be sovereign and indefeasible. The long usurpation of that right by a foreign people and government has not extinguished the right, nor can it ever be extinguished except by the destruction of the Irish people. In every generation the Irish people have asserted their right to national fre

134

... of the world, we hereby proclaim the Irish Republic as a Sovereign Independent State, and we pledge our lives and the lives of our comrades-in-arms to the cause of its freedom, of its welfare, and of its exaltation among the nations.

The Irish Republic is entitled to, and hereby claims, the allegiance of every Irishman and Irishwoman. The Republic guarantees religious and civil liberty, equal rights and equal opportunities to all its citizens, and declares its resolve to pursue the happiness and prosperity of the whole nation and of all its parts, cherishing all the children of the nation equally, and oblivious of the differences carefully fostered by an alien government, which have divided a minority from the majority in the past.

Until our arms have brought the opportune moment for the establishment of a permanent National Government, representative of the whole people of Ireland and elected by the suffrages of all her men and women, the Provisional Government, hereby constituted, will administer the civil and military affairs of the Republic in trust for the people.

We place the cause of the Irish Republic under the protection of the Most High God, Whose blessing we invoke upon our arms, and we pray that no one who serves that cause will dishonour it by cowardice, inhumanity, or rapine. In this supreme hour the Irish nation must, by its valour and discipline and by the readiness of its children to sacrifice themselves for the common good, prove itself worthy of the august destiny to which it is called.

Signed on Behalf of the Provisional Government,

THOMAS J. CLARKE.
SEAN Mac DIARMADA, THOMAS MacDONAGH,
P. H. PEARSE, EAMONN CEANNT,
JAMES CONNOLLY. JOSEPH PLUNKETT.

GREAT IRISH FAMILIES

Barrett

GAELIC: Baróid, Bairéid

This name was introduced into Ireland in the late 12th century by two distinct Anglo-Norman families. One settled in Co. Cork and the other in the Mayo-Galway area. The southern Barretts, who gave their name to Barretts Country in Co. Cork, were more prolific than the northern Barretts, but it was the Connacht family which played a greater role in Irish history. These Barretts founded a sept on the Irish model and in time came to possess much of the land in northern Mayo.

George Barret (1728-1784), Dublin-born landscape painter, was one of the original members of the Royal Academy. He came to London in 1762 and with Burke's influence was appointed master painter to Chelsea Hospital. But his most important work is the decoration of a room at Norbury Park, near Leatherhead. He died on May 29, 1784 and was buried in Paddington Church. His son, also George, about whose life little is known before 1795, was also an accomplished painter. He exhibited regularly at the Royal Academy and was one of the founding members of the Society of Painters in Watercolours. He died in 1842.

Rev. John Barrett (1752-1821), Vice-Provost and Professor of Oriental Languages at Trinity College, Dublin, was noted for his classical studies and, in particular, for his discovery of a 6th century text of the Gospel of St. Matthew.

The American actor Lawrence Barrett (1838-1891) was born in Paterson, New Jersey, the son of an Irish emigrant. In his day he was a famed Shakespearean actor with Booth's Theater in New York. He died on March 20, 1891, and was buried in Cohasset, Massachussetts.

Barry

GAELIC: Ó'Báire, Ó'Beargha

This is one of the names brought to Ireland by the Anglo-Norman invaders in the 12th century. The most prominent of the early Barrys was Philip de Barri, who, in 1179, obtained extensive grants of land in what is now Co. Cork. His descendants prospered and soon became established in the area, forming several septs along Irish lines. Today nearly half the Barrys in Ireland live in Co. Cork and the majority of the rest are also found in the southern part of the country, within the boundaries of the province of Munster.

"Lo" Barry, born in Co. Cork *c.* 1591, is generally regarded as the first Irish dramatist. His fame rests on his comedy *Ram Alley, or Merry Tricks,* produced in London in 1610. Barry's Christian name is thought to be James, but he is called "Lo" – perhaps an abbreviation for "Lording" of "the Honourable" – because his name appeared as Lo Barry on the title page of his play. The date of his death is unknown.

The most famous of the American-Irish Barrys is John Barry (1745-1803), known as the "father of the American navy". Born in Co. Wexford, Barry went to sea as a cabin boy and eventually became master of a merchant ship sailing out of Philadelphia. He

Spangler Barry

settled there around 1770. At the outbreak of the Revolutionary War he offered his services to Congress and, in March 1776, he was commissioned a Captain and put in command of the *Lexington*. One month later the *Lexington* became the first ship of the American navy to capture a British warship and Barry at once found himself a national hero. After the war Barry returned to commanding merchant ships, but he continued off and on to help with the organization of the American navy. He died on September 13, 1803 and was buried in the graveyard of St. Mary's Church in Philadelphia. An Irish postage stamp commemorates Barry and in 1956 the American government erected a monument to him in Wexford town.

Spangler Barry (1719-1772), born in Skinner Row, Dublin, was an Irish actor of "fine voice and figure" who shared the stage with Garrick when he first came to London in the 1740's. Later the two also played in rival performances of Shakespeare plays staged at Drury Lane, Garrick's theater, and Covent Garden, where Barry acted, and it was Barry who often got the nod from the critics. Barry also had a go at setting up theaters in Dublin and Cork, but he subsequently returned to acting in London. He died in that city on January 10, 1772.

James Barry (1741-1805), of Cork, was a promising young painter whose work attracted the attention of Burke in 1763. Burke brought him to London to meet the leading painters of the day and also made it possible for him to study painting on the Continent for four years. He returned to England in 1770 with ambitious plans for painting grand historical subjects, but only one of his large-scale projects was ever realized. This was the decoration for the Society of the Arts in the Adelphi.

John Milner Barry (1768-1822) is known for first introducing vaccination in Ireland. Born in Cork, he studied medicine at Edinburgh. After graduating from there in 1792 he returned to Cork and later founded the Cork Fever Hospital.

Michael Joseph Barry (1817-1889), barrister, poet, and celebrated wit, was born in Cork. He was an enthusiastic Young Irelander until 1848, when he was imprisoned for his part in the uprisings of that year. After being released he changed his politics and profession and became a police magistrate in Dublin. He wrote several volumes of peotry, contributed to *Punch* in its early days, and wrote leaders for the London *Times*.

Blake

GAELIC: Ó Blathmhaic
COMMON VARIATIONS: Blowick

The Blakes were one of the 14 Tribes of Galway. They are descended from Richard Caddell, le Bláca, who was Sheriff of Connacht in 1303. The epithet le Bláca, which means black, became Blake and for several generations was more or less interchangeable with Caddell. For over three hundred years the family appears in the records of the City of Galway either as "Caddell alias Blake" or "Blake alias Caddell". But by the 17th century the name Caddell has been dropped altogether in favor of Blake. The family were extensive landowners in Co. Galway and a branch also settled in

Co. Kildare where they gave their name to Blakestown.

The Blakes played an active part in the civic and religious affairs of the city of Galway, and on a wider scale they were represented at the Assembly of Confederate Catholics at Kilkenny in 1647 by Sir Richard Blake who chaired the Assembly.

The American actor William Rufus Blake (1805-1863) was a descendant of the Blakes of Galway. Born in Halifax, Nova Scotia, he first appeared on stage in America as a light comedian at the old Chatham Theater in New York in 1824. Besides acting, he also had a hand in managing several American theaters, including the Tremont in Boston, the Walnut St. Theater in Philadelphia, and Mitchell's Olympic Theater in New York. He was a member of the stock companies of several New York theaters, but he was most closely associated with Wallack's and is said to have been the highest paid actor on their stock list. Contemporary accounts describe him as "richly humorous" and "so noble in his dignity, so firm and fine and easy in his method, so copious in his natural humor". His "immense rotundity" in later years is said to have "ultimately placed him among the greatest of modern comedians".

Edward Blake (1833-1912), Canadian lawyer and statesman, was the son of William Hume Blake (1809-1870), who emigrated from Ireland and held a chief post in the Canadian judiciary. His son followed in his legal footsteps and was an early authority on the Canadian constitution. In 1871 he was elected Prime Minister of Ontario, and from 1875-1877 he served as Minister of Justice in Alexander Mackenzie's Dominion cabinet. He was leader of the Liberal party from 1880-1887 and from 1892-1907 he represented the Irish nationalists in the British House of Commons where his advice proved helpful on the drafting of the Home Rule Bill of 1893. His greatest contribution to the Irish cause was in raising funds in Canada and the United States to keep the Irish parliamentary party alive. Blake retired in 1907 and died at Toronto in March, 1912.

O'Boyle

GAELIC: Ó Baoighill
COMMON VARIATIONS: Boyle, Boylan

Although the derivation of this name from old Irish is uncertain, it is certainly a native Irish surname. The O'Boyles were a strong sept in Co. Donegal and together with the O'Donnells and the O'Doughertys they commanded the northwest of Ireland. This is still O'Boyle territory. The highest concentration of the name in Ireland today occurs in the Ulster counties of Donegal, Tyrone and Armagh. But the best known Boyles of Ireland came from English stock, and in particular from the Anglo-Irish family fathered by Richard Boyle.

Born in Canterbury in 1566, Richard Boyle went to Ireland in 1588 and there became what has been termed the "first colonial millionaire". He is a prime example of the new magnate type who replaced the lords and chiefs of Ireland. He acquired vast amounts of land, including 12,000 acres owned by Sir Walter Raleigh in Cos. Waterford, Cork and Tipperary, which he left to his large family upon his death in 1643. From 1606 onwards Boyle held high posts for the English government in Ireland and, in 1620, he was named Earl of Cork.

The most well known of the Anglo-Irish Boyles was Robert Boyle (1627-1691), the famous experimental physicist. He was the 7th son and 14th child of Richard Boyle. Born at Lismore Castle, Co. Waterford, on January 23, 1627, he was sent to school at Eton at the age of eight. From 1628 to 1644 he studied on the Continent. When he returned to England his father had just died, but it wasn't until 1652 that he returned to Ireland to visit the estates he had inherited. At that time Boyle found Ireland "a barbarous country, where chemical spirits were so misunderstood, that it was hard to have any hermetic thoughts in it." So he returned to England the next year and set up a private laboratory at Oxford which was then the center of scientific thought in the country. After a few years he moved to London where he was instrumental in the setting up of the Royal Society which was granted a charter by Charles II in 1662. Boyle served as its first President. He is perhaps best remembered for his improvements to the vacuum pump and for the formulation of Boyle's law, which states that "if the temperature and quantity of a gas remain constant, volume varies inversely with pressure." Boyle's only other interest besides science was religion. He wrote many books on religious subjects and in 1684 paid £700 to have the Old Testament printed in Irish for the first time. He died on December 30, 1691, in London and was buried in the Church of St. Martin in the Fields.

Roger Boyle (1621-1679), soldier, statesman, dramatist and first Earl of Orrery, was the most famous of Richard's sons in military and political spheres. He was particularly prominent as a leader of Commonwealth forces during the Cromwell campaign in Ireland. In 1677 he published a *Treatise on the Art of War* and was also a writer of poetry and drama.

The best known of the Gaelic-Irish Boyles was William Boyle (1853-1922). Born in Dromisln, he wrote poetry describing Irish country life. But his fame rests on his accomplishments as a playwright. He was one of the first writers for the Abbey Theater. His plays include *The Building Fund, The Eloquent Dempsey, The Talk of a Town*, and *The Mineral Workers*. He died in London in 1922.

MacBrady

GAELIC: Mac Brádaigh
COMMON VARIATIONS: O'Grady, Brady

The MacBradys were a powerful sept in the ancient territory of Breffny (Cos. Cavan and West Leitrim) whose seat was located a few miles east of Cavan town. Many illustrious MacBrady chiefs were responsible for firmly establishing the name in this area and hence it has come to be traditionally associated with Co. Cavan. It is here where the largest percentage of Bradys in Ireland are found today. There are also several Brady families in east Clare near the village of Tuamgraney. But this is a result of a peculiarity of the O'Grady family in that area who changed their name to the more English-sounding Brady at the time of Henry VIII, whose favor they were courting.

Three MacBradys flourished as Gaelic poets in the early 18th century. These were Fiachra MacBrady and Rev. Philip MacBrady of Co. Cavan, and Phelim Brady, usually referred to as "bold Phelim Brady the bard of Armagh".

Thomas Brady (1752-1827), a farmer's son from Co. Cavan, became a Field Marshal in the Austrian army. His fine looks caught the attention of Empress Maria Theresa and he rose rapidly in the Austrian service, particularly distinguishing himself in battles against Napoleon's forces.

Nicholas Brady (1659-1726) Anglican clergyman and poet born in Co. Cork, was the author, together with Nahun Tate, of a well-known verse translation of the Psalms. He also published a blank verse translation of Virgil's *Aeneid*.

Anthony Nicholas Brady (1843-1913), an Irish-American, made a fortune in railroads and electric lighting companies in Albany and in Brooklyn, New York. His utilities empire included the Municipal Gas Co. of Albany, New York Edison Co., and other power companies in Brooklyn, Memphis, and Chicago. He was also on the board of directors of Westinghouse Electric, American Tobacco, U.S. Rubber, and some thirty other corporations. It was Brady who first spotted the inventing talents of Thomas E. Murray and promoted his early career. When Brady died in 1913 he left an estate of over $100 million – the largest of its day. His son, Nicholas Brady, married Genevieve Garvan, sister of the famous detective Francis P. Garvan, and the couple devoted nearly all their time and energy and a good deal of money to the Catholic church. They were friends and sponsors of the young Francis J. Spellman who was to become Archbishop of New York and Cardinal. It was through his offices that Mrs. Brady received the title Dame of Malta in 1927 and was henceforth known as the Duchess Brady.

MacBride

GAELIC: Mac Giolla Bhrighde
COMMON VARIATIONS: Kilbride, MacGilbride

The Irish form of this name means follower or devotee of St. Brigid, one of the patron saints of Ireland. The name is especially common in Ulster where an ecclesiastical sept of MacBrides settled in Co. Donegal, with a branch later becoming established in Co. Down. Several of the Donegal MacBrides were bishops of Raphoe. In Connacht a variant of the name sometimes appears in the form of Kilbride. MacBride is also a well known name in Scotland.

Although the majority of Irish MacBrides are Catholics, four Ulster Protestants of the name, all of the same family, have been prominent. These include Rev. John MacBride (1650-1718), Presbyterian author; physician and inventor David MacBride (1726-1778), noted for his investigations into "fixed air" (carbon dioxide); John MacBride (1730-1800), admiral in the British navy; and David MacBride (1778-1868), scholar and head of Magdalen College, Oxford.

Alexander MacBride (1708-1852) was a noted miniaturist.

John MacBride (1868-1916), Irish nationalist executed for his part in the Easter Rising of 1916, was the head of another MacBride family which has stood out in modern times in Ireland. His widow Maude Gonne MacBride (1866-1953), an uncompromising republican politician, was a founding member of Sinn Fein. Their son, Sean MacBride (b.1904) founded the republican party Clann na Poblachta which won 10 seats in the Irish Parliament in 1948 and was one of the main strengths behind the Costello Coalition governments of 1948-51. MacBride served as minister for external affairs during the Costello administration.

O'Brien

GAELIC: Ó Briain

The history of this great Irish sept goes back to earliest times but its prominence dates from the 10th century when its chief, Brian Boru, became High King of Ireland. Before he rose to power the family was an unimportant Dalcassian clan in Thomond, the region of northern Munster comprising what is now Co. Clare and some adjacent territory. His greatness firmly established the family as one of the leading septs in Munster and it was from him that they took their name. It was, in fact, just after his death, that the practice of adopting hereditary surnames came into being. In the two centuries following Brian's death the sept divided into several branches which settled in various parts of Munster. Although the name is found throughout Ireland today – with an estimated 20,000 O'Briens in the country, the fifth most common surname in Ireland – it is still most prevalent in its homeland counties of Clare, Limerick, Tipperary and Waterford.

Brian Boru (Boroimhe, "of the tribute") (941-1014) was Ireland's greatest medieval king. A descendant of the 3rd century king Oilill Olum, he succeeded his brother Mahon as chief of his sept and King of Munster in 976. Mahon was slain by Norse invaders who at that time virtually reigned in Munster. Brian's greatest achievement was to drive the Viking invaders out of Ireland and in doing do he re-established country-wide communications, initiated administrative reform, and founded monasteries to promote learning. He has been compared with Alfred, Edgar, and Otto the Great as restorers of Europe after the Scandinavian fury. He proclaimed himself emperor of the Irish and has been called the Irish Charlemagne. In 1001 Brian became undisputed *Ard-ri* (High King) of all Ireland and he maintained his supremacy – no easy task in a country where provincial rivalries still ran strong – until his death in 1014. It is said that he was slain in his tent after defeating the Vikings at Clontarf while returning thanks for the victory.

Murrough O'Brien (d. 1551) Earl of Thomond and direct descendant of Brian Boru, was one of the first great Gaelic chiefs to acknowledge Henry VIII. But this was not until after the Earl had met with O'Neill, O'Donnell, and O'Conor in 1540 to try to organize a united front against Anglo-Irish power in their homeland. Their forces were defeated, however, and this marked the beginning of the end for the Irish chieftains. In 1541 Parliament proclaimed Henry VIII King of all Ireland and Murrough, in return for having his estates restored to him, promised his support to the King.

Murrough O'Brien (1614-1674), 1st Earl of Inchiquin, made his allegiances where they suited him and made his reputation as a ruthless military leader for both Royalist and Parliamentarian sides during the 1641-52 wars. In 1645 he drove the Catholics out of Cork, Youghal and Kinsale, confiscating their goods and burning their houses, thus earning the nickname "Murrough of the Burnings". In 1647 he reduced Cappogquin, Cahir and Cashel, and for a while the entire civil and military administration of Munster was under his control. A royalist at the time when Cromwell came to the fore in 1650, he was forced to flee to France where he remained until the Restoration. He then returned to his homeland where he served as Vice-President of Munster until his death in 1674. He has been described by the Catholics as "the relentless persecutor of themselves and their religion". The Republicans and the Independents denounced him as one whose sole aim was self-aggrandizement and they instanced as justifying these charges his frequent change of sides.

Daniel O'Brien (d. 1690), 3rd Viscount Clare, raised the regiment in James I's Irish Army which later became famous as Clare's Dragoons in the Irish Brigade on the Continent under the command of his son Charles. After the Jacobites were defeated at the Battle of the Boyne, Daniel and his Dragoons went to France where their victories at Ramillies and elsewhere "retrieved the dishonour of their unsteadiness at the Boyne".

Jeremiah O'Brien (1744-1818), the son of Irish parents who settled at Machias, Maine, was an early naval hero in the Revolutionary War. He struck the first blow against the British navy when he, along with his five brothers and forty volunteers, seized a British cargo ship in Machias harbor and captured a small war schooner on June 12, 1775. This was the first naval engagement of the War and the captured vessels became the first ships of the Massachusetts navy and were put under O'Brien's command. He commanded American warships throughout the war and in 1900, in recognition of his services, the American navy named a torpedo boat after him.

Morgan Joseph O'Brien (1852-1937), always called "Judge O'Brien", was the first New York lawyer of Irish Catholic ancestry "to assume a place at the top of his profession comparable to the positions held by Protestants" and it is said that he made it possible for many young Catholic lawyers to find positions in the big "old family" firms downtown. He was also the first prominent New York Irishman to have a summer residence in Southampton, on Long Island's southeastern shore. While still a young lawyer specializing in corporate and civil cases he was elected to the Supreme Court of the State of New York in 1887 at the age of 35, the youngest person at that time ever to sit on that court. He served as a supreme court justice until 1906 when he resigned to resume his private law practice. Always active in the civic affairs of the city, his most notable public service was in leading the campaign to revise the charter of the City of New York. This was overwhelmingly approved in 1936 against desperate opposition to reform put up by Tammany Hall. O'Brien was one of the most prominent Catholic laymen of his time and was a frequent advisor to Cardinals John M. Farley and Patrick J. Hayes. He also aided many Irish causes and in 1920 he organized and headed the American Committee for Relief in Ireland and gave other support to the new Irish Free State. Today, Edna O'Brien, the fiery Irish novelist, typifies her generation.

Browne

NORMAN: De Brún, le Brún

Among the most common of all English surnames, this name in Ireland comes from many different Anglo-Norman sources. From the time of the Anglo-Norman invasion onwards, separate Browne families established themselves in Galway, Killarney, Co. Limerick and Co. Mayo. The Galway Brownes, who were one of the 14 Tribes of Galway, are descended from a Norman, le Brún, who came to Ireland in the 12th century. The Killarney Brownes came to Ireland from England in the 16th century and established themselves by intermarrying with prominent Gaelic families.

The most illustrious of the Irish Brownes is William Brown (1777-1857), who commanded the first Argentine navy. Born in Foxford, Co. Mayo, Brown emigrated with his family to America in 1786. His father died shortly thereafter and he signed on as a cabin boy on a British merchant ship. Eventually he was given command of his own ship, but in 1812 he went to Buenos Aires. At that time the United Provinces of La Plata (Argentina, Uruguay, Paraguay, and Bolivia) were plotting to rebel against their Spanish rulers and in 1814 Brown was offered a naval command by the leaders of the rebellion in Argentina. On March 1, 1814, he was named Naval Lieutenant-Colonel and appointed to take command of the navy of the United Provinces. His command initially included a squadron of three small ships, but he nevertheless managed to raise havoc with the Spanish fleet. In 1826-27 Admiral Brown led the Argentine navy in the war against Brazil and severely defeated the Brazilian fleet. For a short time in 1838 he served as Delegate Governor of Buenos Aires. He is buried in the famous Recolet Cemetary in Buenos Aires, the Glasnevin of Argentina.

Two of the most important men in Galway today are Browns. Most Rev. Michael Browne is Bishop of Galway and Monsignor Patrick Brown in President of University College, Galway and a writer of Gaelic poetry.

Garech Browne (born 1939) is today well known throughout Ireland for his patronage of traditional Irish music and poetry. Realizing it was in danger of extinction under the pressure of twentieth century entertainment he formed a record company to immortalize what is best of Irish folk culture.

Burke

NORMAN: De Burgh
COMMON VARIATIONS: Bourke

This is the most common surname of Norman origin in Ireland. It goes back to the 12th century when William Fitzadelm de Burgo came to Ireland as one of the Anglo-Norman invaders. Dubbed "William the Conqueror" by Irish annalists, he succeeded Strongbow as Chief Governor and by his marriage to an O'Brien princess he soon established a strong position in the western part of the country. The de Burgos, or Burkes, became one of the most influential Norman-Irish families in Ireland. There are some

Edmund Burke

20,000 Burkes in Ireland today, making the name the 14th most common in the country. Because it is so widespread it is unlikely that all the Burkes with Irish ancestry could have descended from the first William. However, it is his descendants who have played such a prominent role in Irish history.

The Burkes acquired vast amounts of land in Connacht and more than any other of the Norman families in Ireland they thoroughly adopted the laws and customs of the native Irish. Like them they had family chiefs and in time several septs were formed. The most important two were located in the present counties of Galway and Mayo. But numerous subsepts were also formed and today the name is common in all parts of Ireland except Ulster.

In the 16th and 17th century wars with England many leading Burkes supported the Crown and after the defeat of James II were forced to flee to the continent where they took positions in the service of France and Spain. A descendant of one of the Mayo Burkes, Raymond Bourke (1773-1847), was made a peer in France and served as a commander in Napoleon's army.

The most famous Burke of the 18th century was statesman and political writer Edmund Burke (1729-1797). Born in Dublin, Burke came to London in 1750 to study law but abandoned that to do his own writing. He developed his classical oratorical style in two early works, *A Vindication of Natural Society* (1756) and *The Sublime and the Beautiful* (1757). In 1765 he entered Parliament as M.P. from Wendover and remained a member for the rest of his life. But, as the son of a Dublin solicitor, Burke was severely handicapped by his humble origins in the aristocratic political environment of London and he never held a high office, nor any office for very long. He lost his seat more than once for advocating the cause of the American colonies, Irish free trade, and Catholic emancipation—even though he himself was a devout Protestant. He also denounced Britain's policy towards India and foresaw the excesses of the French Revolution. Burke has been called one of the great paradoxes of the 18th century for his instinct for supporting right causes for wrong reasons. More an orator than a writer, his speeches on the American questions of 1774 and 1775 are often singled out as prime examples of his polished style. His *Reflections on the Revolution in France* (1790) and *Appeal from the New to the Old Whigs* (1791) contain much of his mature political thought. In his last years Burke was far out of favor and in 1794 was deeply grieved by the death of his only son. He died a destitute and lonely man three years later.

Dr. Thomas Burke (1705-1776), Dominican Bishop of Ossory, was born in Dublin and educated in Rome, where at the age of 14 he was admitted to the Dominican order. He returned to Ireland in 1743 and was made Bishop of Ossory in 1754. His great work is *Hibernia Dominicana,* a history of the Dominicans in Ireland, published in 1762.

Another Dominican, Rev. Thomas Nicholas Burke (1830-1883), attached to St. Saviour's in Dublin, won phenomenal fame as an orator, especially on his tour of America in 1872. While there he managed to raise £100,000 for charities. Pope Pius IX proclaimed him "the prince of preachers".

Galway-born Canon Ulick Bourke (1829-1887) was a pioneer of the Irish language revival.

William Burke (1792-1829), criminal, made his own distinctive contribution to the English language, giving it the verb "to burke", meaning to smother, or cover up. Burke made a living by suffocating people whose bodies he then sold to surgeons for dissection. He was finally hanged for his activities in 1829.

Tipperary-born John Burke (1787-1848), genealogist, was the creator of *Burke's Peerage,* first issued in 1825 as *A Genealogical and Heraldic Dictionary of the Peerage and Baronetage of the United Kingdom.* This was followed in 1833-38 by *A Genealogical and Heraldic History of the Commoners of Great Britain and Ireland,* now known as *Burke's Landed Gentry.* His son, John Bernard Burke (1814-1892), moved to Ireland from London and continued his father's work editing the *Peerage and Landed Gentry.* He also wrote several works on genealogy, the best known of which is *Vicissitudes of Families* (1859).

Robert O'Hara Burke (1820-1861) was the first white man to cross the Australian continent north to south. Born in Galway, he emigrated to Australia in 1853 and settled in the state of Victoria where he became district inspector of police stationed at Castlemaine. He was popular with the people for his brave and dashing manner and in 1860 the State appointed him to lead an expedition to cross the continent over mostly desert territory. The Victorian Exploration Expedition set out from Melbourne on August 20, 1860, and several weeks later Burke, with an advance party, reached the north coast. But the venture cost Burke his life. He died of starvation on the return journey to Cooper's Creek.

O'Brennan

GAELIC: Ó Braonáin, MacBranáin
COMMON VARIATIONS: MacBrennan, Brennan

This is the anglicized form of two different Irish surnames belonging to five unrelated septs. Descendants of two of the five septs have survived in large numbers down to the present day in the area surrounding the original territory of their sept. Hence the name is common in east Roscommon where the MacBranáin sept was situated, and also in north Kilkenny where the principal O Braonáin sept was located.

Rev. John Brennan (1625-1693) Bishop of Waterford and Archbishop of Cashel, friend of Blessed Oliver Plunkett, his periodical reports to Rome contain much valuable information about the state of affairs in 17th century Ireland.

Louis Brennan (1852-1932), Irish-born inventor devised a dirigible torpedo and a monorail railway system. He moved to Australia where he was superintendent and consulting expert with the Government Brennan Torpedo Factory and later took part in government sponsored aircraft research.

Christopher John Brennan (1870-1932), Australian poet born in Sydney of Irish parents. He was lecturer and associate professor of German and Comparative Literature at Sydney University from 1908 to 1925 and was one of the leaders of Sydney's intellectual life. His short, philosophical poems are described as scholarly and often difficult, showing more European than Australian influences.

Francis Brennan (1894-1968), American Roman Catholic cardinal, taught moral theology and canon law in Philadelphia from 1924 until 1940 when he was appointed to the Sacred Rota in Rome – a high court of appeals with jurisdiction in all matters concerning the ecclesiastical rights of individuals. He became the first American dean of the Rota in 1959 and was created a cardinal by Pope Paul VI in 1967.

William Joseph Brennan (b. 1906), associate justice of the United States Supreme Court, first won recognition in the early 1950's as Supreme Court Justice of New Jersey for his role in the nationwide drive to clear up court congestion and delays in litigation. In 1956 Brennan, a Democrat, was appointed to the U.S. Supreme Court by the Republican President Eisenhower. Since then he has written many important majority opinions for the court, including Baker v. Carr 1962, a landmark case which made legislative apportionment open to scrutiny by the federal courts. He also wrote the N.Y. Times Co. v. Sullivan 1964 opinion in which the Supreme Court first imposed limitations on state libel laws, and has written most of the basic opinions on the law of obscenity and several major anti-trust opinions.

O'Byrne

GAELIC: Ó Broin

COMMON VARIATIONS: Byrne

The O'Byrnes are descended from Brian, King of Leinster, who died in 1052. In the next century they were driven from their original territory to what is now Co. Kildare by the Anglo-Norman invaders. By about 1200 they had re-established themselves in the southern part of Co. Wicklow and soon became one of the leading septs in the provine of Leinster. Like their neighbors to the north, the O'Tooles, who had also been driven from their Kildare territory by the invaders, the O'Byrnes are particularly noted for their resistance to English rule. This is the seventh most common surname in Ireland.

Feagh or Fiacha MacHugh O'Byrne (1544-1597), one of the most formidable of the Irish chieftains, is best remembered for his part in the escape of Hugh Roe O'Donnell from Dublin Castle in 1591. He himself made many 'wonderful escapes from his enemies''. ''Every effort to capture him seemed doomed to fail.'' O'Byrne led frequent attacks against the English in the Pale, but was finally caught and killed in 1597.

A branch of the family which settled in France was admitted to the ranks of the nobility there and was a leading family in Bordeaux before the Revolution. They owned extensive vineyards at La Hourange and Macon.

Andrew Byrne (1802-1862), the first Catholic bishop of Little Rock, Arkansas, came to America from Ireland in the late 1820's. He pioneered the establishment of Catholicism in the South among both whites and Indians.

John Byrne (1825-1902), pioneer in electrical surgery, emigrated from Ireland to New York at the time of the Great Famine in the 1840's. He settled in Brooklyn where he made a brilliant career as physician and surgeon and was one of the first to develop a successful method of cauterizing malignant tumors.

Thomas F. Byrnes (1842-1910) had a nationwide reputation as

Inspector Byrnes of the New York police force. Born in Ireland, he was brought to New York as a child. He joined the New York police as a patrolman in 1863 and by 1870 had been made a captain. His first "big job" on the force was rounding up the gang of Manhattan Savings Bank robbers in 1878. After that he was named Inspector Byrnes in charge of the Detective Bureau and in four years his force of forty men had made some 3,300 arrests. He is the originator of "the 3rd degree" method of interrogation. He acted on the theory that it is mental strain, not remorse, that leads the criminal to confess his crimes. Byrnes drew on his experience to write *Professional Criminals of America*, published in 1886.

Alfred Byrne (1882-1956) was ten times Lord Mayor of Dublin.

Butler
NORMAN: De Buitléir

This is an extremely common name both in England and in Ireland. The original English Butler, it is said, was a Norman officer who crossed the channel with William the Conqueror and served as William's butler. In Ireland Butler first came into use as a surname in the late 12th century after Theodbåld Fitzwalter, who accompanied King John on his Irish expedition in 1171, was created Chief Butler of Ireland in 1177. Fitzwalter's descendants were called Butler and they ermerged as one of the great Angle-Norman families in Ireland. They reigned over the ancient territory of Ormonde, comprising what is now much of Co. Kilkenny and north Tipperary. The stronghold of the Ormonde Butlers was Kilkenny Castle. Up until the death of the Great Duke of Ormonde in 1688 the effective government of those parts of Ireland over which England could claim control was in the hands of either the Butlers of Ormonde or the Geraldines. There was a long-standing rivalry between these two great Norman families in Ireland. Today the name is very numerous in all the provinces except Ulster, but it is still most prevalent in Butler homeland of Ormonde.

James Butler (d.1405), 3rd Earl of Ormonde, was an important official of the English government in Ireland. In 1391 he purchased the estate of Kilkenny Castle which from then on was the seat of the Butler family. "Being a mighty strong man, he is styled in some annals the head of the chivalry in Ireland, which kingdom he governed to the content of the king and his good subjects." He subdued many Irish chiefs and was also instrumental in defending the Irish coasts from Scotch and Welsh pirates.

Pierce Butler (1744-1822), signer of the Constitution of the United States, was born in Co. Carlow Ireland in 1744. In 1773 he was stationed in the American colonies as a major in the British army but he resigned his military commission and made his home in South Carolina. He soon became a political leader in the state and was elected to the state legislature in 1778 where he served almost continuously until 1789. He represented South Carolina at the Constitutional Convention in 1787 and was responsible for the clause in it providing for the return of fugitive slaves. In 1789 he was elected U.S. senator and re-elected in 1792. He resigned in 1796 and died in Philadelphia in 1822.

Pierce Butler (1866-1939), United States Supreme Court justice,

James Butler, Ist Duke of Ormonde

was born in a log farmhouse near Northfield, Minnesota in 1866 of pioneer parents who emigrated from Co. Wicklow, Ireland. Butler began his legal career in the 1890's as county attorney in St. Paul and in 1897 he began general legal practice with a firm which was to become Butler, Mitchell and Doherty—one of the great law offices of the Northwest. In 1922 he was appointed to the U.S. Supreme Court by President Harding and became one of the Court's strongest voices in defense of conservative principles and free enterprise. His deep conviction was that a government governs best which governs least. Justice Holmes referred to him as a ''monolith'' in the Supreme Court and the biographer of Charles Evans Hughes states that ''Butler was the most difficult man on the court. Tough-minded and unshakable in his convictions. At the conference table he argued with typically Irish tenacity and force, sometimes with thrusts of wit and eloquence.'' It has also been noted that his inclination was toward protecting the accused, not least in prosecutions under the federal prohibition laws.

O'Callaghan

GAELIC: Ó Ceallacháin
COMMON VARIATIONS: Callaghan, O'Kelaghan, Kealahan

The O'Callaghans are descended from the 10th century King of Munster called Ceallachain. Their original territory was in the barony of Kinelea in Co. Cork, but they were driven out by the Anglo-Norman invaders and re-located near Mallow in the northern part of the county. Under the Cromwellian regime the leading family of the sept were once again dispossessed, and this time they re-settled in east Clare. The village of O'Callaghan's Mills there is named after them. As was usually the case, the smaller branches of the family were not transplanted and for this reason most of the 13,000 or so O'Callaghans in Ireland today are still to be found in Co. Cork. The name O'Callaghan is also found in Oriel (Cos. Armagh, Louth and Monaghan), but as a corrupted form of the completely unrelated name O'Kelaghan which is the anglicized spelling of the Gaelic name O'Ceileacháin. The O'Callaghans are one of the few Irish families who still have a Chief of the Name certified by the Genealogical Office.

In Ireland two O'Callaghans, Edmund O'Callaghan (1797-1883) and John Cornelius O'Callaghan (1805-1883) have stood out as historians and Sir Francis O'Callaghan (1839-1909) was a noted engineer. After the Battle of the Boyne many O'Callaghans settled on the continent, particularly in Spain where they are often mentioned in the national archives.

Morley Edward Callaghan (b. 1903), Canadian writer, met Ernest Hemingway in Toronto in 1925 and followed him to Paris in 1929 where he met a number of American expatriates and became a disciple of Hemingway. His writing has been described as ''intense and clinically observant''. His novels include *Strange Fugitive* (1928), *Such Is My Beloved* (1934), and *They Shall Inherit the Earth* (1935). He has also published three collections of short stories.

Carey

GAELIC: Ó Ciardha

COMMON VARIATIONS: O'Keary, Carr, Keary, MacCary, Currane, Kerin

This is the modern anglicized form of several Irish surnames. O Ciardha, formerly translated into English as O'Keary, was an ancient sept whose chiefs were lords of Carbury in Co. Kildare until they were dispersed by the Anglo-Norman invaders in the late 12th century. The now almost extinct surname MacGhiachra, which belonged to two septs situated in Cos. Tyrone and Galway, was anglicized to Carey as well. The name is also a synomyn for Kerin, for the Irish O Ceirin in Co. Mayo and O Ciarain in Co. Cork. Finally, it is also used to translate Mac Giolla Ceire, which is sometimes further corrupted to Carr in Co. Galway. Because of these many different origins the name Carey is now numerous and widespread in Ireland. But it is more prevalent in the Munster counties of Cork, Kerry and Tipperary than elsewhere.

Three Dublin-born Carey brothers have made the name particularly well known both in Ireland and America. John Carey (1756-1826), classical scholar and inventor of the "shipwreck rocket" moved from Dublin to London where he taught school and edited over 50 volumes of classics in his lifetime. He also wrote many stories and poems. In 1803 he suggested the idea of firing a line to a ship in distress by means of a small rocket and this was soon developed into the so-called "shipwreck rocket".

His brother William Paulett Carey (1759-1839) started out as a painter and engraver and then became a picture dealer and art critic in Dublin.

The third brother, Mathew Carey (1760-1839), author, publisher and political refugee, escaped to America in 1784 after being imprisoned for libel. He settled in Philadelphia where he started the *Pennsylvannia Herald* and then founded his own publishing business. "In his voluminous and spirited writings he made himself the chief advocate of protection for American manufactures." The elder Carey passed on his social, political and economic interests to his son Henry Charles (1793-1879), who continued his father's fame as writer and publisher. He was the American publisher for Thomas Carlyle, Washington Irving, and Sir Walter Scott. Then, at the age of 42, he turned to economic writing for which he earned his reputation as one of the leading and provocative social thinkers of his day. He is considered the founder of a truly American school of political economy and social science. While today he is judged "uncritical in his parade of illustrations from history, and frequently fanciful in the ardor of his pursuit," he is still acknowledged as "not only an original thinker of power, but as the leader of the opposition to the pessimism of the classical schools [of political economy] and also to the socialist group which took rise from the Ricardian *counsel of despair*."

James Carey who was born in Dublin was responsible for informing on his comrades after the Phoenix Park Murders of May 1882. Carey had been a member of a secret organization called the 'Invincibles' and in the following year they shot him for his betrayal.

O'Carroll

GAELIC: Ó Cearbhaill
COMMON VARIATIONS: MacCarroll,
MacCarvill, Carroll

There are two distinct Carroll surnames, O'Carrol and MacCarroll, which taken together number about 16,000 in Ireland today. The great majority of these are in fact O'Carrolls. Before the Anglo-Norman invasion there were six distinct septs of O'Carroll, but by far the most important were the O'Carrolls of Ely O'Carroll (Tipperary and Offaly) and those of Oriel (Monaghan and Louth). The O'Carrolls of Ely O'Carroll derive their name from Cearbhal, Lord of Ely, who was one of the leaders of the army which defeated the Danes at Clontarf in 1014. Their ancestry can be traced back to the 3rd century King of Munster, Oilioll Olum. Today most of the O'Carrolls in Ireland are found in Cos. Kilkenny, Louth and Offaly.

There were two distinct MacCarroll septs, one in south Leinster and one in Ulster, although in Ulster the Irish Mac Cearbhaill is now usually anglicized to MacCarvill. This Ulster sept was situated at Ballymaccarroll and was particularly noted for their musicians.

Maolsuthain O'Carroll (d. 1031), of the Kerry sept, was the confessor of Brian Boru whom he accompanied on his circuit of Ireland in 1004. The priest wrote a short passage in Latin in *The Book of Armagh* which is still legible and which mentions his association with Brian, "imperatus scotroum".

Margaret O'Carroll (d. 1451) is referred to by the Four Masters as "the best woman of her time in Ireland". She was famous for her hospitality, her encouragement of learning, and her contributions for the building of churches, roads and bridges.

John Carroll (1735-1815), first American-born Catholic priest was appointed bishop in the United States and first Archbishop of Baltimore. Born in Maryland, he was educated in Flanders and in France and returned to America after the Jesuits were suppressed in Europe in 1773. In 1776 he was invited by the Second Continental Congress to join Benjamin Franklin, Samuel Chase, and his cousin Charles Carroll in an unsuccessful effort to obtain French-Canadian support for the American Revolution. It was thought that his Catholic faith would help re-assure the French. In 1789 Carroll was created Bishop of Baltimore and he set a precedent in the Catholic church by initiating the custom of public prayers for the government. He was instrumental in the founding of several Catholic colleges, including Georgetown University in Washington D.C. After being promoted to Archbishop Carroll consecrated the first bishops of Boston, Philadelphia and Louisville.

Charles Carroll (1737-1832), known as "Charles Carroll of Carrolltown", which was the way he signed his name on the Declaration of Independence, was born in Annapolis, Maryland to one of the most prominent Roman Catholic families in America. After studying for the law in England he returned to Maryland to supervize his 10,000 acre estate, Carrolltown Manor. As a Catholic he was at first excluded from holding political office but, by 1773, he had entered public life and remained an active participant until his retirement in 1804. In 1776 he was named by the Continental Congress to join in an abortive mission to persuade Canada to support the American Revolution. That same year he helped draft the Maryland Constitution and was elected to the Second Continental Congress. From 1789-1792 he served as U.S. Senator from Maryland and from 1774-1804 was a member of the Maryland Senate. Carroll died in Baltimore in 1832 at the age of 95, the last surviving signer of the Declaration of Independence.

Daniel Carroll (1730-1796) was a delegate from Maryland who signed the U.S. Constitution, was the only Catholic to sign the Articles of Confederation and is credited with having drafted the first amendment to the Constitution. He was elected to the first U.S. Congress in 1789 but served only until 1791 when he accepted an appointment as commissioner of the District of Columbia in charge of drawing up plans for the capitol. He died in Maryland in 1796.

Paul Vincent Carroll (1900-1968), was an Irish dramatist whose work helped revive the fame of Dublin's Abbey Theater as a training ground for new Irish playwrights. Born at Blackrock, Co. Louth, he was a schoolmaster in Glasgow, Scotland from 1921-1937, after which he devoted himself completely to writing. His reputation rests on his two most successful plays, *Shadow and Substance* and *The White Steed*, both first produced in the late 1930's and both of which won the New York Drama Critics Circle Award.

MacCarthy

GAELIC: Mac Cárthaigh
COMMON VARIATIONS: Carthy

The MacCarthy sept has been described as "the most eminent by far of the noble families of the south". Their origins can be traced back to the 3rd-century King of Munster Oilioll Olum. One of his two sons, Eoghan, inherited the territory of south Munster and the families which descended from Eoghan were known as the Eoghanacht. The MacCarthys were the chief family of the Eoghanacht and one of the leading septs in Munster. They take their name from a lord of Eoghanacht called Cárthach, who, it is said, died when a house he was staying in was deliberately set on fire in 1045 by one of the Lonergans, a sept in north Munster.

There are some interesting facts associated with the name. One is that it is the most common "Mac" name in Ireland. (It is also among the 12 most common surnames in the country.) Another is the preponderance of certain Christian names associated with the name. A vast number of Justin MacCarthys have played prominent roles in the history of Ireland. Justin is the anglicized form of the Gaelic name Saorbreathach, which was the name of Carthach's father. Two other Christian names also popular among the MacCarthys are Finghin, anglicized to Fineen or Florence, and Cormac, which is the Gaelic equivalent of Charles.

Several branches of the MacCarthy sept were formed in south Munster, occupying territory in the present counties of Cork and Kerry. The principal residence of the chief of the Muskerry branch in Co. Cork was the famous Blarney Castle. Almost two-thirds of the MacCarthys in Ireland live in Co. Cork.

Cormac MacCarthy, 12th-century King of Munster, had the

Eugene MacCarthy

first Romanesque church built in Ireland between 1127-1134. He brought masons over from the continent to build his chapel at Cashel in Co. Tipperary.

Cormac Laidhir Oge MacCarthy (d.1536), sept chieftain and Lord of Muskerry, was the son of Cormac Laidhir who founded the castles of Blarney and Kilcrea. The younger Cormac joined forces with the English of Munster in 1510 and subsequently became head of the coalition against the Fitzgeralds. In 1520 Cormac was in command of the troops which completely routed the Fitzgeralds at the Battle of Mourne, near Mailow, and as a result the Butlers became supreme rulers in Munster. Described as a "sad, wise man", Cormac died in 1536 and was buried at Kilcrea.

Fineen (Florence) MacCarthy (1562-1640), chief of the MacCarthy Reagh branch of the sept, after serving for a while in the army of Queen Elizabeth, spent much of the remainder of his life in the Tower of London where he wrote a history of ancient Ireland.

Justin Count MacCarthy (1744-1812), born in Co. Tipperary, was a famous book collector in France ennobled by Louis XVI in 1776. His library was one of the finest and richest in Europe.

Justin MacCarthy (1830-1912), novelist, historian, and politician born in Cork, was already an established novelist in 1879 when he was elected a member of the British Parliament for Co. Longford. His parliamentary career lasted for the next 21 years. After the fall of Charles Stewart Parnell in 1890 he was chairman of the Irish Home Rule Party—the anti-Parnellites—for six years. His most important literary work is *A History of Our Own Times* (1879-97) in 5 volumes beginning with the accession of Queen Victoria. He also wrote *Lady Judith* (1871), *Dear Lady Disdain* (1875), *Miss Misanthrope* (1878), and other novels. He wrote biographies of Pope Leo XIII (1896) and of William Ewart Gladstone (1897), and an autobiography, *The Story of an Irishman* (1904).

There have been numerous prominent Irish-American MacCarthys. Col. Daniel E. MacCarthy was the first American soldier to set foot in France during the First World War. Governor C. J. MacCarthy was President of the Pan Pacific Union at the beginning of this century. Today Eugene MacCarthy, politician, and Mary MacCarthy, novelist, are perhaps the most prominent carriers of the name, a name which unfortunately was sullied by the infamous Senator Joseph from whose persecutions the word "macarthyism" stems.

O'Casey

GAELIC: Ó Cathasaigh
COMMON VARIATIONS: Casey, MacCasey

There were at one time six separate, unrelated septs of this name in different parts of Ireland. Two of these were dispersed at an early date, however, and today the name is found chiefly in two regions where the other four septs had their home territories. Two of them were situated in southwest Munster, one at Liscannon in Co. Limerick, and the other near Mitchelstown in Co. Cork. The remaining two were in north Connacht, at Tirawley in Co. Mayo and in the barony of Athlone in Co. Roscommon.

Sean O'Casey

The most famous O'Casey in Irish history is Sean O'Casey (1880-1964), the playwright, one of the giants of modern theater. He is best known for his plays about the working people of the Dublin slums during the Irish "troubles" of 1916-1923. In spite of the subject matter, his early pieces are full of comic vitality and are notable for their idiosyncratic characters. Born John Casey in Dublin in 1880, O'Casey was forced to go to work at the age of 14 by his father's death. He worked as a laborer until 1925 when he devoted himself entirely to writing. Both as a worker and a writer O'Caseys primary concern was to reveal and improve the conditions of Irish workers. In 1913 he helped form the Irish Citizen Army – a militant arm of the Irish trade union movement – and he served as its first secretary. But he resigned in 1914 because the socialist aims which he favored were being subjugated to nationalist ideals. O'Casey's first play, *The Shadow of a Gunman*, was produced by the Abbey Theater in Dublin in 1923. This was the first of several plays on the Irish "troubles" in which O'Casey concentrated on the comic and pathetic aspects of war rather than its patriotic and glorious sides. This aroused the wrath of Irish nationalists and in 1926 the production of his *The Plough and the Stars* resulted in riots, after which O'Casey left Dublin for London. His professional links with Ireland were severed for good in 1928 when the Abbey rejected *The Silver Tassie*. From then on his plays, which were becoming more and more symbolical and allegorical, were largely neglected or badly produced. Today, however, O'Casey's work is looked upon as among the most influential in modern drama. In addition to his plays he also published a six-volume autobiography collectively titled *Mirror in My House*, 1956.

O'Clery

GAELIC: Ó Cleirigh
COMMON VARIATIONS: Clarke, Clerkin, MacCleary, Cleary, MacAlary

This is one of the earliest hereditary Irish surnames, dating from the middle of the 10th century. The O'Clery sept originated in Lilmacduagh, Co. Galway, but by the middle of the 13th century their power had declined and they were driven out of their original homeland. Branches spread to several parts of the country, but by far the most important was that which became established in Cos. Donegal and Derry. They were noted mainly for their poets and antiquaries. Following the Plantation of Ulster in the early 1600's the name O'Clery there was changed to the common English surname Clarke. Today there are some 20,000 Clarkes and Clerys throughout Ireland, but the majority of them are concentrated in Munster and in Dublin.

Three O'Clerys together with Ferfeasa O'Mulconry were responsible for the compilation of the great 17th century Irish chronicle which has come to be known as the *Annals of the Four Masters*. Two of the O'Clerys, Michael and Conary, were brothers, the sons of the chieftain Lughaigh O'Clery who was himself an historian. Michael, a monk in the order of St. Francis, spent nearly 18 years collecting and transcribing ancient manuscrips in monasteries throughout Ireland, while Conary's contribution was mainly as a scribe or copyist. Their cousin, Cucory was an historian and head of the Tirconnell sept of O'Clerys. Of the fourth annalist, Ferfeasa O'Mulconry, nothing is known except that he was an hereditary antiquary and a native of Co. Roscommon. The *Annals,* written by these four men in the monastery of Donegal between 1632 and 1636, have been called "the most important single contribution ever made to the study of Irish history", though the notices of the events it records are "in the main bald, and entirely wanting in colour or picturesqueness."

Arthur Patrick O'Clery (1841-1915), a Limerick-born historian, is best known for his *History of Ireland to the Coming of Henry II.*

Julie and Desirée Cleary (1781-1860), daughters of an Irish merchant in Marseilles, became respectively Queens of Spain and Sweden during the reign of Napoleon. Their father became acquainted with Joseph Bonaparte and his younger brother Napoleon at Marseilles in 1794 at the height of the reign of terror. The two brothers fell in love with the two sisters and engagement followed. Joseph eventually married Julie while Napoleon, discouraged by family opposition to his marriage to Desirée, and fascinated by his new acquaintance Josephine de Beauharnais, broke off the engagement after a year. In 1798 Desirée married General Bernadotte, Napoleon's great rival for military supremacy, who acceded to the throne of Sweden. She was crowned queen of the country in 1829. Her sister Julie became Queen of Spain in 1808 when her husband was made King of Spain by the Emperor Napoleon. Joseph's kingship was brought to an end in 1813, however, by the French defeat at the Battle of Vittoria.

O'Connell

GAELIC: Ó Conaill

In medieval times there were several distinct and unrelated septs of this name but by far the most important was that which originated in Co. Kerry. Their ancestry can be traced back to Aengus Tuirmeach, a king of Ireland around 280 B.C. They became established in the barony of Magunihy in East Kerry but in the 11th century some of them were forced by the powerful O'Donoghues to move westward to the Atlantic coast where they became hereditary castellans of Ballycarbery under the MacCarthy Mor chiefs. Magunihy, however — where Killarney is located — remains the homeland of the leading O'Connell family in Ireland today.

Daniel Count O'Connell (1743-1833), "the last colonel of the Irish Brigade", was born at Darrymarne, Co. Kerry, the youngest of twenty-two children by one marriage. He entered the French army at the age of fourteen as a lieutenant in Lord Clare's regiment of the Irish Brigade. After fighting in the Seven Years' War in Germany he was attached to the Corps de Génie and became one of the best engineers in France. He was appointed Inspector-General of the French Army, but returned to Ireland at the outbreak of the Revolution. On a visit to France in 1802 he was imprisoned by Napoleon and not released until the restoration of the Bourbons in 1814, when he was promoted to general and allowed to reassume his estates in France.

Daniel O'Connell (1775-1847), known as "The Liberator" of the

Daniel O'Connell

Irish Catholics, was born in Co. Kerry and trained as a lawyer. After a speech made at Dublin in early 1800 at a meeting held to petition against union with England, O'Connell was singled out as one of the most promising and energetic of the younger Catholic leaders. He actively campaigned for the repeal of laws which placed civil restrictions on Catholics and in 1823 founded the Catholic Association which carried on active agitation in spite of government attempts to quash it. The main grievance of the Association was that Catholics could not sit in Parliament without taking an oath which they considered contrary to conscience. O'Connell managed to muster enough support to get the Catholic Emancipation Bill passed in 1829 which allowed him to take up the seat he had won from Co. Clare two years earlier. He became the leader of the Irish party in the House of Commons and was idolized by his Catholic countrymen as their liberator. In 1842 O'Connell began urging repeal of the union between Great Britain and Ireland, but his influence was on the decline with the rise of the new Young Ireland party which advocated more radical measures than those favored by O'Connell's "moral force" policy. He died on a trip to Italy in 1847.

Maurice O'Connell (1727-1825), squire, patriarch, autocrat, smuggler and the uncle of Daniel the Liberator, was a celebrated Irish character known as "Hunting Cap".

William Henry O'Connell (1859-1944) Archbishop of Boston, was one of the most influential Catholics in the United States when he was created Cardinal by Pope Pius X in 1911. Born in Lowell, Massachusetts, he became rector of the North American College in Rome in 1895 and in 1901 was appointed bishop of Maine. His appointment as Archbishop of Boston came in 1907.

O'Connolly

GAELIC: Ó Conghaile, Ó Coingheallaigh
COMMON VARIATIONS: Connolly, Connelly

Most of the Connollys and O'Connolly stem from three Gaelic septs which were situated in Connacht, Monaghan and Munster — corresponding to the present counties of Galway, Monaghan and Cork. The name is still most heavily concentrated in these areas but it is also common in Fermanagh and Meath. In early times the most important sept was the one in Co. Monaghan. It was one of the "four tribes of Tara", a group whose kingship and worship centered around the Hill of Tara in Co. Meath. But this sept was forced out of its original territory by the Anglo-Norman invaders. It moved to the north and re-settled in Co. Monaghan.

William Connolly (1660-1729), M.P. from Co. Kildare and Speaker of the House of Commons, was reputedly the richest man in Ireland in his lifetime. He rose to power and wealth as commissioner of revenue and Lord Justice for the English Government in Ireland before being elected a member of Parliament. It is said that at his funeral the custom of wearing linen scarves first came into being and was continued to help encourage the linen trade.

James Connolly (1870-1916) was the first active socialist in Irish history and one of the seven leaders in the Easter Rising of 1916. Born in Co. Monaghan, Connolly grew up in Edinburgh,

James Connolly

Scotland in conditions of extreme poverty. A self-educated Marxist, he returned to Ireland and worked for socialist causes in Dublin from 1896-1903 and then in New York from 1903-1910. Back in Dublin, he helped organize the Irish Transport and General Workers Union and was one of the leaders of the general strike in Dublin in 1913. After the failure of the Dublin strike Connolly set up the Citizen Army and commanded it in the 1916 Easter Rebellion. For his part in the rebellion he was shot by the British on 12 May 1916.

Maureen Connolly (1934-1969), was an American tennis star from San Diego, California. Nicknamed "Little Mo", she became a tennis sensation at the age of 16 when she defeated Shirley Fry at Forest Hills for the U.S. Women's Singles Championship in 1951. She also won this title in 1952 and 1953, won for three years running at Wimbledon from 1952-1954, and in 1953 also took the French and Australian women's tennis championships. As a member of the winning U.S. Wightman Cup team from 1951 to 1954 she won every match she played. But her tournament career was cut short by a horseback riding accident in 1954 which crushed her leg. She died in Dallas in 1969.

Henry Connolly (1800-1866), first elected governor of New Mexico by its citizens in 1850 before it became a territory of the United States, was a pioneer born in Kentucky of Irish ancestry. He was appointed by Lincoln to continue as governor in 1861 when New Mexico came under U.S. jurisdiction.

MacCormack

GAELIC: Mac Cormaic
COMMON VARIATIONS: MacCormac, MacCormick, O'Cormack, O'Cormacan

This name is very common and widespread throughout Ireland. There was a recognized sept of the name in Co. Longford, but on the whole the name appears to have come into existence independently in several different places at a fairly late period when sons of fathers whose Christian name was Cormac (the Gaelic equivalent of Charles) described themselves as MacCormaic. This was then kept as a surname by subsequent generations. Other examples of this tendency are seen in the surnames MacTeige and MacShane. In the Middle Ages several prominent MacCormacks of Fermanagh are mentioned in the Annals of Irish history, and in Elizabethan times MacCormacks were among the leading gentry in Co. Cork.

Two MacCormacs, father and son, were outstanding 19th century doctors. Belfast physician Henry Cormac (1800-1886) was one of the first doctors to advocate fresh air treatment for tuberculosis. Also an enthusiastic linguist, he is said to have had knowledge of 20 languages. His son, Sir William MacCormac (1836-1901), after being in charge of an Anglo-American ambulance in the Franco-Prussian War, became a surgeon at St. Thomas's Hospital, London, in 1873. He was knighted in 1881, served as president of the Royal College of Surgeons, was a consulting surgeon during the Boer war, and wrote extensively both on his war experiences and medicine.

John Count McCormack (1884-1945), Irish tenor, achieved great popularity in America as a singer of Irish folksongs and ballads. He made his operatic debut at Covent Garden, London in 1907 and in New York with the Manhattan Opera Co. in 1909. In 1913 he turned to the concert stage and from then on spent most of his time in America. He became a U.S. citizen in 1919. He was made a papal count in 1928 and retired in 1938, seven years before his death.

John McCormack (b. 1891), Democratic member of the U.S. House of Representatives since 1929 from Massachusetts, succeeded Sam Rayburn as Speaker of the House in 1962. Trained as a lawyer, McCormack is a moderate known for his sharp wit and his influence in the Democratic party.

O'Connor

GAELIC: Ó Conchobhair

COMMON VARIATIONS: O'Conor, Connor, Connors

This name rivals O'Neill, O'Brien, O'Donnell and O'Kelly for the title of most illustrious Irish surname. At one time there were six distinct O'Connor septs situated in different parts of the country, four of which have survived in great numbers. The most important of these was the O'Connor sept of Connacht. They are descended from Conchobhar, King of Connacht (d.971), and two of their ancestors were the last two high kings of Ireland—Turlough O'Connor (1088-1156) and Rory O'Connor (1116-1198). Another important O'Connor sept held sway in Munster. Their chief, known as O'Connor Kerry, was lord over an extensive territory in north Kerry. This is the most numerous O'Connor clan in Ireland today. Of the 30,000 O'Connors in the country the vast majority of these are from Kerry or the adjacent counties of Cork and Limerick. The two other surviving families are the O'Connors of Corcomoroe, a barony in north Clare on the Atlantic coast, and the O'Connors of Offaly, who trace their origins back to Cathaoir Mor, and century king of Ireland. A fifth sept, the O'Connors of Glengiven (Derry), who trace their origins back to a son of Oilioll Olum, 3rd century king of Munster, was overpowered and dispersed by the O'Kanes in the 12th century. A few descendants of this royal family are still found in that part of Ulster where their ancestors were once very powerful.

Roderic or Rory O'Connor (1116-1198), last High King of Ireland, succeeded to the throne of Connacht on the death of his father Turlough O'Connor in 1156. After ten years of successful warring against other powerful Irish septs he was inaugurated Ard Ri or king of all Ireland in 1166. When Henry II made his tour of Ireland in 1171 after the first wave of Anglo-Norman invaders hit the Irish shores Roderic refused to submit to him. But in 1175 he concluded a treaty by which he was to continue to rule Connacht and be head of the kings and chiefs of Ireland under Henry's sovereignty. In 1186 he was dethroned by his son, who was in league with the English, and driven out of Connacht. He was king again for a short time after the death of his son in 1189, but was soon deposed by Cathal O'Connor and retired to a monastery where he died, thus bringing to an end the last high kingship of Ireland.

Later O'Connors of Connacht were prominent in the 1641-52 wars in Ireland and in the 18th century several of them became distinguished officers with the Irish Brigades on the continent. Two important authors of this clan where Mathew O'Conor (1773-1844) who wrote a *History of the Irish Catholics* and Charles Owen O'Conor (1838-1906), President of the Royal Irish Academy and of the Society for Preserving the Irish Language and author of *The O'Conors of Connacht*.

The Kerry O'Connors also contributed a number of officers to the Irish Brigades in France, the best known of whom was Arthur O'Connor (1763-1852) who was a general in Napoleon's army. Three notable Irish-Americans stemmed from this sept – the brothers Michael O'Connor (1810-1872) and James O'Connor (1823-1890), both Catholic bishops in the United States, and Patrick Edward Connor (1820-1871), frontiersman, Indian fighter and Confederate soldier in the Civil War.

Another Irish-American, John Francis Xavier O'Conor (1852-1920) was remarkable for the breadth of his learning. An ordained priest and professor of philosophy and rhetoric at the College of St. Francis Xavier, he lectured on subjects ranging from cuneiform inscriptions to early Greek and Christian art, to Wagnerian operas. He also was a voluminous writer of articles, short stories, plays, poetry and hymn verses. His books include *Christian Art* (1885), *Life of St. Aloysisu* (1892), *Rhetoric and Oratory* (1898), *Education in the Schools of New York* (1901), and *The Crusade of Children* (1916).

Costello

GAELIC: Mac Oisdealbhaigh
COMMON VARIATIONS: MacCostello, Nagle

This is the anglicized form of the surname Mac Oisdealbhaigh which is taken from Oistealb, a song of the famous 12th century Norman invader Gilbert de Nangle. Thus the Costellos are related to the great Norman family of Nangles. This was the first Norman family in Ireland to assume a "Mac" name, although the prefix has subsequently been dropped. Their territory was in east Co. Mayo where the barony of Costello is named after them. It is here and in Co. Galway that the name is most prevalent today.

In the aftermath of the upheaval of the old Gaelic order in the 17th century the Costellos were one of the many great Irish families which produced famous rapparees, or irregular soldiers. One of them, Duley Costello, who was an officer in the army of the Confederate Catholics in 1642 and was forced to seek exile in Spain, returned to Ireland after the Restoration and "devoted the rest of his life to wreaking vengeance on the new Cromwellian proprietors."

Two English-born Costellos of Irish stock, brother and sister Arthur Dudley Costello (1803-1865) and Louis Stuart Costello (1799-1870) were noted 19th century novelists and travel writers.

John A. Costello (b. 1891) became Prime Minister of the Republic of Ireland when de Valera resigned the premiership in 1948. He served until 1951 and again from 1954-1957. His most notable accomplishment was the Republic of Ireland Act, passed in December 1948, which established Eire as a republic outside the British Commonwealth.

Conroy

GAELIC: Ó Conraoi, Ó Conaire, Ó Maolchonaire
COMMON VARIATIONS: O'Conry, MacConry

This name derives from several different septs, the majority of which were situated in Connacht. The most important of these was O Maolconaire (O'Mulconry) whose patrimony was the parish of Clooncraf near Strokestown in Co. Roscommon. They were hereditary poets and chroniclers to the O'Connors, kings of Connacht. Two other important Connacht septs were O Conraoi, a branch of the Ui Maine in east Galway, and Mac Conraoi who were situated at Moycullen on the shores of the Bay of Galway. The surname of King is often used as a synonym for the Moycullen MacConroys because of the similarity in sound of this Mac name with the phrase "Mac an Righ" which is Irish for "son of the king". In the late 17th and 18th centuries the name was often mistakenly translated into English as King. Conroy is a name also found in Leix and Offaly where there was a sept called O Conratha, alias Mac Conratha, related to the MacCoughlans of Offaly.

Fearfasa O'Mulconry was one of the four compilers of the most famous book of Irish history, the *Annals of the Four Masters*, completed in 1636. Little is known of him, other than that he was an hereditary chronicler in the principal family of Connacht O'Mulconrys. Another member of this family, Maurice O'Mulconry, is known for his beautiful manuscript copy of the "Book of Fenagh" completed in 1517. Rev. Florence Conry (1561-62), also a member of this sept, was Archbishop of Tuam and one of the founders of the Irish College at Louvain. He served as chaplain in the Spanish Armada and was chaplain to Hugh O'Donnell at his death.

Padraic O'Conaire (1883-1928) of Galway, was one of the best known modern writers in Irish.

MacConway

GAELIC: Mac Connmhaigh, Mac Conmidhe, Ó Conbhuidhe, Ó Connmhachháin
COMMON VARIATIONS: O'Conway, Conboy

Conway is the anglicized form of several different but similar Irish surnames which belonged to septs scattered throughout the country. The most important of these were Mac Connmhaigh of Thomond, Mac Conmidhe of Co. Tyrone, O Connbhuidhe in the

161

parish of Easky, Co. Sligo, and O Connmhachain of Co. Mayo. The Mayo sept, which is a branch of the O'Haras, has had their name variously anglicized as O'Conoughan, later as Kanavaghan, and more recently as Conway and Convey.

Thomas "Count de" Conway (1735-1800), soldier of fortune in the Irish Brigade in France rose to the rank of major general in the French army and at one time was governor over all the French possessions in India. In 1777 he went to America to fight for the colonies and was made a brigadier general by the Continental Congress. One of his first moves was to instigate a plot known as the "Conway Cabal" to remove Washington as Commander in Chief of the Continental Army and replace him with General Horatio Gates, the victorious commander at Saratoga. But the intrigue miscarried and Conway was forced to resign from the army. In 1779 he rejoined the French army, was commissioned a major general, and later appointed governor of the French Possessions in India. After the outbreak of the French Revolution he was driven into exile by the revolutionists and died in obscurity in England.

His Eminence William John Conway (1913), was appointed Archbishop of Armagh and Primate of All Ireland in 1963 and was created Cardinal in 1965. From 1942-57 he was professor of moral theology and canon law at St. Patrick's College, Maynooth. He is the author of several books, including *The Church and State Control* (1952), *Problems in Canon Law* (1955), *The Child and the Catechism* (1959), and *Youth Problems* (1960).

O'Daly

GAELIC: Ó Dalaigh

COMMON VARIATIONS: Daly

This is one of the greatest names in Irish literature, for the O'Dalys have produced scores of Gaelic writers and poets. The parent sept originated in the barony of Magheradernon in Co. Westmeath, but several branches spread to other parts of the country where they continued their literary calling. Indeed, it was as poets that they were often able to become established in a new area. An O'Daly was made official poet of the MacCarthys of West Cork and thus acquired lands and privileges for his family in the barony of Carbery. The O'Dalys in Co. Cavan were similarly attached to the Breffny O'Reillys. There was also an O'Daly branch in Co. Galway where they became Barons of Dunsandle and achieved great wealth and power in the 18th and 19th centuries. Most of the 16,000 O'Dalys in Ireland today are found in these areas. It is the 24th most common name in the country.

One of the most famous of the O'Daly bards was the 13th century Donough Mor O'Daly, born at Finvarra, Co. Clare. He has been called "the Irish Ovid" for the smoothness of his poetry, most of which deals with religious themes developed at great length.

Aengus O'Daly, a 16th century Gaelic poet, was employed by the English to disparage his countrymen in verse. The result was "The Tribes of Ireland", a bitter satire which was translated into English in 1852. While it condemns, it also contains much local

Richard Daley

Denis Daly

color reflecting the manners and the customs of the times. The poems proved O'Daly's undoing, as he was stabbed by one of the O'Meagher's in 1617 for some lines in his satire which were unfavorable to that family.

Rev. Dominic O'Daly (1595-1665) left his native Ireland for Portugal where he became a key figure in the religious and political life of that country in the 17th century. In 1634 he founded a college at Lisbon and gained favor in the court, playing an important part in the 1640 revolution which freed Portugal of Spanish rule. He was envoy to Charles I and II, ambassador to Louis XIV, confessor to the Queen of Portugal and president of her Privy Council. Denis Daly (1747-1791) was Member of Parliament for Galway who opposed proposals for parliamentary reform proposed by Flood.

Marcus Daly (1841-1900), Irish-born American capitalist, built up a mining empire in Montana based on the Anaconda copper mine. Daly immigrated to the United States in the 1850's and started out as a miner in several Western states. Eventually he got financial backing to acquire the Anaconda Silver Mine and when the silver ore was soon exhausted he was able to buy out the other shareholders. This left him sole owner of the immense copper veins which were later found under the worked-out silver deposits. Also included in Daly's Montana holdings were coal mines, timber tracts, banks, power plants, irrigation systems, and a railway.

Richard Joseph Daley (b. 1902), mayor of Chicago and leader of Illinois Democrats, was born on Chicago's West Side in 1902 of Irish descent. Trained as a lawyer, in 1936 he was elected to the Illinois legislature and worked in close association with Governer Adlai E. Stevenson. In 1950 he became clerk of Cook county and in 1952 succeeded Jacob M. Avery as Cook county Democratic chairman. Daley was elected mayor of Chicago in 1955 and re-elected in 1959, 1963 and 1967 by large majorities. As mayor of Chicago he is credited with having reduced political graft in city government and reformed the fire and police departments. But in the late 1960's he was being pressed by leaders of the black community to end discrimination in Chicago. An extremely powerful and influential Democrat, Daley's support was crucial to the Democratic presidential nominations won by Stevenson, John F. Kennedy, and Hubert Humphrey. In 1968, Daley suffered a considerable loss of public sympathy when, after violent clashes between students and police, he gave unstinting praise to law enforcement officers despite their obvious brutality.

O'Dempsey

GAELIC: Ó Diomasaigh

COMMON VARIATIONS: Dempsey

The O'Dempseys are a branch of the O'Connors of Offaly and were a powerful sept in Clanmalier on the borders of Leix and Offaly. Their chief was one of the few who won a battle against Strongbow, leader of the Anglo-Norman invaders, in 1172. Later, as supporters of James II, they were ruined as a sept and dispossessed of their lands following the Jacobite defeat at the Battle of the Boyne.

Jack Dempsey

Dermot O'Dempsey (d. 1193), chief of the sept, founded the Cistercian Abbey at Monasterevan. The place takes its name from St. Evin who was the patron saint of the O'Dempseys.

Jack Dempsey (b. 1895), American boxer, was world heavyweight champion from 1919-1926. Born in Manassa, Colorado, his first fights were fought around Utah and Colorado mining camps. On the 5th of July, 1919, he won the heavyweight crown from Jes Willard in Toledo, Ohio, flooring his taller and heavier opponent seven times in the first round and knocking him out in the fourth. The "Manassa Mauler", as Dempsey was nicknamed, lost his title seven years later to Gene Tunney in a fight at Philadelphia on 23 September 1926. He lost again to Tunney a year later in Chicago in the famous "long count" bout in which he failed to retire immediately to his corner after flooring Tunney in the second round and Tunney was down for a good 15 seconds. Five of Dempsey's fights in the 1920's drew million dollar gates and in 1954 he was one of the first to be elected to boxing's Hall of Fame. Today he is a successful New York restauranteur.

John H. Dempsey (b. 1915), Democratic Governor of Connecticut from 1961-1970 started his political career as mayor of Putnam, Connecticut, and has twice served as chairman of the New England Governor's Conference.

MacDermot

GAELIC: Mac Diarmada

There are three branches of this important sept which springs from Tulough O'Connor who was King of Connacht prior to the Norman invasion. The main branch was situated in Co. Roscommon where their territory centered around Moylurg. A second branch settled in Co. Galway, and a third, also in Connacht, declined in importance after early succumbing to English domination. The MacDermots are one of the few septs whose head is recognized by the Irish Genealogical Office and is therefore entitled to be called "The MacDermot". The name is among the hundred most common in Ireland and besides its prevalence in Cos. Galway and Roscommon, it is also frequently found in Cos. Donegal and Tyrone. In some parts of Connacht the name has been corrupted to Kermode due to the aspiration of the initial D of MacDiarmada in spoken Irish.

Brian MacDermot (d.1592) was a scholar remembered as the owner of the famous manuscript *The Annals of Loch Ce*.

Hugh Hyacinth O'Rorke MacDermot (1834-1904), "The MacDermot" of his generation, was a prominent barrister and politician. He served as solicitor and attorney general under the liberal governments of 1885 and 1892-94.

Peter Rowe MacDermot was a prominent but underrated nineteenth century American poet who fought in, and wrote about the American Civil War. His moving verse well reflects the miseries in the South immediately after the war.

Martin MacDermott (1823-1905), Young Irelander and early contributor of a few fine poems to the *Nation*, was trained as an architect. In 1866 he was hired as an architect by the Egyptian government and was responsible for the rebuilding of Alexandria after the bombardment of 1882.

O'Devlin

GAELIC: Ó Diobhilin
COMMON VARIATIONS: Devlin

This was a leading Ulster sept whose chiefs were lords of the territory known as Munsterdevlin on the shore of Lough Neagh in Co. Tyrone. Four-fifths of the Devlins in Ireland today come from Ulster, and most of these from Co. Tyrone. In former times there was another distinct O'Devlin sept in Co. Sligo, but they were dispersed and most of their descendants have died out.

Anne Devlin (1778-1851), faithful servant of Robert Emmet, the insurrectionist was hanged for his part in the uprisings of 1798 and 1803. His servant was imprisoned and tortured but refused to give any information about him.

Denis Devlin (1908-1959), Irish poet. His *Collected Poems* were published in 1964.

Bernadette Devlin (b.1947), fiery young civil rights leader from Northern Ireland became the youngest member of the British House of Commons in 1969. In her maiden speech she broke with tradition by speaking only after being sworn in on a controversial subject—she lashed out at the Unionist politicians who, she said, had controlled Ulster for half a century by encouraging religious antagonism to preserve their privileged positions. Still she maintains that religion is less to blame for the problems in Ireland than basic social and economic discrepancies between different classes of people. Born to a poor family in Cookstown, Co. Tyrone, she has written in her book *The Price of My Soul* that "I'm not a socialist because of any high-flown intellectual theorizing; life has made me one." Although she is currently one of the main forces in Northern Ireland politics she has no intention of making her career in politics. "I hope instead," she says "to be a very good psychologist" adding that she would always be interested and involved in politics and that her hobby would continue to be "making mincemeat of politicians".

Bernadette Devlin

Dillon

GAELIC: Diolún

This name was brought to Ireland by a family of Anglo-Norman invaders in the 12th century. They soon acquired power and influence and since then they have featured very prominently in Irish history. Their main territory was a large tract of land known as Dillon's Country in what is now Co. Westmeath. A branch of the family also settled in Co. Mayo. Today the name is found chiefly in Meath, Westmeath and Roscommon.

Up until the fall of the Stuarts at the end of the 17th century many Dillons held high government office. Afterwards their main claim to fame was as Colonel-Proprietors of Dillon's Regiment in the French army. In 1711 the Dillons in France were created counts and descendants of this noble family are still found in France today.

Three generations of a Roscommon Dillon family have been prominent in Irish politics. John Blake Dillon (1816-1866) was one of the founders of the Young Ireland party and of its weekly

newspaper, the *Nation*. His son, John Dillon (1851-1927), M.P. and Irish nationalist like his father, has been called Charles Stuart Parnell's "ablest lieutenant". After the divorce scandal which ruined Parnell he joined the anti-Parnellite wing of the Irish party and in 1896 became their chairman. In 1900 he supported John Redmond, a Parnellite, as chairman of a re-united Irish party and was his close associate in managing the nationalist movement. He succeeded Redmond as party chairman in 1918, but the Sinn Fein victory in the general election that year liquidated the Irish party and Dillon lost his east Mayo seat to Eamon de Valera. One of Dillon's sons, James, has twice been Minister of Agriculture for the Republic of Ireland.

James Dillon's brother Myles was a scholar of great repute. He held several professorships on both sides of the Atlantic and was for a time Professor of Celtic Studies and was director of the Celtic School in Dublin's Institute for Advanced Studies.

O'Doherty

GAELIC: Ó Dochartaigh
COMMON VARIATIONS: Dougherty, O'Dogherty

This large and powerful sept descends from the same stock as the O'Donnells. They originated in the barony of Raphoe in Co. Donegal and by the 14th century the O'Doherty chiefs had extended their territory and increased their power to the point of being made lords of Inishowen. But in 1608 their holdings were reduced to almost nothing when the chief of the sept, Sir Cahir O'Doherty, led a revolt against the English which ended in failure. As a result the entire peninsula of Inishowen was taken from O'Doherty rule and annexed to the confiscated territory of Tyrconnell. The great majority of O'Dohertys in Ireland today come from this northwest corner of the country.

John Doherty (1783-1850), M.P., was notorious as Crown prosecutor in the Doneraile Conspiracy case and subsequently was made Lord Chief Justice of Ireland.

Dennis Joseph Dougherty (1865-1951), American Roman Catholic archbishop and cardinal, was born at Girardville, Pennsylvania and ordained at the North American College at Rome in 1903. The first of his priesthood he served as missionary bishop to the Philippines. He was appointed bishop of Buffalo, New York in 1915, and three years later named archbishop of Philadelphia. Over a period of some thirty years in this post he created 112 parishes and saw to the building of 145 parochial schools, 53 high schools, 4 colleges, 12 hospitals and 11 homes for the aged. In 1921 he was made a cardinal.

Paul Dougherty (1877-1947), American painter born in Brooklyn, is best known for his seascapes of the New England coast.

Charles Joseph Doherty (1855-1931), Canadian Minister of Justice 1911-1921 was Canada's delegate to the Paris Peace Conference and signer of the Treaty of Versailles. He also represented Canada at the assembly of the League of Nations between 1920 and 1921.

O'Dolan

GAELIC: Ó Dúbhláin

COMMON VARIATIONS: Dolan, Doolan, Dowling

This is a common name in Connacht in the counties of Roscommon and Galway where the O'Dolan sept originated. Several members of the family migrated to the northeast, so the name is now also prevalent in Ulster, especially in the Catholic areas of Leitrim, Fermanagh and Cavan.

Thomas Dolan (1834-1914), a well-known Irish-American capitalist, was one of the largest textile producers in the United States. He also had interests in several utility companies.

Francis James Dolan (1893-1933) was president of the College of the Holy Cross in Worcester, Massachusetts.

Michael J. Dolan (d.1953) was a noted actor in the Abbey Theatre in Dublin.

MacDonnell

GAELIC: Mac Domhnaill

Today there are nearly 10,000 MacDonnells in Ireland whose origins can be traced back to three distinct sources. Most of them are descendants of a Scottish clan which came to Ireland from Argyle in the 13th century and served as gallowglasses, or mercenary soldiers, to become the most powerful chiefs in northern Ireland. In time they acquired their own territory and by the middle of the 15th century they had firmly established themselves in the region known as the Glens of Antrim. At the same time there was a distinct native sept of MacDonnells in west Ulster, in Co. Fermanagh, but it is almost extinct now. Survivors of another Gaelic sept of MacDonnells can still be found in Co. Clare where before the English invasion they were bards to the O'Briens of Thomond. This sept descended from Dohmnall, son of King Murtagh Mor O'Brien—hence the Irish form of the name Mac Domhnaill, which means son of Domhnall.

Sorley Boy MacDonnell (1505-1590), son of a Scottish laird, became chief of the Scots-Irish sept of MacDonnells in Co. Antrim and was a lifelong foe of the English. He raised havoc with Queen Elizabeth's forces in northern Ireland for many years until he was finally forced to submit in 1586 and relinquish his claims to Ulster.

Seán Clárach MacDonnell (1691-1754) was acknowledged by his contemporaries as the supreme poet of Munster.

Alexander MacDonnell (1798-1835), Belfast-born textile merchant and chess player was recognized as the best British chess player of his day. In 1834 he played a marathon match with the secretary of the Paris Chess Club, de Labourdonnai which went on for 88 games before the Frenchman was recalled to Paris. Mac Donnell died before the match could be resumed.

In Australia the name MacDonnell is best known as applied to the Macdonnell Ranges, a mountain range in the Northern Territory which were named after an early Irish settler.

O'Donnell

GAELIC: Ó Domhnaill

This is one of the most famous names in Irish History, made so mainly by the principal sept of O'Donnells of Tirconnell (Co. Donegal). But there were two other prominent septs of the name as well. One was a Thomond sept which became established at Corcabaskin in what is now west Clare, and the other was a branch of the Ui Maine in Co. Galway. All of these septs trace their name back to some ancestor named Domhnall and hence are called O Domhnaill in Irish. In the case of the Tirconnell O'Donnells, their eponymous ancestor, who died in 901, was a descendant of Niall of the Nine Hostages, the powerful 4th century Ard Ri, or High King of Ireland. The Tirconnell O'Donnells first rose to prominence in the 13th century, but they are especially known for their outstanding 16th and 17th century leaders. The O'Donnells in Ireland today number nearly 13,000 and are found chiefly in those areas where the three leading septs originated.

Hugh Roe O'Donnell (1571-1602), chief of the Tirconnell O'Donnells, has been described as the last of the old Gaelic kings. The power of his clan was especially feared by the English, who captured "Red Hugh", as he was called, when he was sixteen and imprisoned him in Dublin castle. He escaped five years later, returned to Tyrconnell and immediately re-asserted his power in his territory by driving out the English sheriff and his officers. By 1597 he had control of Connacht from Sligo to Leitrim and the following year he was at the peak of his power when he played a major part in the Irish victory over the English at Yellow Ford. But disaster followed in 1601 when O'Donnell and Tyrone together with the Spanish commander Juan del Aquila were crushed by the English at Kinsale. This battle marked the end of the old Gaelic order in Ireland. O'Donnell fled to Spain and is said to have been poisoned there by an English agent.

Leopold O'Donnell, Duke of Tetuan (1809-1867), of an exiled Irish family which settled in Spain, joined the Spanish army and supported Maria Christina, the queen mother, in her struggles against the Carlists. By intrigue he managed to have himself appointed governor of Cuba in 1843. But he returned to Spain in late 1840's and though his career was clouded for a time by an abortive attempt to lead an insurrection he came into favor again in 1856, being made war minister under Espartero, and Prime Minister in 1858. In 1859 he led a successful expedition against the Moors and as a result was created Duke of Tetuan.

In Ireland, the O'Donnells were actively involved in politics. Paeder O'Donnell, born in 1893 in Donegal was a leading left wing activist as well as a considerable literary figure.

Frank Hugh O'Donnell (1848-1916), M.P., member of the Irish parliamentary party, brought a famous libel suit against the London *Times* in 1888 claiming £50,000 damages for certain statements made against him in the so-called "Parnellism and Crime" articles published by the *Times*. Although O'Donnell lost the action it was mainly as a result of the case that the Parnell Commission was set up two months later.

In American politics, Kenneth O'Donnell rose to prominence as a senior member of J. F. Kennedy's staff, throughout his career as Congressman, Senator and President.

Two princes of the O'Donnells

MacDonagh

GAELIC: Mac Donnchadha
COMMON VARIATIONS: MacDonogh,
Donaghy, MacDonough

This name sprang up in two different parts of Ireland – in Co. Cork, where the MacDonoghs were a branch of the MacCathys and held the castle of Kanturk, and in Connacht where they were an off-shoot of the great MacDermot clan and whose chiefs were lords of Corran in Co. Sligo.

In America the Irish-born John MacDonogh (1779-1850) was a philanthropist best known for his efforts on behalf of slaves. Another Irish-American Thomas MacDonough (1783-1825), was an officer in the American navy who won fame for his defeat of the British fleet at the battle of Plattsburg on Lake Champlain in 1814. This victory, which forced the British to retreat into Canada, was one of the most decisive of the War of 1812. For his performance MacDonough was promoted to captain and eventually had command of the American squadron in the Mediterranean.

In Ireland the poet Thomas MacDonagh (1878-1916) was a leader of the Easter Rising of 1916 and afterwards a victim of the executions which followed. His books of poetry include *Songs of Myself* (1910) and *Lyrical Poems* (1913). Donagh MacDonagh (1912-1968) was another Irish poet. Also a playwright, his *Happy as Larry* was produced in 1946.

O'Donnelly

GAELIC: Ó Donnghaile
COMMON VARIATION: Donnelly

Nearly all of the 10,000 Donnellys and O'Donnellys in Ireland today are descended from the Ulster O'Donnelly sept which was a branch of the O'Neills. They take their name from Donnghaile O'Neill who was 17th in descent from Niall of the Nine Hostages. Though originally situated in Co. Donegal, the O'Donnellys later moved further east into Co. Tyrone and established themselves in the district around Ballydonnelly which is named after them. Here is where the name is still most prevalent. The O'Donnellys were noted soldiers and their chief served as hereditary marshal of the O'Neill's military forces.

Ignatius Donnelly (1831-1901), American writer, reformer, and politician, was born in Philadelphia, studied for the law there and moved to Minnesota in 1856 where two years later at the age of 28 he became lieutenant governor of the state. In 1863 he was elected to Congress and achieved considerable popularity as a radical Populist reformer. From 1874-1878 he was a member of the Minnesota State Senate and in 1900 was Vice Presidential nominee of the Populist party. As well as editing two political journals, the *Anti-Monopolist* and the *Representative,* Donnelly also wrote an extremely popular novel entitled *Caesar's Column: A Story of the Twentieth Century* (1891). He is best remembered, however, for his book *The Great Cryptogram* (1888) in which he attempted to prove by an elaborate word cipher that Francis Bacon wrote the plays of William Shakespeare. His sister, Eleanor Cecilia Donnelly (1838-1917), wrote many Catholic devotional works.

Charles Francis Donnelly (1836-1909), was a famous Catholic lawyer in America.

O'Donoghue

GAELIC: Ó Donnchadha
COMMON VARIATIONS: Donoghue, Donohoe

This is one of the most common names in Ireland today and one of the most eminent in Irish history. There were several septs of O'Donoghue in early times but three in particular stood out from the rest. The most important of these was the Desmond sept, whose original homeland was in Co. Cork. They were driven west, however, by the MacCarthys into Co. Kerry during the 11th century where they settled in the district now called Onaght O'Donoghue. They are descended from Domhnall, son of an early 11th century King of Munster. This family eventually split into two branches and the head of one of them is one of the few Chiefs of the Name still officially recognized as such and entitled to be called "The O'Donoghue". Of the two other prominent O'Donoghue septs, one was a branch of the Uí Máine in Co. Galway and the other was situated in Co. Cavan. In these two places the modern spelling of the name is usually Donohoe. Here and in Co. Kerry is where the name is most prevalent today.

Geoffrey O'Donoghue "of the Glen", was a foremost Gaelic poet and scholar of the 17th century.

In the 18th century many O'Donoghues gained recognition as Wild Geese in the Irish Brigades of the continental armies. In Spain, where the name became O'Donoju, Juan O'Donoju (1755-1821) rose to the rank of captain general in the Spanish army and was the last Spanish ruler of Mexico.

Patrick Donohoe (1811-1901) was founder and first editor of the Irish-American newspaper the *Boston Pilot*.

David James O'Donoghue (1866-1907) is known for his book on *The Poets of Ireland* and John O'Donoghue (1900-1964), Irish novelist, wrote *In a Quiet Land*.

In the world of sport the name was immortalized by Stephen – 'Steve' – Donoghue (1884-1925) who was perhaps the greatest flat racing jockey of all time. In the years between 1915-1925, he rode no less than six Derby winners beating Fred Archer's long established record of five wins in the event.

O'Donovan

GAELIC: Ó Donnabháin

The O'Donovans are one of the best documented families in Ireland with a verified pedigree extending back to Gaelic times. The sept originated in Co. Limerick, but a short time after the Anglo-Norman invasion they were forced to migrate to the

Steve Donoghue

John O'Donovan

southwest into Co. Cork. Here they were a leading sept until the end of the 17th century, when, as supporters of James II, they fell from power after the Jacobite defeat. O'Donovan's Infantry was one of the top-ranking regiments of King James's Irish army. After the defeat many O'Donovans crossed the Channel and joined up with the Irish Brigades in the continental armies. A branch of the O'Donovan family settled in Co. Kilkenny, but of the 9,000 or so O'Donovans in Ireland today, most of them are concentrated in Co. Cork.

Jeremiah O'Donovan (1831-1915), the most famous O'Donovan in Irish history, was imprisoned for supporting the Fenian cause and after his release went to America. His funeral at Glasnevin cemetery in Dublin is said to have been one of the largest ever witnessed there.

John O'Donovan (1809-1861), archaeologist born in Co. Kilkenny, is best known for his edition of *The Annals of the Four Masters*, 1848-1851. He wrote extensively on Irish history and antiquities and also wrote an authoritative *Grammar of the Irish Language*, 1845.

William Rudolf O'Donovan (1844-1920), American sculptor and painter, was commissioned to do many public statues but is best known for his portraits, an example of which is that of General Joseph Wheeler in the National Gallery of Art, Washington D.C.

William Joseph Donovan (1883-1959), New York attorney and major general in the United States army, organized and directed the Office of Strategic Services (OSS) during World War II. This was the military precursor of the Central Intelligence Agency. From 1953 to 1954 he served as U.S. Ambassador to Thailand.

Richard Frank Donovan (b. 1891), American composer, conductor and teacher, joined the Yale faculty in 1928 after studying with organist and composer Charles Widor in Paris. He was assistant conductor of the New Haven orchestra from 1936-1951, and from 1928-1966 was organist and choirmaster at Christ Church.

Doyle

GAELIC: Ó Dubhghaill
COMMON VARIATIONS: MacDowell

The Irish Doyles are descended from pre-Norman Vikings who settled in southwest Leinster (the present day counties of Wicklow, Wexford and Carlow) where the name is still most prevalent today. With some 21,000 Doyles in Ireland, the name is the 12th most common in the country. The Irish form of the name— O Dubhghaill—comes from dub-ghall, meaning dark foreigner, which was the Gaelic word used to denote a Norseman or Scandinavian. In Ulster, Doyle is sometimes found as a synonym for MacDowell.

Sir Arthur Conan Doyle (1859-1930), creator of Sherlock Holmes, was born in Edinburgh, Scotland, but is descended from a talented Dublin family. After studying medicine and then practicing for a few years in Southsea, England, he began writing short stories in the late 1880's and in 1891 the first installments of "The Adventures of Sherlock Holmes" began appearing in the *Strand Magazine*. The renowned detective became so popular

Sir John Doyle

with the reading public that Doyle was even forced to revive him after he had become so bored with the character that he had killed him off. In addition to the Sherlock Holmes stories Doyle also wrote plays and several historical romances and, in the last years of his life, he wrote and lectured extensively on spiritualism after receiving what he believed to be personal messages from a son killed in World War I.

John Doyle (1797-1868), grandfather of Arthur Conan Doyle, was a Dublin born painter and caricaturist who, under the anonymous initials "H.B.", contributed a popular series of political caricatures to *Punch* between 1829-51. His gentle satiric style became a model of how to handle political comment and criticism in an incisive but restrained manner.

James Warren Doyle (1786-1834) Bishop of Kildare and Leighlin was champion of the Catholic cause in Ireland and his polemical and political writings carried enormous influence in their day. He first emerged as a politician and controversialist in the early 1820s when he rebutted the charge of the Protestant archbishop of Dublin that "the Catholics had a church without a religion, and the dissenters a religion without a church." Doyle established Catholic schools in every parish in his diocese and waged a vehement campaign against the established Church of England. It was said of him that it was impossible not to admire "the cunning of fence, the grace of action, and the almost irrestible might" of his argument.

O'Duffy

GAELIC: Ó Dubhtaigh
COMMON VARIATIONS: Duffy, Dowey, O'Diff

There were several distinct septs of this name in different parts of Ireland. In what is now Co. Donegal the O'Duffy family were followers of the 7th century Saint Dubhtaach. They were situated in the parish of Lower Templecrone in the diocese of Raphoe. Another sept of O'Duffy's has its seat at Lissonuffy – or Lissyduffy – near Strokestown in Co. Roscommon. This Connacht family is especially known for their contributions to church art, most famous of which is the Cross of Cong, a particularly fine example of 12th century Irish craftsmanship. Traditionally these O'Duffys are believed to have come from east Leinster, from the same stock as the O'Burnes and the O'Tooles. This origin is also claimed for another sept of O'Duffy which settled in Monaghan.

Sir Charles Gavan Duffy (1816-1903) started out as a journalist in Dublin in 1835. He became increasingly involved in the nationalist movement together with men like Thomas Davis and John Blake Dillon and in 1842 they founded *The Nation,* the weekly newspaper which became the organ of a new political party, the Young Irelanders. Their paper attracted the best literary talent of the day and it became a powerful weapon and wielded enormous influence. In it the Irish people found for the first time a vehicle of self-expression. It has been said that this periodical marks "the renaissance of Anglo-Irish literature. It was the authentic forerunner of the Gaelic League, the Celtic renaissance, Sinn Féin and 1916." The end of the Young Ireland Party and

The Nation came in 1848 when its leaders were arrested for planning an uprising. Duffy, among them, was transported to Tasmania. After his release from prison there (in 1855), he emigrated to Australia, entered politics and eventually became prime minister. In 1880 he returned to Europe and settled in London where he was president of the Irish Literary Society. An author himself, he wrote *Young Ireland* (1880), *Four Years of Irish History* (1883), *The Life of Thomas Davis* (1890), and *My Life* (1898). He died in Nice in 1903.

Edward Duffy (1840-1868) during his short life devoted himself to spreading Fenian principles in Connacht. His is described as "the life and soul of the movement west of the Shannon". He was arrested for his activities in 1868 and died the same year in Millbank prison in London.

James Duffy (1809-1871) founded the famous Duffy publishing firm in Dublin. They published many works by the Young Irelanders, including Duffy's *Library of Ireland*, and played an important role in the 19th century revival of Irish literature.

O'Dwyer

GAELIC: Ó Duibhir

COMMON VARIATIONS: Dwyer

The O'Dwyers of Klanmanagh were an important sept whose lands lay in the mountainous region of central Tipperary. They are especially noted for their resistance to English aggression. Michael Dwyer (1771-1825) led a band of insurgents in Emmets uprising of 1798 and for five years afterwards defied the English forces until he finally surrendered and was transported to Australia where he became a policeman.

Joseph O'Dwyer (1841-1898) was an American physician, a pioneer in the treatment of diphtheria. Born in Cleveland and practicing in New York, he was the first to use intubation for asphyxia in diphtheria cases.

William O'Dwyer (b. 1890), mayor of New York and U.S. Ambassador to Mexico, came to America in 1910 from Co. Mayo, Ireland. He worked as a laborer, bartender and patrolman, attending evening classes at Fordham University Law School. Starting out in private law practice in 1926, he was Judge of the Brooklyn Adolescent Court from 1932 until 1939 when he was appointed Brooklyn District Attorney. As District Attorney he became widely known for his prosecution of the gang known as "Murder Inc". In 1941 he lost the mayoralty election to La Guardia but, four years later, was elected mayor of New York by the largest popular vote ever cast for one candidate for the office. O'Dwyer had a reputation for honesty and "house cleaning" which dissociated him from Tammany politics. But his career was ruined by the 1950 hearings of the Kefauver Committee which exposed corruption in his administration although he was said to be innocent. In 1950 he was appointed Ambassador to Mexico by President Truman but resigned the post in 1951 and then resided in Mexico in self-imposed exile. He has been called "the most controversial figure since Jimmy Walker" in New York.

William O'Dwyer's younger brother Paul also reached promi-

Paul O'Dwyer

nence in political circles and gained a reputation as a leading liberal in New York. Having stood for several political posts, he was elected president of New York City Council in 1973.

MacElroy

GAELIC: Mac Giolla Rua
COMMON VARIATIONS: Kilroy, Gilroy, MacGilroy

The MacElroy sept originated in Co. Fermanagh on the east shore of Lough Erne. The name is now prevalent in that county as well as in Co. Leitrim where it is often spelled MacGilleroy. The name is also found in Connacht, but the "Mac" has been dropped and the modern spelling of the name there is either Kilroy or Gilroy. The Irish form of the name, Giolla Rue, means red-heaired youth.

Rev. John MacElroy, S.J. (1782-1877), a native of Fermanagh, was famous as a Jesuit missionary priest and builder of churches in America. Described as "a gigantic fellow, wiry and red-faced," MacElroy betrayed the Presbyterian United Irishmen and escaped to America in 1803. In 1806 he joined the Society of Jesus as a lay brother in Georgetown. He soon won fame as a forceful preacher and retreat master, giving missions throughout Virginia, Maryland, and Pennsylvania. After serving as chaplain in the Mexican War 1846-48 he was assigned to St. Mary's Church in north Boston. This became the largest Catholic Church in Boston under his rectorship and he was an influential leader in the city despite his advanced age.

O'Farrell

GAELIC: Ó Fearghail
COMMON VARIATIONS: Farrell, O'Ferral

With some 13,000 Farrells and O'Ferrells in Ireland this is the 35th most common surname in the country. Most of these come from Leinster, particularly Co. Longford and the adjacent area, for this was the ancient territory of the O'Farrell sept. Their chief was the Lord of Annaly and his seat was called Longphuirt Ui Fhearghaill, or O'Farrell's fortress.

One family of O'Ferralls, three brothers, became prominent officers in the Irish Brigade in France after their father Ceadagh O'Ferrall of Annaly was killed at the Battle of the Boyne in 1690.

Sir Thomas Farrell (1827-1900) was a noted sculptor, many of whose statues are to be found in Dublin.

James A. Farrell (1863-1943), the "Steel King", started out as a mechanic in a Pennsylvannia steel mill and rose to become head both of the United States Steel Company and the Farrell Steam-of the United States Steel Company and the Farrell Steamship Line.

James T. Farrell (b.1904), the American novelist is best known for his Studs Lonigan trilogy. Born in Chicago, Farrell drew most of the material for his novels and short stories from the life of Irish-

Americans in that city from the turn of the century to the 1930's Depression. His frank descriptions of city life have earned him a reputation as a powerful realistic writer. He describes himself as "a literary naturalist, interested in content rather than technique". Among his other series of books are the Danny O'Neill pentalogy, which describes the spiritual growth of a sensitive, intelligent youth, and the Barnar Carr trilogy, based on Farrell's own experiences as a writer in New York in the 1930's.

Fitzgerald

GAELIC: MacGerailt

This is one of the great families which came to Ireland as part of the Anglo-Norman invasion. The Fitzgeralds are all said to have descended from Maurice Fitzgerald who accompanied Strongbow on his invasion of Ireland in 1170. The Geraldines were experienced warriors and rulers and in Ireland they saw the opportunity to increase their domain. Because of their superior fighting skills they easily overcame the native Irish and Maurice even boasted that, if his superiors in Wales and England had allowed it, he and his companions could have conquered all of Ireland and established an independent Norman monarchy in the country. But as it turned out the Geraldines had to settle for their own territory in the two southern provinces of Leinster and Munster. The two main branches of the family, the Fitzgeralds of Kildare in Co. Kildare and the Fitzgeralds of Desmond in Co. Kerry, were two of the most influential noble families in Ireland. The Fitzgeralds in Ireland today number nearly 13,000 and are found mainly in Cos. Cork, Kerry, Kildare, and Limerick.

Maurice Fitzgerald (d.1177), as mentioned above, was one of the most prominent of the Anglo-Norman invaders in Ireland and founder of the Geraldine clan there. He was the son of Gerald of Windsor, constable of Pembroke in Wales, and Nesta, Princess of Wales. He helped Strongbow secure Dublin for the English and in 1172 was appointed by Henry II Warden of the city under Hugh de Lacy. In 1176 he was made a grant of the barony of Offaly and the territory of Offelan, comprising the present towns of Maynooth and Naas. He died the following year. He is described in contemporary words as a "modest man, with a face sun-burnt and well-looking, of middle height; a man of few words, but of full weight, having more of the heart than of the mouth; a sober, modest, and chaste man; constant, trusty, and faithful; a man not altogether without fault, yet not spotted with any great or notorious crime".

Thomas Fitzgerald (1513-1537), known as "Silken Thomas", Lord of Offaly and 10th Earl of Kildare, was born in England and lived there until 1534 when, at the age of 21, he was appointed Deputy-Governor of Ireland by his father, the 9th Earl of Kildare, and went to Dublin to take up his office. Soon after he arrived there rumor reached him that his father had been executed in the Tower. In retaliation Thomas summoned the council and appeared before them with a band of 140 gallowglasses, or mercenary troops, heavily armed and with silken fringes on their helmets. This touch of extravagance earned him his nickname. In front of the council Thomas renounced his allegiance to England and declared war against the government of Henry VIII. "I am none of Henrie his Deputie," he said. "I am his fo. I have more mind to conquer than to governe, to meet him in the field than to serve him in office." Thomas's war against the English lasted for 14 months until he finally surrendered on August 18, 1535. He was taken to the Tower and on February 3, 1537, and after 16 months in prison he was executed, at the age of 24 along with his five uncles. A contemporary account describes him as "tall and personable; in countenance amicable; a white face, and with all somewhat ruddie, delicately in eche lymme featured; a rolling tongue, and a rich utterance, of nature flexible and kinde; verie soon caryed where he fansied; easily with submission appeased, hardly with stubbornnesse weyed; in matters of importance an headlong hotespurre, yet nathelesse taken for a young man not devoyde of witte; were it not, as it fell out in the ende, that a fool had the keeping thereof."

Lady Elizabeth Fitzgerald (1528-1589), generally known as "The Fair Geraldine", born in Maynooth, the daughter of Gerald, 9th Earl of Kildare. While still an infant she was taken by her mother to England where she was brought up at Hunsdin with the Princesses Mary and Elizabeth. Famed for her fair features, her beauty was celebrated in verse by the Earl of Surrey, Michael Drayton, and Sir Walter Scott. Lord Edward Fitzgerald (1764-1798) was Member of Parliament for Athy who later became military leader of the United Irishmen. He was betrayed just before the 1798 insurrection and died from wounds.

George Robert Fitzgerald (1748-1786), known as "Fighting Fitzgerald", was a "noted duellist and lawless desperado". Born in Co. Mayo, he was a descendant of the Desmond branch of the Fitzgerald family. One account of him relates that "he brought one young wife to an early grave, mourned for her in an extravagant manner, and before long married a second. An account of his wild freaks and lawless excesses would fill a small volume. Most of his life was spent on his paternal estate in Co. Mayo. There he hunted by torchlight, terrified his friends by keeping a bear and other ferocious animals as pets, erected a fort and set the law at defiance, and even held his father to ransom for a sum of £3,000. On 12 June 1786 he was executed at Castleton, with two accomplices, for the murder of an obnoxious attorney."

John Francis Fitzgerald (1863-1950), long-time mayor of Boston, political boss and U.S. Congressman, called "Honey Fitz", personified the Irish talent for politics and oratory, a talent which was inherited by his Kennedy grandchildren. He once told an audience: "Having been wined and dined by all the high potentates of Europe, I return to the old North End, where every cobblestone beneath my feet seems to say, 'Welcome home, John F. Fitzgerald, welcome home . . .'"

Barry Fitzgerald (1888-1961), an actor often cast in quarrelsome but lovable roles, won an academy award in 1945 for best supporting actor in *Going My Way*. Born William Joseph Shields in Dublin on March 10, 1888, Fitzgerald was trained for the civil service and for several years pursued a dual career as civil servant and actor, appearing with the Dublin Abbey Players. In 1929 he appeared in the London production of *The Silver Tassie* which Sean O'Casey had written for him, and five years later he made his New York debut in another O'Casey play, *The Plough and the Stars*. He then went to Hollywood and appeared in such notable films as

Lord Edward Fitzgerald

The Long Voyage Home (1940), *How Green was My Valley* (1941) and *The Quiet Man* (1952). He died in Dublin on January 4, 1961.

F. Scott Fitzgerald (1896-1940), American novelist and short story writer, has been hailed as the spokesman and embodiment of the Jazz Age, a term which he coined. He was more popular for the way he lived than for what he wrote. In 1920, with the publication of his first novel *This Side of Paradise,* he was made instantaneously famous and momentarily rich. He married Zelda Sayre in the Spring of that year and their New York honeymoon was, in Fitzgerald's words, "the greatest, gaudiest spree in history". "With their good looks, their wit, and their charm", they quickly achieved the success they had dreamed of. But Fitzgerald had to struggle to maintain the style of life he had become accustomed to, and the success was never long-lasting. After his second novel, *The Beautiful and the Damned,* he went to live in Paris in 1924 and the next year published *The Great Gatsby,* a critical success but a financial failure. From that point on the going was mostly downhill. His wife had a mental breakdown in the late 1920's from which she never recovered. Fitzgerald began complaining of "emotional bankruptcy" and in 1934 moved to Hollywood to write for the movies. The theme of surrender and defeat which ran through his novels ran through his life. He was fascinated by wealth, but at the same time disgusted with the moral turpitude that seemed to accompany it. He was working on *The Last Tycoon,* a novel, when he died of a heart attack in Hollywood in 1940.

Fitzgibbon

GAELIC: Mac Giobúin

COMMON VARIATIONS: MacGibbon, Gibbons

The surname Gibbons (and its variants) in Ireland is of Anglo-Norman origin and, apart from English settlers of the name who came to Ireland after 1600, it can be traced back to two separate sources. One is the family first known as MacGibbon Burke which became established in Co. Mayo and were a branch of the great Norman-Irish family of Burkes in that county. The other is the Fitzgibbon family of Co. Limerick. Prior to 17th century their territory was the southeast corner of Co. Limerick near Co. Cork and the head of the family was one of the three hereditary knights in Desmond known as The White Knight. The other two were the Knight of Kerry and the Knight of Glin who were Fitzgeralds. In Co. Limerick the "Fitz" is often dropped and an "s" tacked on to the end in speech though seldom in writing.

John Fitzgibbon (1749-1802), Lord Chancellor of Ireland (1789-1802), was one of the most hated men in Ireland of his day for championing British rule and Protestant ascendancy. Born near Donnybrook, he was trained as a barrister and entered the Irish Parliament in 1778 as a moderate patriot. But in the 1780's he became a leading advocate of union with Britain, an event which he ultimately saw accomplished in 1801, the year before his death.

James Gibbons (1834-1921), Cardinal and Archbishop of Baltimore, known especially for his support of the growing labor movement in America and his close friendship with many U.S.

Presidents. In 1917 Theodore Roosevelt wrote to him: "Taking your life as a whole, I think you now occupy the position of being the most respected and venerated and useful citizen of our country." He was very successful in interpreting the United States to church officials in Rome, notably in the controversy over the so-called heresy of Americans in the late 19th century. He was equally successful at interpreting the church to the American people and his most famous book, *The Faith of Our Fathers,* which is a simple and clear explanation of Catholic doctrine, has sold over two million copies. Cardinal Gibbons also wrote a considerable number of articles on public questions relating to religion and morals and several other books besides *Faith of Our Fathers,* including *Our Christian Heritage, Discourses and Sermons,* and *A Retrospect of Fifty Years.*

Fitzpatrick

GAELIC: Mac Giolla Phádraig
COMMON VARIATIONS: MacGilpatrick, MacKilpatric, MacIlpatrick, Kilpatrick

This is the only "Fitz" name in Ireland which is of native Irish origin. The others are all Norman. Up until the 17th century the name usually appeared as MacGilpatrick or MacKilpatrick. (The Irish Mac Giolla Phadraig means follower or devotee of St. Patrick). The Fitzpatricks take their name from Giolla Padraig, a 10th century chief in the territory of Ossory (present-day Co. Kilkenny and adjacent areas). Later on the head of the family became Lord of Upper Ossory ruling over the counties of Leix and Kilkenny. It is in this area where most of the 10,000 Fitzpatricks in Ireland today are found. The name is also common in Fermanagh, however, where the Fitzpatricks are said to be related to the MacGuires.

Brian Fitzpatrick (1585-1652) Vicar Apostolic of Ossory who was murdered by Cromwellian soldiers, transcribed the "Book of the O'Byrnes" and thus saved it from destruction.

Thomas Fitzpatrick (1799-1854), American fur trapper, frontier guide and Indian agent, was born in Co. Cavan, Ireland, and came to the United States in his youth. In 1823 he pioneered the opening of the beaver country in the central Rocky Mountains and in 1830 he organized the Rocky Mountain Fur Co. which he headed for four years. After the fur trade declined he guided the first emigrant wagon train over the Oregon Trail in 1841 and was chosen by John C. Fremont as guide for his 1843-44 exploring expedition to Oregon and California. His next guide post was with General Stephen W. Dearny and his Dragoons on their tour of the western mountains in 1845 and in 1846 served as guide to Kearny's Army of the West in the first year of the Mexican War. In 1847 he became the first Indian agent to the tribes of the Upper Platte and Arkansas rivers and in 1851 negotiated the Ft. Laramie peace treaty with the largest assembly of Indians ever held. Two years later he negotiated a treaty with the hostile Comanche and Kiowa tribes. Fitzpatrick died of pneumonia on 7 February, 1854, in Washington, D.C.

Another Thomas Fitzpatrick (1832-1900) was a well known physician in Ireland.

Hugh Johnson Kilpatrick (1836-1881), Civil War general and diplomat, commanded the cavalry of Sherman's army in the march from Savannah to Atlanta in 1864 and in 1865 was appointed minister to Chile. He was re-appointed to this post in 1881 and died that year in Valparaiso.

William Heard Kilpatrick (1871-1965), American educator often called the "father of progressive education", applied the theories of John Dewey to education and originated the "project method" of teaching. Born in White Plains, Georgia, he taught philosophy of education at the Teachers College of Columbia University in New York. His books include *Education for a Changing Civilization* (1926), *Education and the Social Crisis* (1932) and *Philosophy of Education* (1951).

O'Flaherty

GAELIC: Ó Flaithbheartaigh

COMMON VARIATIONS: Flaverty, Laverty, O'Laverty

The O'Flaherties rose to power and prominence following the Anglo-Norman invasion. In the 13th century they were forced to leave their ancestral territory on the east banks of Lough Corrib. They moved across the lake into Connemara, the territory which became known as Iar-Connacht. This western district, at its largest, extended from Killary Harbour to the Bay of Galway and included the Aran Islands. In this almost inaccessible land the O'Flaherties reigned supreme for several centuries. With the neighboring Normans they earned themselves a reputation as a fierce and ferocious sept. The Norman "Tribes of Galway" inscribed the West Gate of their city, built in 1577, with the supplication "From the Ferocious O'Flaherties, God Defend Us". A Breton nobleman, arriving in Galway in the late 18th century for his "Rambles through Ireland", wanted to see the land to the west. The Galwegians thought him mad. The place was impossible, they said, with inhabitants as "savage as the Iroquois".

Some fifty years later the people of Connemara appear to have mellowed somewhat, enough to allow William Makepeace Thackeray to include the O'Flaherty domain in his Grand Tour. Thackeray was captivated by the land and described it as "one of the most wild and beautiful districts that it is ever the fortune of the traveller to examine."

A love for the land and its history was also instilled in the last recognized Chief of the Name for the sept, the celebrated historian Roderick, or Rory, O'Flaherty (1629-1718). His *Ogygia* is a chronological account of Irish events collected from ancient documents. O'Flaherty proudly wrote that "No nation in the world with more assiduity has preserved its antiquities from the earliest eras thereof, or transmitted to posterity with greater precision its chronological and genealogical accounts, the achievements of its heroes, their propagation, the boundaries of their principalities, their laws – in short, everything relative to their antiquity . . .

I have entitled my book *Ogygia* for the following reasons given by Camden: 'Ireland is justly called *Ogygia*, i.e. *Very antient* according to Plutarch, for the Irish date their history from the first eras of the world; so that in comparison with them, the antiquity of all other countries is modern, and almost in its infancy.' "

Two O'Flaherties were distinguished priests in this century. The Rev. Colman E. O'Flaherty, brother of the first O'Flaherty mayor of Galway, was born in Carroroe in 1874 and ordained at Sioux Falls, South Dakota in 1901. As a church builder he established a record, erecting seven churches in nine years in the western part of the state. He was also instrumental in the development of Columbus College at Chamberlain and of Notre Dame Academy at Mitchell. During the First World War he went to France as Chaplain to the 28th Infantry of the American Expeditionary Force and was killed there on October 1, 1918.

The Rt. Rev. Mgr. Hugh O'Flaherty, born in Kerry, became known as "The Scarley Pimpernel of the Vatican" for his work in helping thousands of allied soldiers escape from German-occupied Italy during World War II. He disguised escaped allied prisoners as priests, nuns and bus drivers and organized escape routes for them. After the war he was named Notary of the Holy Office, the first Irishman ever to receive that honor. In 1960 he retired and returned to Cahirciveen, Co. Kerry, where he died in 1963.

Dublin-born author Oscar Fingal O'Flahertie Wills Wilde was so named because his father claimed that he was descended on the maternal side from the ancient chieftains of Connemara. The Wilde family had blood links with the West and had a fishing lodge on the wooded peninsula Illaunroe which juts into Lough Fee, near the Galway coast.

Liam O'Flaherty, author and novelist, was born in the Aran Islands in 1897. Educated at Rockwell College, Blackrock College, and University College, Dublin, his best known work is *The Informer*, a novel written in 1926 and later made into a film.

The poet "Eva" of *The Nation* was born Mary Eva Kelly in the home of her O'Flaherty grandfather, in Headford, Co. Galway. She is known for her patriotic poems and prose essays which she contributed to the Young Ireland party newspaper *Nation* under the name Eva. Her husband was the equally fervant Young Irelander, Kevin Izod O'Doherty.

Millionaire industrialist Stephen O'Flaherty, born in Passage East, Co. Waterford in 1905, introduced the Volkswagen into Ireland in 1950. It was the first time this car was assembled outside Germany.

O'Flanagan

GAELIC: Ó Flannagáin

COMMON VARIATIONS: Flanagan

This is an especially common surname in Co. Roscommon and the western seaboard counties of Mayo, Galway and Clare. It was in this part of Connacht where the most important sept of O'Flanagans originated. They stem from an O'Connor called Flanaga whose descendants served as stewards or "royal lords" to the O'Connor

Kings of Connacht. Two minor O'Flanagan septs were located at Toorah in northweat Fermanagh and in the barony of Ballybrit in Offaly. Descendants of these two families are still to be found in these places today.

Edward Joseph Flanagan (1886-1948), Roman Catholic priest, was founder of Boys Town. Born in Co. Roscommon, Flanagan came to the United States in 1898 at the age of 18. In 1912 he was ordained priest for the archdiocese of Omaha, and 10 years later founded his reclamation center for delinquent boys 11 miles west of the city. His work at Boys Town won him a world-wide reputation. After World War Two he served as a consultant in setting up youth programs in Japan and Korea.

John Flanagan (1865-1952) American sculptor born at Newark, New Jersey, his works include portrait busts, plaquettes, and commemorative medals. He designed the monumental clock of the Library of Congress as well as the U.S. quarter dollar bearing the likeness of George Washington.

John Bernard Flannagan (1895-1942), American sculptor is known for his small primitivistic animal figures.

O'Flynn

GAELIC: Ó Floinn

COMMON VARIATIONS: Flynn, O'Lynn

This is the name of several septs which originated in different parts of Ireland. Consequently the name is widely distributed, but it is especially prevalent in two main areas: Cork and Waterford in the south, and in the north along the borders of Connacht and Ulster where the counties of Roscommon, Leitrim and Cavan meet. Two O'Flynn septs were prominent in Co. Cork, while one family of O'Flynns in north Connacht held high positions under the royal O'Connor family. There was also a famous O'Flynn sept which occupied the territory in southern Antrim between Lough Neagh and the sea. Their ancestry can be traced back to the 4th-century King Colla Uais. In northern Ireland the name has become O'Lynn due to the aspiration of the F in modern Ulster Irish.

Numerous though they were, few Flynns have achieved a place in Irish history. Several, however, figured prominently in the Irish Brigades in France and many have made their mark in America.

William James Flynn (1867-1928), New York detective, headed the United States Secret Service from 1912-1917 and afterwards became head of the F.B.I.

Edward Joseph Flynn (1891-1953) Democratic boss of the Bronx, played a major role in the four presidential election victories of Franklin D. Roosevelt. He became a close friend of Roosevelt's during his term of office as New York Secretary of State from 1929-1939. From 1940-1943 he was Democratic national chairman and under orders from Roosevelt helped engineer the nomination of Truman as Roosevelt's running .mate in 1944. Educated and urbane, Flynn was far from being the usual type of city political boss. In 1947 he published a defense of his political philosophy in a book called *You're the Boss*.

Elizabeth Gurley Flynn (1890-1964), a leader of the Communist

Errol Flynn

party of America, helped found the American Civil Liberties Union in 1920 and remained prominent in that organization until 1940 when she was asked to resign because of her Communist affiliation. Her family settled in New York in 1900 and while she was still in her teens she became an active Socialist and well-known labor agitator. After joining the Communist party in 1937 she began writing a column for the *Daily Worker* and in 1961 was elected chairman of the party's national committee. She died in Moscow, September 5, 1964.

Errol Flynn (1909-1964), actor, born in Tasmania the son of a biology professor, was brought to Hollywood in 1934 "to fill the void left by the death of Rudolph Valentino". His early reputation was made as a swashbuckling hero in such films as *Captain Blood*, *The Charge of the Light Brigade*, and *The Adventures of Robin Hood*. Later he starred in *The Sun Also Rises* (1957) and *The Roots of Heaven* (1958). Known for his romantic escapades and financial jams, Flynn once said, "I never worry about money so long as I can reconcile my net income with my gross habits."

MacGee

GAELIC: Mag Aoidh

COMMON VARIATIONS: McGee, McGhee, Magee

This is an Ulster name which comes from the Irish "Mag Aodha", which means son of Aodh, or Hugh. A prominent Magee sept was situated in Co. Antrim where the large isthmus east of Lough Larne, Island Magee, is named after them. Other Magee septs were scattered about in northwest Ulster, some of them of Scottish origin, in the counties of Donegal and Tyrone. There was also a sept of Magees in Westmeath in early times but they were dispersed after the Anglo-Norman invasion. On the whole the early history of the Magees is obscure but several persons of the name were prominent in the 18th and 19th centuries.

Rev. William Magee (1766-1831), mathematician and Protestant Archbishop of Dublin, roused the ire of the Catholics in Ireland when he declared in a sermon in 1822 that "the Catholics had a church without a religion, and the dissenters a religion without a church". He pursued an aggressive policy of protestant propaganda and his polemical preaching generated considerable discussion of the points of the Protestant controversy.

Martha Maria Magee (1755-1846), foundress of Magee University College, Londonderry, inherited a fortune from her two soldier brothers, half of which she left to the Irish Presbyterian mission in India while the other half was put in a trust for the erection and endowment of a college for the education of the Irish Presbyterian ministry.

Two John Magees (1750-1809 and 1780-1814), father and son, were famous for the undaunted journalism of their newspaper *The Dublin Evening Post*.

In America there have been several prominent Magees of Irish extraction in the last century and in the early years of this century. Among them are the geologist William John McGee (1853-1912);

Charles McClung McGhee (1828-1906), financier; the politician and philanthropist Christopher Lyman Magee (1848-1901) who was owner of the Pittsburgh Times, member of the Pennsylvania State Senate and a delegate to the Republican National Convention from 1876-1896.

Gallagher

GAELIC: Ó Gallchobhair

The O'Gallaghers claim to be the chief family of the Cineal Connaill, a group of families traditionally said to be descended from Conall Gulban, son of Niall of the Nine Hostages. Their territory extended over a large area in the baronies of Raphoe and Tirhugh in Co. Donega. They were one of the leading septs in this region and their chiefs served as military marshals to the O'Donnells. The name ranks 14th on the list of most common surnames in Ireland. It is found mainly in the northwestern counties of Ulster and Connach, and in Co. Donegal where the sept originated.

The O'Gallaghers have produced an exceptional number of priests. Six of them were bishops of Raphoe in the 15th and 16th centuries. In the 18th century Most Rev. James O'Gallagher (1681-1751), Bishop of Raphoe and later of Ossory, was famous for his sermons which were usually preached in Irish. When published they ran to twenty editions.

Hugh Patrick Gallagher (1815-1882), frontier priest in America, was born in Killygordon, Ireland and came to America in 1837. He was ordained in 1840 and became the leader of Irish priests and congregations in the Western United States. He helped build churches in various mining camps and frontier towns and began the Church of Immaculate Conception in Oakland, California. He helped build St. Mary's Cathedral in San Francisco and in 1853 founded the *Catholic Standard*, the first Catholic newspaper on the West Coast. Father Gallagher is credited with the introduction of the parochial school system into California. Also the founder of St. Mary's hospital in San Francisco, he died there on March 10, 1882.

Michael James Gallagher (1886-1937) was bishop of Grand Rapids and Detroit.

William Davis Gallagher (1808-1894), American journalist and poet, was the son of an Irish refugee. From 1839-1850 he was associated editor of the Cincinnati *Gazette*. He published two books of poetry, *The Wreck of the Hornet* (1835) and *A Golden Wedding, and Other Poems* (1881).

Gorman

GAELIC: Mac Gormáin
COMMON VARIATIONS: MacGorman,

The original territory of this sept was the barony of Slievemargy in Co. Leix near the town of Carlow. They were driven out by the Anglo-Norman invaders, however, and two branches of the sept were formed when they resettled in Ibrickan in west Clare and in

Co. Monaghan. The Ibirckan branch fared the better of the two, as their chiefs became hereditary marshals to the Thomond O'Briens. In the 15th century they were especially noted for their "wealth, hospitality and for their patronage of the Gaelic poets". Gorman was originally a "Mac" name, but the prefix was generally dropped in the 18th and early 19th centuries when the native Irish were under almost complete English domination. When prefixes were restored during the ensuing period of national revival the Gormans mistakenly took up the "O" prefix instead of the proper "Mac". As a result few MacGormans are found today except in Co. Monaghan, while O'Gormas are prevalent in Co. Clare and plain Gorman is the variant common in Co. Tipperary. The man responsible for the mistaken substitution of the "O" for the "Mac" was "the celebrated gigantic Chevalier Thomas O'Gorman" (1725-1808). An exile vineyard owner in France, he was ruined by the French Revolution and made a new occupation of drawing up Irish pedigrees.

Finn MacGorman, bishop of Kildare from 1148-1160, is famous as the compiler of *The Book of Leinster*.

Two O'Gormans have been active in Irish politics. Nicholas Purcell O'Gorman (1778-1857) was secretary of the Catholic Association and Richard O'Gorman (1820-1895) was a member of the Young Ireland party.

In America James A. O'Gorman was the first Irish Catholic elected to the United States Senate.

O'Grady

GAELIC: Ó Grádaigh

COMMON VARIATIONS: Grady, Brady, Gready

This was a Dalcassian sept which originated in Co. Clare and later migrated to Co. Limerick where the Chief of the Name ("The O'Grady"), one of the few still recognized as such, still presides over the territory of Kilballyowen. Nevertheless, the majority of the 4,000 or so Gradys and O'Gradys in Ireland today are found in Co. Clare, but a significant number are also found in Mayo where a branch of the original Dalcassian sept is thought to have settled. A peculiar fact about this name is that it was changed to Brady by the leading O'Grady family in the 16th century during the reign of Henry VIII, presumably in an attempt to court Henry's favor by having a more English-sounding name.

Standish O'Grady (1766-1840), prosecuting counsel at the trial of Robert Emmet, succeeded in getting his man hanged for his part in the insurrections of 1798 and 1803. Standish Hayes O'Grady (1832-1915) has been called "the last of the grand old scholars of Ireland." And yet another Standish O'Grady wrote historical novels in the late 19th and early 20th centuries based on Cú Chulainn and other legendary figures of ancient Ireland. His work, more intended to arouse great patriotic feeling than achieve literary acclaim, includes *Red Hugh's Captivity*, *The Flight of the Eagle*, and *The Coming of Cuculain*.

More recently Desmond O'Grady, who was born in Limerick, has distinguished himself as a poet and journalist.

In America, Henry O'Grady was an eminent 19th century

journalist on the staff of the New York *Herald*. He was noted for his brilliant reporting in the years immediately following the American Civil War and for his liberal views on the Negro problem in the South where he was born and educated.

Frank O'Grady, born in Australia in 1909, is Vice-President of the Irish Historical Society there and the author of several novels, including *The Golden Valley* and *The Sun Breaks Through*.

The popular children's song "O'Grady Says" is reputedly based on an O'Grady who served abroad with the British army.

MacGrath

GAELIC: Mag Raith

COMMON VARIATIONS: McGrath, Magrath, Magraw, MacGra, MacGraw

This is the name of two distinct septs which originated in Thomond and in Ulster. The Thomond sept were hereditary poets to the O'Briens and were situated in what is now Co. Clare. A branch of this sept migrated to Co. Waterford and the name is now more common there than in the original territory. The Ulster MacGraths were centered around Termon MacGrath near the Fermanagh-Donegal border in Fermanagh, but they too eventually moved away from their home territory into the adjacent county of Tyrone where the name is now more prevalent than in Fermanagh. Descendants of the Ulster sept are also found in Co. Down where their name is often spelled MacGraw, and in Donegal where MacGragh is the common variant.

The most remarkable and notorious bearer of the name was Miler MacGrath (1523-1622) of the Fermanagh sept. He began his religious career as a Franciscan friar, later changed faith and became Protestant Archbishop of Cashel while still holding the Catholic bishopric of Down. Not a man to be outdone, in 1604 he held four bishoprics and seventy livings and was twice married.

Joseph McGrath is a leading racehorse owner in Ireland and organizer of the Irish Hospitals Sweepstakes.

In America, Andrew Condon Magrath (1813-1893), Confederate Civil War veteran and judge, became governor of Carolina. James Howard McGrath (b. 1903), governor of Rhode Island and U.S. Senator in the 1940's, was U.S. Attorney General under President Truman. His term of office was a stormy one, as he clashed with the President's special investigator in a clean-up job to oust corrupt officials, and he resigned in 1952.

MacGuire

GAELIC: Mag Uidhir

COMMON VARIATIONS: Maguire

This name is associated exclusively with Co. Fermanagh. The Maguires were a leading sept in that county and one of the most important ruling septs in Ulster. Their prominence dates from the beginning of the 14th century and they maintained their high position in the Gaelic aristocracy of northern Ireland for the next 300 years. Then, for their part in the wars against the English in the 16th and 17th centuries, they were dispossessed of their lands by the Plantation of Ulster in the early 1600's and later on in the century by the confiscations ordered by Cromwell and William. As a result, the Maguires of Fermanagh, along with the Mac-Mahons, the O'Neills, and the O'Donnells, disappeared from the landed aristocracy of the North. Many of them went to the continent where, as Wild Geese, they took positions in the service of France and Austria. In spite of the ultimate English victory in the North, it wasn't an easy one. The Maguire family provided some of the strongest opponents to the invaders.

Hugh Maguire (d.1600), Lord of Fermanagh, was the first of the Northern chiefs to resist the English in their attempt to penetrate Ulster in the closing decade of the 16th century. He succeeded his father as chief in 1589 and promptly defied the English government to appoint a sheriff in his lands. In 1594 he defeated a small English force at the "Ford of the Biscuits" near Enniskillen, marking the beginning of the great rising of Northern chiefs. Four years later he was in command of the cavalry at the Battle of the Yellow Ford where the English suffered their only major defeat against the Irish at this period. In 1600 he died of wounds received in a skirmish near Cork.

Cuconnaught Maguire, brother and successor of Hugh, is said to be the one who procured the ship for The Flight of the Earls in 1607. He accompanied them into exile and died in Genoa the following year.

Conor Maguire (1616-1645), Baron of Enniskillen, was one of the group of Ulster nobles who plotted to seize Dublin Castle and instigate a general uprising against the English in Ulster in 1641. The date fixed for the rebellion was October 23. The day before, the plot to take the castle was revealed, but the insurrection went off according to plan in Ulster and with it began the Rising of 1641. But it was soon put down, and for his part in it Maguire was arrested, removed to the Tower of London, tried, convicted, and executed in 1645.

Thomas Maguire (1792-1847), "Father Tom", was parish priest of Drumreilly and Ballinamore and belonged to one of the highest families of the Knockninny Maguires. Besides being an ardent controversialist, "he used to boast that he was the best shot, the best coarser, the best quoit-player, the best breeder of greyhounds, pointers, and spaniels and the best brewer of 'scaltheen' in the whole of county Leitrim," according to the Gentleman's Magazine's obituary notice of him.

Another Maguire priest, Charles Bonaventure McGuire (1768-1833) laid the cornerstone of St. Paul's Church on Grant Hill in Pittsburgh in 1829. When finally completed under his successor it was one of the largest churches in America. Born in Dungannon, Co. Tyrone, McGuire was forced by the penal laws to flee the country. After studying at Louvain he was ordained a Franciscan friar and for several years led an adventurous life in and out of the hands of French revolutionaries and Bonapartists until he went to America in 1817.

Hunter Holmes McGuire (1835-1900), a descendant of a Co. Kerry man who settled in Virginia in 1747, was personal physician to Stonewall Jackson and chief surgeon for his troops during the

Civil War. After the war he became Professor of Surgery at Virginia Medical College and was instrumental in setting up the College of Physicians and Surgeons in Richmond in 1893, later named University College of Medicine. Always an ardent Southerner, Dr. McGuire is commemorated by an heroic-size statue of him in Capital Sq., Richmond.

MacGuinness

GAELIC: Mag Aonghusa, Mag Aonghuis
COMMON VARIATIONS: Guinness, MacGenis, Magennis

There are over 22 variants of this name, but the most common English spelling is McGuinness, which means literally "son of Angus". (The Scottish counterparts are Innes, Innis and Macinnes.) Originally the McGuinnesses were Kings of Ulster, but their power waned and it was not until the twelfth century that their fortunes and power were restored and they became the principal territorial lords of Iveagh in Co. Down. The subsequent history of the county is one of fighting to regain land from the English, fending off the O'Neills of Tyrone to the west, and trying to keep out the Scots. But in the 17th century, following the ill-fated rebellion which broke out in 1641 and the Battle of the Boyne with the English in 1690, the McGuinnesses were dispossessed of their lands and, like many of their fellow countrymen, many of them fled to the Continent. Of those who joined with Sarsfield as Wild Geese, the best known was Brian Magennis, second Viscount Iveagh, who was colonel of Iveagh's Regiment in the Austrian Imperial Army and was killed in 1703. His brother, Roger, third Viscount (died 1709) served in both France and Spain.

The McGuinnesses staunchly supported the Irish cause during the Battle of the Boyne but, for a short period about a century earlier, the sept showed some Protestant leanings. Two conforming bishops were McGuinnesses—one of the diocese of Down, the other of Dromore.

The name McGuinness is of course most famous for the form it appears in on those little brown bottles from Dublin. The founder of the Guinness Brewery was Arthur Guinness, born in 1725 in Leixlip, Co. Kildare. His father, Richard, was agent and receiver to the Archbishop of Cashel. Arthur moved to Dublin in 1759 and with a legacy of £100 he set up on December 31 of that year what was later to become the largest brewery in the world. The Guinness Brewery presently covers more than 60 acres in Dublin and employs about 4,000 people. Its present chairman is Viscount Elvedon, the fifth direct descendant of the founder.

Charles Donagh Maginnis, the well known architect, was born in Derry City in 1867. Trained in Dublin, he went to the United States where he became associated with Edmund Wheelwright in Boston in 1885 as a designer. He eventually founded his own firm in 1898. Maginnis was three times awarded the gold medal of the American Institute of Architects and served as its president in 1937-38. He received the Laetar Medal in 1924, became a Knight of Malta in 1945, and received honorary degrees from Boston

College, Harvard, Holy Cross and Tufts. Among his outstanding monuments are: the National Shrine of the Immaculate Conception and Trinity College chapel in Washington; the Cathedral in Baltimore; campus buildings of Boston College, Holy Cross and Notre Dame; the Carmelite Convent in Santa Clara; the bronze doors of St. Patrick's Cathedral, New York; and many churches, schools and hospitals throughout the United States. He died in Boston in 1955.

O'Hara

GAELIC: Ó hEaghra

This sept goes back to earliest times in Irish history when Eaghra, of the family of Olioll Ollum, King of Munster, became chief of Leyn in Co. Sligo. His descendants called themselves O hEaghra, or O'Hara as the anglicized version of the name is written. About the middle of the 14th century two divisions of the sept were formed in Co. Sligo and later a branch migrated to Co. Antrim. Most of the O'Haras in Ireland today are found in these two counties.

Kane O'Hara (1712-1782), born in Co. Sligo, is famous as the author of *Midas,* a burlesque which he wrote to parody the Italian burletta which was the rage in Dublin around the middle of the century. The piece was a hit both in Dublin and in London and was still being performed nearly a century after it first appeared.

Rev. William O'Hara (1816-1899) was the first bishop of Scranton, Pennsylvania. Born in Derry in 1816, he emigrated with his parents to Philadelphia at the age of four. After deciding that he wanted to enter the priesthood, he went to Rome to study and was ordained in 1843. He returned to Pennsylvania and by 1860 had become vicar-general of Philadelphia. He was consecrated bishop of Scranton in 1868.

James O'Hara (1752-1819) was a revolutionary soldier and early industrialist in Pennsylvania. He emigrated from Ireland to Philadelphia in 1772 and soon found work in Pittsburgh with a firm which traded with the Indians. At the outbreak of the Revolutionary War he volunteered as a private and later became captain of his own company of volunteers. From 1781-83 he was assistant quartermaster for General Greene. After the war O'Hara was a private contractor for the government and in 1792 was appointed quartermaster of the United States army by President Washington. He is even credited with "saving the army" by his efficient business methods and remarkable understanding of the Indian mentality. Around the turn of the century he founded the first glassworks in Pittsburgh. Another one of his ventures was as a pioneer in the cotton trade to Liverpool. Very prominent in the affairs of Pittsburgh, he was also director and finally president of the Pittsburgh branch of the Bank of Philadelphia.

Theodore O'Hara (1820-1867) was a journalist and soldier born in Danville, Kentucky, the son of Kean O'Hara who escaped from Ireland after being implicated with Lord Edward Fitzgerald in the Irish conspiracy of 1798. O'Hara studied to become a lawyer, but finding the legal life too tame for him he turned to journalism and soldiering. During the Mexican War he served from 1846-48

Maureen O'Hara

as captain and assistant quartermaster of a group of Kentucky volunteers. The following year he joined Narciso Lopez's expedition to liberate Cuba. In the 1850's there was a lull in his fighting activities and he took editorial positions with the Louisville *Times* and the Mobile *Register*. At the outbreak of the Civil War he raised the Mobile Light Dragoons and in January, 1861, seized Fort Barrancas in Pensacola Harbor. He later became colonel of the 12th Alabama Infantry. O'Hara had the Irish gift of oratory and he is remembered for his poem "The Bivouac of the Dead" commemorating Kentucky soldiers killed in the battle of Buena Vista. He also wrote a short dirge for Daniel Boone and a eulogy of William Taylor Barry which is regarded as a masterpiece of Southern oratory.

Maureen O'Hara, the titian-haired Hollywood actress once called the "Queen of Technicolor", was born in Dublin on August 17, 1921. The daughter of a merchant farmer and a part-time actress at the Abbey Theatre, she herself was already acting with the Abbey Players by the age of 14. In 1938 she was brought to Hollywood by Charles Laughton and the following year he played opposite her in *Jamaica Inn* and *The Hunchback of Notre Dame*. From then on she was on the way to becoming one of Hollywood's leading ladies, starring in *How Green was my Valley* (1941), *The Miracle on 34th Street* (1947), *The Quiet Man* (1952), *The Long Gray Line* (1955) and *Our Man in Havana* (1959). She became a United States citizen in 1946.

Novelist John O'Hara was born on January 31, 1905, in Pottsville, Pennsylvania. He has been called "the self-appointed chronicler of the 'hangover generation'" — the post — F. Scott Fitzgerald biographer of the Ivy League graduate and his girl friend. When his father died in 1925 he went to work at a variety of odd jobs and gradually drifted into journalism, writing for newspapers in Pennsylvania and New York, and finally for *Time* and the *New Yorker*. His first novel, *Appointment in Samarra*, appeared in 1934, followed a year later by *Butterfield 8*, *Pal Joey* (1940), *Ten North Frederick* (1955) and *From the Terrace* (1958). The money theme runs strong through all his novels perhaps because O'Hara has always felt slighted that his father died without leaving him enough money to go to Yale.

O'Hennessy

GAELIC: Ó hAonghusa
COMMON VARIATIONS: Hennessy, Henchy

There were several distinct septs of this name which is now very common in Munster. The principal sept had their territory in the northern part of Co. Offaly. A branch of this family settled in the border region between the counties of Meath and Dublin, and other branches spread into Tipperary and Clare. (In Co. Clare they are now called Henchy.) Finally, there was a sept of O'Hennessys situated near Ross Bay in Southwest Cork. Today the name is found mainly in the counties of Cork, Limerick and Tipperary. The Irish form of the name—O hAonghusa—means descendant of Aonghus, or Angus.

The French Hennessys, famous for their cognac, are of Irish

descent. They came to France in the 18th century as Wild Geese. Richard Hennessy (b.1720) of Ballymacmoy, Co. Cork, was an officer in Dillon's Regiment in France and settled in Cognac about 1750. His son James was a member of the French Chamber of Deputies and became a peer of France. He married a Martell, thus linking himself with another famous cognac family in France.

Sir John Pope Hennessy (1834-1891) was the first Catholic Conservative Irish member of the British House of Commons.

In America William John Hennessy (1839-1917) became a well known landscape and genre painter after studying at the National Academy of Design in New York. He later moved to London.

Rev. John Hennessy (1825-1900) was Archbishop of Dubuque.

Jean Hennessy (b.1874), French journalist and political leader, was director of the newspaper *Le Quotidien* and president of the French League of Nations Society.

Henry

GAELIC: Mac Éinrí, Ó hInnereirghe
COMMON VARIATIONS: O'Henry, MacHenry

The majority of Irishmen with some form of the surname Henry today stem from an Ulster sept, O'Inneirghe, which was situated at Cullentra in Co. Tyrone. There are, however, a few additional sources of the name. The MacHenrys of Co. Limerick are descendants of the MacInneirghe sept whose seat was in the barony of Upper Connelloe in that county. In Co. Wexford the name Henry appears as an abbreviation of the Norman name Fitzhenry. A branch of the Fitzhenrys settled in Connacht where they eventually came to be called MacHenry.

Three James McHenrys were prominent in America in their day. James McHenry (1753-1816) of Ballymena, Co. Antrim, became private secretary to George Washington. In 1771 he joined the throng of emigrants leaving Ulster for Philadelphia. There he studied medicine under Benjamin Rush and, when the Revolutionary War broke out, he joined the army as a surgeon "because of his pronounced hostility to England". His efficiency soon drew the attention of his superior officers and in 1778 Washington appointed him his private secretary. In 1781 he was elected to the Maryland Senate and served as Maryland's delegate to the Constitutional Convention. His private record of the Convention has proved an invaluable historical document. McHenry served as Secretary of War under Washington and Adams from 1796-1800. But he fell out with Adams, resigned the post and retired to his estate at Fayetteville near Baltimore where he died in 1816.

Another James McHenry (1785-1845) also emigrated from Co. Antrim to Philadelphia, in 1817, and also studied medicine there. As well as becoming one of the city's leading physicians he was active as a merchant, political leader, magazine editor, poet and critic. But for all his many talents, it has been said, "his sole contribution to American letters was his portraiture of the Ulster Irishman, who in conduct, beliefs, and religious tenets resembles the lowland Scot." In 1843 he was appointed American consul in Londonderry, and after two years in office died in his native town of Larne.

The son of the above, also James (1816-1891), was an American financier and patron of the arts and letters. At the time of the Great Famine in Ireland he introduced Indian corn to replace the diseased potato.

Miler Fitzhenry was one of the chief Anglo-Norman invaders of Ireland. In 1199 he was appointed Lord Justice of Ireland by King John, a post which he held until 1208. During his time he dispossessed many native chieftains in Connacht and acquired large tracts of land there. He is described by a 19th century historian as being "of a dark complexion with black eyes and a stern, piercing look. Below the middle height, for his size he was a man of great strength. Broad-chested and not corpulent, his arms and other limbs were bony and muscular, and not encumbered with fat. An intrepid and adventurous soldier, he never shrank from any enterprise, whether singly or in company, and was the first in the onset, the last in retreat. He would have deserved the highest praise if he had been less ambitious of worldly honours, and had paid due reverence to the Church of Christ."

Higgins

GAELIC: Ó hUigín

COMMON VARIATIONS: O'Higgin

The O'Higgins sept was a branch of the southern O'Neills which moved westward into Co. Sligo where they acquired large estates. They were still extensive landowners in the 19th century, holding estates in nearly all the western counties. Today O'Higgins are still found mainly in Co. Sligo.

A remarkable fact about this sept is the number of outstanding poets it produced in the three hundred years beginning with Tadhg Mor O'Huigin, who died in 1315, to Tadhg Dall, who died in 1617. They seemed to average one a generation. A poem by the 16th century Pilib Bocht O'Huigin was the first to be printed in the Irish language. Their achievements were not restricted to literature, however. John Higgins (1676-1729) was a famous doctor in Spain.

By far the most famous O'Higgins is Bernardo O'Higgins (1778-1842), "Liberator of Chile" who is ranked with Bolivar and San Martin as one of the great liberators of South America. Born in Chillán, Chile, the son of Ambrosio O'Higgins, an Irish soldier and trader who, after 1788, served as captain general of Chile, Bernardo was sent to England for his education. He returned to Chile in 1802 and in 1810 joined the Chilean revolutionists. In 1813 he was appointed head of the Chilean army but was defeated by the invading Spanish army the following year and had to flee across the Andes to Argentina. In 1817 O'Higgins was one of the chief lieutenants of the liberating army under San Martin who marched back into Chile and defeated the Spaniards at Chacabuco. As a result of this victory O'Higgins was made dictator of Chile after San Martin declined. Under his rule Chile's independence was formally declared and the Spaniards were driven out. Many of his proposed democratic reforms, however, were opposed by the aristocratic party and O'Higgins was deposed in 1823. He then went to Lima, Peru, where he spent the remainder of his life.

O'Holohan

GAELIC: Ó hUallacháin

COMMON VARIATIONS: Hoolahan, Houlihan, Holland, Mulholland

This is the name of two prominent septs which arose independently in the Co. Clare area of Thomond and the Offaly region of Leinster. In time both migrated to the south, so that the name is now most prevalent in Co. Kilkenny—where it is spelled Holohan—and in west Munster—where it is spelled Houlihan. In all, some 17 variant spellings of this name have been recorded. Many of the Houlihans who reached Co. Cork in their southward migration from Clare and Offaly adopted the name Holland as the English equivalent of their surname.

John Philip Holland (1840-1914), Irish-American inventor, was born in Co. Clare and emigrated to America in 1973. He designed the first submarine which was able to run underwater for extended lengths of time, thus making it an important element in sea power. This was launched in 1898 and purchased by the United States Navy in 1900. Holland also built submarines for Britain, Russia and Japan.

O'Hurley

GAELIC: Ó hUrthhuile

COMMON VARIATIONS: Hurley, O'Herlihy

This very common surname is the anglicized form of two distinct Gaelic names, Ó hUirthile of Thomond and Ó Muirthile or Ó Murghaile of Co. Cork. The Thomond Hurleys are now found mainly in Co. Limerick although their original homeland was in Co. Clare. The vast majority of Hurleys in Ireland today, however, come from Co. Cork and are sometimes, though rarely, called Murley. Their ancestral territory was situated near Kilbritain in Carbery East, Co. Cork.

Dermot O'Hurley (1519-1584), Archbishop of Cashel, is noted for his act of martyrdom in defiantly refusing to acknowledge the "Queen's religion" in Ireland. Born in Co. Limerick, he was educated at Paris and Louvain and in 1581 appointed to the see of Cashel. But soon after he arrived to take up his post he was arrested "bearing treasonable papers" and subjected to excruciating torture. "The executioners placed the Archbishop's feet and calves in tin boots filled with oil; they then fastened his feet in wooden shackles, or stocks, and placed fire under them. The boiling oil so penetrated the feet and legs that morsels of the skin, and even flesh, fell off and left the bone bare." The Archbishop reluctantly refused to purchase a cessation of his torments by acknowledging the Queen's supremacy in matters of religion. An end was put to his sufferings by his being hanged on a tree outside Dublin, 19 June 1584.

Patrick Hurley (d.1700) led an adventurous and infamous career as an informer and self-styled "Count of Mountcallan".

Joyce

GAELIC: Seoigh

This name was brought to Ireland in the second half of the 13th century by a Welshman, Thomas de Jorse, or Joyce, who married the daughter of O'Brien, Prince of Thomand. The marriage was undoubtedly a judicious move on the Welshman's part, for it linked him with one of the most prominent and powerful Gaelic families in southern Ireland. But Joyce did not remain in O'Brien territory. He took his bride across Galway Bay into West Connacht and there settled in the mountainous region between Galway and Mayo. Although the family was at first tributary to the O'Flahertys, they soon became established in their own right. They adopted the native Irish custom of having a Chief of the Name and the territory they inhabited became known as Joyce's Country. They were one of the 14 Tribes of Galway and several Joyces have been mayor of that city. The Joyces are still prominent in this part of Ireland today with over 80% of the persons by that name in the country coming from Galway or Mayo.

James Joyce (1882-1941), the writer whose original and varied styles have had immeasurable influence on 20th century literature, was born in Dublin on February 2, 1882, the eldest son of John Stanislaus Joyce, member of an old Cork family. Joyce was a master craftsman with words and an innovator of language. He worked with words, trying, as he has Stephen Dedalus say in *A Portrait of the Artist as a Young Man*, "to forge in the smithy of my soul the uncreated conscience of my race". Joyce wrote only two more works after this was published in 1916. *Ulysses*, a Joycean version of the *Odyssey*, spans one day in the life of several Dubliners and is a record of both the conscience and consciousness of those people. Because of its frankness of description and language the book was banned for 11 years after its publication in 1922. But it has since come to be recongized as one of the greatest works of literature. After completing *Ulysses*, Joyce spent the next 17 years working on *Finnegans Wake,* which is written in a language Joyce invented to try to portray the world of dreams. This time it was a form he forged to try to express the subconscious thought of the race.

Although Joyce wrote about the Irish and Ireland, he could not write there, and after leaving the country in 1904 with his wife-to-be, he spent the remainder of his life on the Continent in self-imposed exile. He taught English in language schools in Pola and Trieste until World War I and then moved to Zurich. It was here that he suffered his first attack of glaucoma, the eye disease which was to trouble him for the rest of his life. In 1920 he and his family moved to Paris and stayed there until 1939. Then Joyce moved back to Zurich where he lived until his death in 1941.

Patrick Weston Joyce (1827-1914), scholar and historian, born in Ballyorgan, Limerick, is best known for his classic volume *Irish Names of Places*. He also published a collection of folk songs and music. His brother, Robert Dwyer Joyce (1830-1883), started out life as an English teacher, then decided to become a physician. He took his M.D. degree in 1865 and the following year emigrated with his family to America where he settled in Boston. He was elected a member of the Royal Irish academy and wrote many ballads, songs, and sketches for the *Pilot* and other Irish journals.

James Joyce

His best work is "Deirdré"—and epic poem published in 1876. He also published *Legends of the Wars in Ireland* (1868), *Fireside Stories of Ireland* (1871), and *The Squire of Castleton* (1879), an historical novel.

Issac Wilson Joyce (1836-1905) was a famous Methodist revivalist preacher in America.

Kavanagh

GAELIC: Caomhanach

COMMON VARIATIONS: Keevan, Kevane

The Kavanaghs were a famous branch of the MacMurrough sept. The name, which means follower of St. Caomhán, was applied to Donal MacMurrough whose descendants then became known as Kavanagh. His father, Dermot MacMurrough, King of Leinster, was the man immediately responsible for the Anglo-Norman invasion through his deals to gain military support from the Welsh marcher lords. The Kavanagh territory was situated in that part of Leinster which is now Counties Wexford and Carlow. It is still in this area where most of the Kavanaghs in Ireland today can be found.

The Kavanaghs were particularly noted for their stature. In the second half of the 17th century when many members of the family fought on the side of King James, Brian Kavanagh is said to have been the tallest man in King James's army. After the Jacobite defeat at the Battle of the Boyne in 1691 many Kavanaghs had to flee to the continent where they reached high positions as officers in the Irish Brigades in France and also distinguished themselves in court circles in Austria. Morgan Kavanagh, who became Governor of Prague in 1766, is reputed to have been the "biggest man in Europe" in his day. Joseph Kavanagh had his moment of glory in France as the leader of the attack on the Bastille July 14th 1789. A pamphlet written at the time describes in detail the "Exploits glorieux du célèbre Kavanagh, cause première de la Révolution."

Arthur MacMurrough Kavanagh (1831-1889) was a remarkable man and M.P. for Cos. Wexford and Carlow from 1865-1880. Although he had only stumps of arms and legs, he became an expert horseman, angler, writer, painter, and yachtsman and traveled extensively in Europe and Asia. He was also instrumental in introducing lace-making into his constituencies.

Another Morgan Kavanagh, father of Julia, was a writer and eccentric. He was born in Tipperary in 1800 and became known for his poems and novels.

In literature, the Kavanagh women were far more prominent during the 19th century than were their male contemporaries. The most illustrious of these was Julia Kavanagh (1824-1877) who spent her youth in Paris and traveled widely. She achieved an international reputation both as a novelist and a travel writer.

Edward Kavanagh (1795-1844), the son of an Irish immigrant to Maine, rose to become governor of that state for a brief period before his early death in 1844 at the age of 48. His father James was one of the builders of St. Patrick's Church at Damariscotta Mills, Maine—the oldest Catholic church still standing in New

Julia Kavanagh

England. After first serving in the State Legislature, Kavanagh was elected to Congress in 1831 and was a loyal supporter of the Jackson administration. In return for his support, Jackson appointed him chargé d'affaires in Portugal, a post which he held for six years. He then returned to Maine and was elected to the State Senate. In March, 1843 he became governor, but he died after only a few months in office.

The stronghold of the Wexford Kavanaghs was the Castle of Enniscorthy which stands to this day and houses an interesting folk museum.

Many of the monasteries which lie in ruins in counties Wicklow and Wexford were also built by Kavanaghs.

Keane

GAELIC: Ó Cathain, Ó Cein
COMMON VARIATIONS: O'Kane, O'Cahan

Keane, Kane and O'Kane are the modern anglicized variants of the Gaelic name Ó Catháin which belonged to two separate and unrelated septs in Ulster and Connacht. (The earlier anglicized form of this name was O'Cahan.) Kane and O'Kane are the variants most commonly found in Ulster where the chiefs of this sept were lords of Keenaght in Co. Derry until the Plantation of Ulster in the early 1600's. Though ruined as a sept by the Plantation, the family still thrives in Counties Derry and Tyrone. The Mac-Closkeys of Derry are an offshoot of these O'Kanes, being descended from Bloskey O'Kane who killed the heir to the throne of Ireland in 1196. The other Ó Catháin sept, usually anglicized to Keane, was a branch of the Ui Fiachrach located in Co. Galway. Though they never achieved great prominence, they were prolific and their descendants are numerous in this area today. Keane, or Kean, is also the anglicized form of another Irish surname, O Cein, which was a sept situated between Kilmacthoms and Bunmahon in Co. Waterford.

Echlin O'Kane (1720-1790), an Ulsterman though born in Drogheda, was one of the most famous Irish harp players of the 18th century, playing in several European courts.

Edmund Kean (1787-1833), English tragic actor born in London of Irish ancestry. His highly successful career dates fron his first appearance at the Drury Lane Theatre in the role of Shylock. He was praised by William Hazlitt and Charles Lamb and Coleridge once said, "To see Kean act is like reading Shakespeare by flashes of lightning". He specialized in tragic Shakesperian roles and was the foremost actor of his day in England. He visited the U.S. in 1820, appearing on the stage in New York, Boston and Philadelphia. Five years later his career suffered a severe setback when he was named co-respondent in a divorce case, and he never fully regained his former prominence. His son, Charles John Kean (1811-1864), manager of the Princess Theater, London, greatly influenced the art of play production by using imaginative settings and paying close attention to historical detail.

John Joseph Keane (1839-1918), Irish American bishop, was selected in 1884 to organize the Catholic University and became its first rector in 1889. In 1900 he was made archbishop of Dubuque.

Edmund Kean

Kearney

GAELIC: Ó Catharnaigh, Ó Cearnaigh
COMMON VARIATIONS: Carney, O'Kearney,
Keherney, McCarney

This is the anglicized form of two Gaelic surnames: O Cearnaigh and O Catharnaigh. O Cearnaigh is the name of two septs, one a branch of the Ui Fiachrach in Co. Mayo, and the other a branch of the Cal Cais who migrated to Cashel in Co. Tipperary. Kearney and Carney—the alternative spelling of the name in Connacht—are still common names in these counties today. The most important Kearney sept, however, were the O Catharnaighs of Teffia in Co. Meath. Because of an ancient tradition of referring to their chief as Sionnach, or "the fox", the Meath Kearneys are usually called Fox.

John Kearney of Fethard was secretary to James II. After the Jacobite defeat his family settled in France where they became prominent in French court and legal circles in the 18th century.

Stephen Watts Kearny (1794-1848), general in the American army on the Western frontier who commanded the troops which conquered New Mexico at the start of the Mexican-American War. He also fought in the Battle of San Pascual in California and after occupying Los Angeles was made governor of California in March, 1847. In June he rejoined the army in Mexico and stayed there until the end of the war.

Lawrence Kearny (1789-1868), cousin of Stephen Watts Kearny, was an officer in the American navy. After 1840 he served as commander of the East India squadron and had an important part in the conclusion of the first commercial treaty (1844) between the United States and China.

Dennis Kearney (1847-1907), Irish-American labor leader, was president of the Workingmen's Party of California. Born in Co. Cork, Kearney went to sea in 1858 and settled in San Francisco ten years later. He became foreman of the stevedores there and in 1877 formed the Workingmen's Party which spoke out against the land and railroad trusts and urged opposition to Oriental labor. In 1879 his party succeeded in getting legislation passed (though later repealed) to exclude Chinese from holding property. The party held its large mass meetings on a sandlot next to the new city hall. By 1880, however, the "Kearney Movement" was fading and Kearney retired from public activity.

O'Keeffe

GAELIC: Ó Caoimh

The O'Keeffes originated in Co. Cork and though they were forced from their original territory by the invading Normans in the early 13th century they resettled not far to the west, still within the present-day boundaries of Co. Cork. They became so firmly established in their new territory that it became known as Pobal O'Keeffe. The name in Irish, O Caoimh, is derived from a 10th-century chieftain whose father was King of Munster. O'Keeffe is

one of the few Irish "O" surnames which has consistently retained the prefix.

This was one of the many Irish families forced into exile after the defeat of James II. Constantine O'Keeffe (1671-1745) was an officer in the Irish Brigade in France and because of his distinguished Irish lineage he was admitted into the French aristocracy. General Patrick O'Keeffe (1740-1809) joined Dillon's Regiment in France, fought in the Seven Years' War and was with a French expeditionary force which fought on the side of the Colonies during the American Revolutionary War. In 1783 he was created Knight of St. Louis for his bravery in battle. Back in France he was a supporter of the Revolution and in 1795 was made general of a brigade and commandant of Besançon. He retired from active service in 1807.

In Ireland many O'Keeffes emerged as painters and dramatists. Daniel O'Keeffe (1740-1786) was a painter trained at the Dublin Society's drawing school who later exhibited at the Royal Academy in London. His brother John O'Keeffe (1747-1833) was a comic actor and writer who worked at the Smock Alley theater in Dublin. He turned more and more to writing as his sight failed him and he could no longer act, and though completely blind by 1797 he still kept up a steady output of humorous plays and much verse. His plays, which were produced in England as well as throughout Ireland, include *Tony Lumpkin In Town, The Castle of Andalusia*, and *Wild Oats*. Many of the songs from his comic operas remained popular for years and some, such as "Amo Amas" (I Love a Lass), are still sung today. In 1826, seven years before his death, he wrote his autobiography entitled *Recollections*. His portrait, by Thomas Lawrenson, now hangs in the National Portrait Gallery in London. Another John O'Keeffe (1797-1838) was a distinguished heraldic artist.

In America Georgia O'Keeffe (b. 1887) is an abstract painter whose works are characterized by their Oriental simplicity. Her favorite subjects are simple natural objects—rocks, bones, clouds, flowers and desert landscapes. (Since 1946 she has lived in New Mexico.) Two of her best known paintings, Black Iris (1926) and Black Flower and Blue Larkspur (1926) are hanging in the Metropolitan Museum of Modern Art in New York.

O'Kelly

GAELIC: Ó Ceallaigh

COMMON VARIATIONS: O'Keily, Kelly, Queally, MacKelly

The surname Kelly or O'Kelly is the second most common in Ireland, outnumbered only by the name Murphy. One recent estimate puts the number of Kellys now living in Ireland at 50,000, with countless thousands of others scattered throughout the world. There are about 25,000 Kellys and O'Kellys in the United States today and nearly that many in Canada. One would assume from the preponderance of the surname that not all of its bearers have sprung from one ancestor and, in fact, at least ten separate septs can be distinguished. The various septs are:

1. The O'Kellys of Uí Maine, in Connacht, from the eastern part of Co. Galway and the southern part of Co. Roscommon.
2. O'Kellys of Breagh, whose territory covered a large portion of Co. Meath and the northern part of Co. Dublin.
3. O'Kellys of Ulster, originating in the Barony of Loughinsholin, Co. Derry, where the name is still prominent.
4. O'Kellys of Leighe, now Lea, in Co. Laois.
5. O'Kellys of Magh Druchtain, Co. Laois.
6. O'Kellys of Gallen, Co. Laois.
7. O'Kellys of Uí Teigh, in the northern part of what is now Co. Wicklow.
8. O'Kellys of Ard O gCeallaigh, in the Parish of Templeboy, Co. Sligo.
9. O'Kellys of Corca Laoighdhe, in the southwest portion of Co. Cork.
10. O'Kellys of Clanbrasil MacCoolechan, Co. Down.

The O'Kellys of Uí Maine are by far the most prominent sept and its members are frequently mentioned in the annals of Irish history. In 1518 they were among the "dangerous" Irish septs proscribed by a by-law of Galway, a city then inhabited by "tribes" of Norman invaders. It was decreed that "neither O' ne Mac shall strutte ne swaggere thro' the streets of Gallway" and more specifically that citizens should not receive into their homes "any of the Burks, M'Williams, the Kellies, nor no cepte elles." The most famous Co. Galway O'Kelly of those times was Col. Chares O'Kelly (1621-1695), who fought in the 1641 Rebellion, was a commander under Sarsfield in 1690, and represented Co. Roscommon in the Parliament of 1689. He is best known, however, as the author of the contemporary history *Excidium Macariae*.

The list of illustrious O'Kellys since then is impressive.

In the 18th century Dennis O'Kelly (1720-1787), popularly known as "Count" O'Kelly, became the most renowned host of his day. He emigrated from Ireland and started off in London as a billiard room marker and a tennis court attendant. Falling into debt, he spent three years in Fleet Prison, but after his release he quickly regained social favor and later became part-owner of the famous racehorse Eclipse. With his friend Charlotte Hayes the Count built a home on Clay-hill near Epsom, and there they lavishly hosted their guests. O'Kelly claimed to be descended from Irish chieftains and always declared himself equal by birth to the greatest men in Europe. The story of his colorful life is told in *The Genuine Memoirs of Dennis O'Kelly commonly called Count O'Kelly*, published in London in 1788.

An equally colorful, if less fortunate Kelly, was Ned Kelly, the leader of Australia's bush-ranging "Kelly Gang". He was hanged in Melbourne on November 11, 1880.

In America John Henry Kelly fathered what was to become one of the most remarkable Irish-American families, "the Kellys of Philadelphia." John Henry was born in Co. Mayo and emigrated to America at the age of twenty. He began work as an unskilled laborer and eventually built up his own flourishing insurance business. Of his six sons, John Brendan (Jack) was a highly successful New York contractor and in 1920 became the first American to win an Olympic gold medal in sculling. His daughter, the actress Grace Kelly, is now Princess Grace of Monaco, after her marriage to Prince Rainier in 1956. Another son of John Henry was the Pulitzer Prize-winning writer George Kelly. He achieved

Princess Grace 'Kelly'

huge success with his post-World War I plays *Craig's Wife* and *The Show Off*.

Eugene Kelly (1808-1894) distinguished himself as a banker and philanthorpist in America, and his son, Thomas Hughes Kelly (1865-1933) followed in his father's philanthropic footsteps, directing the fortune left by his father. He donated the Lady Chapel of New York's St. Patrick's Cathedral.

The poet "Eva" of *The Nation* was born Mary Eva Kelly in the home of her O'Flaherty grandfather in Headford, Co. Galway. She is known for her patriotic poems and prose essays which she contributed to the newspaper *The Nation* under her pen name Eva.

Another poet and author of the same branch of the Kelly family as "Eva" of *The Nation* was Patrick Kelly, born near Mount Talbot, Co. Roscommon in 1879. He was raised in Cashel and after his years in Dublin as a Civil Servant and in France as a soldier, he returned to Cashel in 1922. His best known work is the volume of poems entitled *The Sally Ring*. Most of his poetry describes the land and the people of his beloved Connemara. Many of his essays and articles were published in the *Dublin Magazine*. He died in 1940.

Sir David Kelly, author and diplomat, was born in Adelaide, South Australia, on September 14, 1891. He was educated at St. Paul's School, London, and Magdalen College, Oxford and entered the Diplomatic Service in 1919. From 1949-1951 he was British Ambassador in Moscow. His books include his memoirs, *The Ruling Few; Beyond the Iron Curtain;* and *The Ungry Sheep*. He died in 1959.

Catherine Kelly, according to the *Guinness Book of Records,* was the shortest Irish adult dwarf. Born in 1756, she was known as "the Irish fairy" and stood 34 inches tall and weighed 22 lbs. She died at Norwich, Norfolk, England, on October 15, 1785.

Kennedy

GAELIC: Ó Cinnéide

COMMON VARIATIONS: O'Kennedy

This sept takes its name from Cinneide, or Kennedy, a nephew of Brian Boru. Their original territory was near Killaloe in East Clare. Under mounting pressure from their powerful neighbors the O'Briens and the MacNamaras, the Kennedys were forced to move eastward across the Shannon where they settled in Upper and Lower Ormond – what is now north Tipperary. Here they soon established their own base of power and from the 11th to the 16th centuries they were the ruling lords of Ormond. The name is now numerous and widespread throughout all of Ireland, but the greatest proportion of the 18,000 Kennedys in the country today are still found in Co. Tipperary. The name is the 16th most common surname in Ireland.

In spite of the great numerical strength of this sept, surprisingly few Kennedys have been prominent in Irish history. Those who have, have usually been associated with the literature of the country. Patrick Kennedy (1801-1873), for instance, kept Irish literary tradition alive in 19th century Dublin where he established a small lending library and bookshop on Anglesea Street.

Jack Kennedy

He was the author of an entertaining manual on Gaelic folklore — *Legendary Fictions of Irish Celts* — and he also wrote English versions of old Irish folk tales collected in *The Banks of the Boro*, *Evenings in the Duffrey*, and *Legends of Mount Leinster*.

Matthew Kennedy (1652-1735) was a colorful literary figure in Paris, noted for his enthusiasm for the Irish language. Born in Co. Limerick, he went to France after the capitulation of Limerick in 1691 and remained there for the rest of his life. Connected with the court in Saint Germain-en-Lay, he wrote *A Chronological, Genealogical and Historical Dissertation of the Royal Family of the Stuarts* in which he tried to prove that the Stuarts were of Irish descent. But he was more noted for his linguistic skills than for his insights as a genealogist and historian. One of his favorite pastimes was to have verse-writing competitions in Irish with an exiled abbe from Breffny also living in Paris. "Dr. Kennedy was my great friend," wrote the abbe, "and was surprised how I kept my Irish, being so long a time out of Ireland. He was jealous with me, for he thought no man a greater master of Irish than himself and published in all the courts of Saint Germain that he knew but me alone who could compare with him."

Patrick John Kenedy [sic] (1843-1906) maintained the family literary tradition in America. He was a Catholic book-seller and publisher in New York City and his firm P. J. Kenedy and Sons was one of the chief publishing houses in the English-speaking Catholic world.

The name is most well known, of course, through the famous Kennedy clan of Boston. Fathered by financier and ambassador Joseph P. Kennedy, they have become one of the most outstanding political families in America. They trace their roots back to Patrick Kennedy who left Co. Wexford, Ireland, in 1848 and came to Boston. His son Patrick J. (1862-1929) called "P.J." in the family, acquired some wealth in the saloon and banking businesses and was active in local politics. As a member of the Massachussetts legislature he became acquainted with John F. "Honey Fitz" Fitzgerald, the colorful longtime mayor of Boston, and in 1914 P.J.'s son Joseph P. and Honey Hitz's daughter Rose Fitzgerald were married. The Fitzgeralds and the Kennedys were part of the tradition of Irish control of Boston politics and when Joseph P. Kennedy amassed his fortune in the 1920's he was determined that his sons should achieve greatness in the political sphere. He destined his first son Joe Jr. to become president but when he was killed in action in the Second World War in 1944 the burden passed on to his younger brothers. Politics and Presidential ambitions were a matter of course among the Kennedys. "Just as I went into politics because Joe died, if anything happened to me tomorrow, my brother Bobby would run for my seat in the Senate. And if Bobby died, Teddy would take over for him," said John F. Kennedy before becoming the first Catholic President of the United States. After he was assassinated in office in 1963, his brother Robert, who had served as his attorney general, was killed by an assassin's bullet while campaigning for the Presidency in 1968. He once quipped while his brother Edward lay critically injured in a hospital after a plane crash in 1964, "I guess the only reason we've survived is that there are too many of us. There are more of us than there is trouble." Teddy is now Senator from Massachusetts and it remains to be seen if he will take over the presidential ambitions of his brothers.

O'Leary

GAELIC: Ó Laoghaire
COMMON VARIATIONS: Leary

This name is associated exclusively with Co. Cork where the O'Leary sept ruled as chiefs under the Muskerry MacCarthys in the remote territory of Inchigeela, at the eastern base of the Kerry Mountains. The O'Learys played a prominent part in the English wars fought in Munster and exiled members of the family later rose to high-ranking positions in the Irish brigades on the Continent.

Several O'Learys are known for their contributions to Irish culture, including the poetess Ellen O'Leary (1831-1889), Joseph O'Leary (1795-1855), the song-writer, and Father Peter O'Leary (1839-1919), better known as Peadar O Laoghaire, who was one of the first Irish writers of the Gaelic revival and in his day was called "the greatest living master of Irish prose."

The most famous of all the Irish O'Learys was the Fenian leader John O'Leary (1830-1907) who went to America in 1859 to drum up support for the advanced Fenian movement and then returned to Dublin to edit the Fenian weekly *Irish People*. This was seized by the government in 1865 and O'Leary was arrested and thrown in prison for nine years. In 1874 he retired to Paris and stayed there until 1885 when he returned to Ireland and became prominent in Dublin literary society. His enthusiasm for Irish literature was a particularly strong influence on W. B. Yeats at the time. "From O'Leary's conversation, and from the Irish books he lent or gave me," Yeats has written, "has come all I have set my hand to since." It was with O'Leary's support and influence that Yeats founded the National Literary Society in Dublin in 1892.

Mrs. O'Leary's Cow, as the legend goes, is supposed to have caused the fire which devastated Chicago in October, 1871. On October 1, a cow in Patrick Leary's barn on De Koven St. kicked over a lantern, starting a blaze which swept through hundreds of acres of frame buildings and is said to have produced a heat that was felt in Holland, Michigan, a hundred miles away across the lake.

MacLoughlin

GAELIC: Mac Lochlainn
COMMON VARIATIONS: MacLauchlin

MacLoughlin is the anglicized form of the names of two distinct Gaelic septs, both of which were fairly important at one time. One of these septs was called O Maoilsheachlain in Irish, a name which was always anglicized O'Malaghlin up until the end of the 17th century. They take their name from Maoilsheachlainn, better known as Malachy II, King of Ireland from 980-1002 when he was dethroned by Brian Boru. Their territory lay in what is now Co. Westmeath where most of the descendants of the sept are to be found today.

The other Irish sept whose name was anglicized to Mac-

Victor MacLoughlin

Loughlin was Mac Lochlainn. They were a senior branch of the Ulster O'Neills and had their territory in Inniṣhowan in Co. Donegal. The name is now very common in Donegal and Derry where it is usually spelt MacLaughlin. There were some minor MacLoughlin septs in Connacht related to the MacDermots and the O'Connors.

John McLoughlin (1784-1857), called the "Father of Oregon" was a Canadian pioneer and fur trader born in Riviere du Loup, Canada, of Irish ancestry. In 1821 he was made a chief factor in the Hudson Bay Company and was sent to administer its Columbia River territory. In 1825 he built Fort Vancouver – now Vancouver, Washington – in the Oregon Country and this remained his headquarters for the next 20 years. He resigned his post in 1846 and retired to Oregon City where the McLoughlin Institute was established in 1907 in his memory.

Maurice Evans McLoughlin (b. 1890), Pacific Coast tennis star nicknamed the California Comet, is credited with having changed the whole temper and style of the game and was largely responsible for starting tennis on its way to becoming a national sport in America. He was a dazzling and spectacular player and a member of the U.S. Davis Cup team in 1909, 1911, and 1913. He also wrote a book on the game, *Tennis as I Play It*, published in 1915.

Another eminent American member of the family was Victor MacLoughlin, movie star, who is best remembered for the *Informer*, set in Ireland in which he played the title role.

Lynch

GAELIC: Ó Loingsigh
NORMAN: de Lench

This surname, which is among the hundred most common in Ireland, is of dual origin. It can be traced back to the native Gaelic name Ó Loignsigh and also to the Norman name de Lench. Even though the Norman Lynches came to Ireland after the Ó Loingsighs had long been established there, and although they remained far outnumbered by the latter, nevertheless they have been more prominent in Irish history because of the leading role they played among the Tribes of Galway. It was a Norman Lynch who procured the charter for this city from Richard III in 1484 and, until 1654, when Catholics were debarred from holding civic offices, 84 mayors of the city came from the Lynch family. The family was also prominent in ecclesiastical spheres, with a number of priests, bishops and religious writers to its credit.

The Gaelic Lynchs were dotted throughout the country in several small independent septs. Although their overall influence was perhaps less great than that of their Norman namesakes, they did produce several notable individuals. For example, Clare – born Patrick Lynch (1757-1818), the linguist and Gaelic scholar. And John Joseph Lynch (1816-1888) of Breffny who became archbishop of Toronto in 1869. He started his missionary career in Houston, Texas, in 1847, and gradually worked his way northward until he crossed the border into Canada and was nominated coadjutor to the bishop of Toronto in 1859. A vigorous and eloquent writer, he strongly supported home rule for Ireland and it is said that his sermons had much influence on public life in Canada. He was the first Roman Catholic bishop since the reign of James II to attend a royal levee.

Another Breffny-born Lynch, Patrick Neeson Lynch (1817-1882) also became a Roman Catholic bishop, this time in Charleston, South Carolina. He emigrated with his parents to America in 1818. In 1847 he became rector of the newly-built cathedral in Charleston and later vicar-general and bishop. In the first year of the Civil War the cathedral and much of the church property was destroyed by fire. When South Carolina seceded from the Union Lynch became an ardent supporter of the Confederacy and in 1863 he went to Rome to see the Pope, bearing a letter from Jefferson Davis. When he returned in 1866 he found his diocese in ruins and he began visiting many cities in the North to raise money for re-building. In doing this he was not only successful but instrumental in promoting better feeling between North and South.

Little is known about the Irish background of Patricio Lynch (1825-1886), the Chilean naval hero born in Valparaiso. It is said that he was the son of a "wealthy Irish merchant". His early experiences at sea were with the British navy and he fought in the war against China in 1841-1842. In 1847 he returned to Chile and became a lieutenant in the Chilean navy. Although he retired in 1854, he returned to service in 1865 and was active in the campaign against Spain as governor of Valpariso, organizer of the National guard, and commander of his own ship. In 1879 he was appointed first Chilean governor of the Peruvian territory of Tarapaca and two years later he led an expeditionary force to the north of Peru. For his services he was appointed commander of the Chilean army and was also promoted to vice-admiral of the navy. In 1885 he was sent as minister to Spain, but died on the return voyage a year later near the Canary Islands.

After the 1847 famine, a colony of Irish including the Brownes, Dillons and Lynches grew up in Buenos Aires. Madame Elizabeth Lynch was a notorious and colorful figure who went to Paraguay with Francisco Lopez II. Lopez was the son and heir to the dictatorship of Paraguay and, while he was waiting to take office, kept Madame Lynch in great splendor.

Thomas Lynch (1749-1779), a third generation Irish-American, was the youngest signer of the Declaration of Independence. His great-grandfather had emigrated from Ireland to South Carolina shortly after the settlement of that colony. The Lynch family became prominent landowners and public office holders in South Carolina. Thomas Lynch was sixth delegate from that colony at the Continental Congress when the Declaration of Independence was adopted and signed.

The term "lynch law" is said to be named after one Charles Lynch (1736-1796) whose father emigrated from Ireland and became a member of the Virginia House of Burgesses. Lynch, who was appointed justice of the peace in Bedford Co., Virginia in 1766, evidently presided over his own extra-legal court and meted out his own justice when the ordinary state of affairs was disrupted by the Revolutionary War. But another account traces the term back to the mayor of Galway who in 1493 had his own son executed for murder.

Today the most eminent bearer of the name is undoubtedly Jack Lynch, lawyer, sportsman and the first Prime Minister of Ireland not to have been actively engaged in the 1916 revolution.

Jack Lynch

MacMahon

GAELIC: Mac Mathghamhna, Mac Mathbna
COMMON VARIATIONS: Mahon, Vaughan

This is one of the best known names in Ireland and is said to be derived from the ancient Irish word for bear. It is the name of two distinct and important septs. The more prolific of the two is descended from Mahon O'Brien, grandson of the great 10th century high king of Ireland Brian Boru. Their territory was located around Corcbaskin in west Clare. Today the name outnumbers all others in that county. It is also common in Co. Monaghan where descendants of the other sept of MacMahons are found. This sept originated in Ulster where until the 13th century its chiefs were lords of Oriel.

MacMahons have been very prominent in Irish history. They contributed many active leaders to the cause of the Confederate Catholics in the 1640's, including Heber MacMahon (1600-1650), Bishop of Clougher, Hugh McMahon (1606-1644), the last chief of the Ulster sept, and Col. Brian MacMahon who took part in the Battle of Benbub in 1646 which completely routed the Anglo-Scottish army. In the 18th century one family of MacMahons produced three archbishops of Armagh: Bernard MacMahon (1680-1747), his uncle Hugh MacMahon (d. 1737), and his brother Ross Roe MacMahon (1698-1748).

After the Stuart defeat at the Battle of the Boyne many MacMahons who had fought in King James's Irish Army went to France where they took up service in the Irish Brigade. The most notable descendant of these MacMahons in France was Comte Marie Edmé Patrice Maurice de MacMahon (1808-1893), marshal in the French army and second president of France from 1873-1879 under the Third Republic.

Bernard McMahon (1775-1816), one of America's first and foremore horticulturalists, came from Ireland to Philadelphia in 1796. He started a seed and nursery business there and set up an experimental garden for the cultivation of rare flowers and plants. Many of the new varieties of plants brought back from the west by Lewis and Clarke after their 1804-1806 expedition were cultivated in McMahon's greenhouses. In 1806 he published the *American Gardener's Calender*, the first important horticultural work to be produced in the United States. It remained a standard reference book for over 50 years.

Edward McMahon is one of the best known faces on American television. Born in Philadelphia, son of Irish immigrant parents, he is best known as an announcer and companion of chat-show compere Johnny Carson.

O'Mahony

GAELIC: Ó Mathghamhana
COMMON VARIATIONS: Matthews

This was a leading sept in west Munster (Co. Cork) where the name is still prevalent today. The powerful O'Mahony chiefs ruled as princes over a territory extending from the modern barony of Kinelmeaky to the sea where they had a fortified castle called Rosbrian on an island off the coast of southwest Cork. The modernized Irish spelling of the name – O'Mahúna – is derived from an ancestor called Mathghamhan, who was a grandson of Brian Boru, the great high king of Ireland who was killed in 1014. (Mathghamhan is the Irish word for bear.) O'Mahúna, which is among the 100 most common surnames in Ireland, is sometimes, but rarely, anglicized to Matthews.

Count Daniel O'Mahony (d. 1714), a general in the Irish Brigade in France, was the hero of the battle of Cremona. By repelling the Austrian attack on the town he is credited with saving the French army in Italy. Known as "le fameux O'Mahoni" on the continent, he was enobled by Louis XIV and later appointed by Philip V of Spain, Louis' grandson, to command a regiment of dragoons in Spain. He spent the remainder of his life in the Spanish service.

John O'Mahony (1816-1877) was a Celtic scholar who founded the Fenian Brotherhood in 1868. This was one of the many underground resistance movements which led to the victorious Rising of 1916.

O'Malley

GAELIC: Ó Máille

COMMON VARIATIONS: Melia, Mailey

Although the O'Malleys were never a very large sept, they were one of the most illustrious. Situated on the west coast of Connacht in what is now Co. Mayo, the family is one of the few clans of Ireland celebrated in the native histories as seafarers. Their motto is "terra marique potens", and many O'Malleys won fame, or at least notoriety, for their daring and sometimes unscrupulous naval exploits. This is one of the few Irish "O" names from which the prefix was seldom dropped. The O'Malleys today are still heavily concentrated in Connacht, and in particular in Co. Mayo.

Grania or Grace O'Malley (1530-1600), a legend in her own time in the province of Connacht, was a famous and formidable feminine sea captain celebrated in song and story. Like her father before her, she was a leader of "piratical expeditions" with her base of operations located at Clare Island. The English Viceroy at Galway called her a "notorious woman in all the coasts of Ireland" and "more than a master's mate" to her husband. Less respectfully the Governor of Connacht denounced her as "a notable traitress and nurse of all rebellions in the province for forty years". She is said to have paid a visit to Queen Elizabeth at Westminster just so that the Queen might have the opportunity of being introduced to her. Described as "a dark lady, tall and commanding", she died about 1600 and was buried on Clare Island.

Rev. Thaddeus O'Malley (1796-1877) was the self-proclaimed "Father of Federalism in Ireland". Born at Garryowen near Limerick, he combined both religious and political preaching. He made his debut as a political activist in the 1830's by advocating the introduction of a poor law in Ireland and by favoring a system of national education. He also gave strong support to the Home Rule movement inaugurated by Isaac Butt in 1870. For this he wrote a small volume entitled *Home Rule on the Basis of Federalism* which ran into a second edition. He also had published anonymously a book called *Harmony in Religion* which, among other things, advocated marriage of the priesthood. O'Malley was strongly censured by his brothers of the robe when it was discovered that he was the author. He died in Dublin in 1877 and was buried in Glasnevin Cemetery.

Frank Ward O'Malley (1875-1932) was regarded as one of the most entertaining humorous writers and one of the best reporters of his generation. Born in Pittsburgh, he began his writing career with the *Morning Telegraph* in New York in 1902 where his humorous treatment of trivial happenings made him an instant success. But he also stood out for his accurate and dramatic reporting of serious events and in 1906 he went to work as a reporter for the New York *Sun* where he remained for 14 years. From 1920 to 1932 he wrote humorous and satirical articles for the *Saturday Evening Post*, most of them dealing with aspects of American and European life. Two articles of his appeared in the *American Mercury* for May and September, 1929, on the virtues and weaknesses of the Irish in America. It is said that "his only bitterness was directed at prohibition", which he denounced publicly and privately with vehemence and to which he attributed his long stays in Europe. He died in Tours, France in 1932, leaving a wife and son and daughter.

O'Malone

GAELIC: Ó Maoileoin
COMMON VARIATIONS: Malone

This is an ancient sept related to the O'Connors of Connacht. For centuries they were associated with the Abbey of Clonmacnois before it was united with Armagh. But today most of their descendants are found in Co. Clare. Many Malones are also found in Co. Wexford, but their origin is obscure.

One family of Malones produced three outstanding figures in the 18th century. Anthony Malone (1700-1776) was active in politics and became Chancellor of the Exchequer. His brother, Edmund (1704-1776) was an Irish M.P. and judge in Ireland. The latter's son, also Edmund (1741-1812), lived in London and was a noted Shakespeare critic. He also belonged to the famous London literary "Club" and was friends with Johnson, Boswell, Burke, and others. He is said to have helped Boswell with his *Life of Johnson*. Malone devoted his entire life to investigating and elucidating the works of Shakespeare and to book collecting. His famous collection is now at the Bodleian Library at Oxford. "Mr Malone died, principally from over study and sedentary habits, 25th May 1812, aged 70."

Two Malones made their reputations as priests. Rev. William Malone (1586-1659) was Superior of the Jesuit Mission to Ireland and Rev. Sylvester Malone (1822-1906), vicar-general of Kilruch, wrote the *Church History of Ireland*, which has become a standard work.

Martin

GAELIC: Mac Máirtin, Ó Martáin
COMMON VARIATIONS: MacMartin, Gilmartin

This name was brought to Ireland from England at the time of the Anglo-Norman invasion and it is now as common and widespread there as in its original country. The first Anglo-Norman Martins in Ireland settled at Galway where they were included in the "14 Tribes" of that city. There were also several minor native Irish septs whose names were anglicized to Martin distributed throughout the country. An Irish sept of O'Martins became established in Westmeath. In Co. Tyrone the MacMartins were an offshoot of the O'Neills. The MacGilmartins also originated in Co. Tyrone, but they were gradually forced westward into Cos. Leitrim and Sligo where most of their descendants are found today.

Richard Martin (1754-1834), Irish M.P. for Co. Galway, was the main force behind the prevention of cruelty to animals act which was passed by Parliament in 1822. Because of his passionate concern for the welfare of animals, Martin was popularly known as "Humanity Dick". It is said that he was first called this by his close friend George IV. He was one of the founders of the Royal Society for the Prevention of Cruelty to Animals which came into being in 1824. Along with his concern for animals Martin also had a fondness for duelling which earned him the second nickname of "Hair Trigger Dick".

Edward Martyn (1859-1923), dramatist, was a pioneer of the Irish dramatic movement. Together with W. B. Yeats and Lady Gregory he co-founded the Abbey Theater. He also helped found the nationalist movement Sinn Fein and from 1904-1908 served as president of the Sinn Fein party. Two of his most well known plays are *The Heather Field* and *Maeve*.

Edward Martyn

Molloy

GAELIC: Ó Maolmhuaidh
COMMON VARIATIONS: Mulloy, Miley, Maloy, MacCloy

Technically speaking this is the name of an important sept in central Leinster (Co. Offaly) related to the southern O'Neills and traditionally said to be descended from Niall of the Nine Hostages, the famous 4th-century King of Ireland. But Molloy is also used as the anglicized form of several other Irish names found in east Connacht, Kerry and the Ulster counties of Donegal and Monaghan. For the most part, however, the modern day Molloys are found in Cos. Roscommon and Offaly.

Albin O'Molloy (d.1223) was Bishop of Ferns and one of the officiating prelates at the coronation of Richard I. He is best remembered for a sermon he preached in Christ Church, Dublin, in 1186 in which he attributed all the ills of Ireland to the English and Welsh clerical intruders. He attended the Council of Rome in 1215 and a year later made another bold move in excommunicating the Earl of Pembroke.

Rev. Francis Molloy, 17th century Franciscan born in Co. Meath, was Professor of Theology at St. Isidore's in Rome and agent at the papal court for Irish catholics. In 1676 he published his *Grammatica Latino Hibernica*—the first printed Irish grammar.

James Lynam Molloy (1837-1909), composer born in Cornelare, King's Co., is known for his many popular ballads and songs, among them "The Kerry Dance" and "Darby and Joan" and especially "Love's Old Sweet Song".

O'Moran

GAELIC: Ó Moráin, Ó Moghráin
COMMON VARIATIONS: Moran, Morahan, Morrin

This is the anglicized form of two Gaelic surnames, O Morain and O Moghrain, belonging to several distinct septs which arose independently in different parts of Connacht. Chiefs of these two septs resided at Criffon in Co. Galway, Ballina in Co. Mayo, Ballintober in Co. Roscommon, and one was situated in Co. Leitrim. The majority of Morans in Ireland today are found in these four counties.

James O'Moran (1739-1794), born in Co. Roscommon, rose to become a general in the French army. He started his military career in France as a cadet in Dillon's regiment of the Irish Brigade in 1759. With them he saw service in the closing years of the Seven Years' War in Germany, and later in America during the War of Independence. When the Revolution came in France he was made general of a division and appointed governor of Conde. But in 1793 his fortune turned when he was falsely accused of plotting against the French government. In a letter protesting the accusations against him he wrote that he still cherished the dream of freeing his native land "from the tyrannical oppression of the savage English government." His protests were in vain, however, and he was guillotined on 6 March 1794.

Michael Moran (1794-1871), "the last gleeman" of Ireland, was a popular Dublin street singer. Blind from birth, he sang ballads and recited pieces such as "Zozimus", from which he took his nickname.

Cardinal Patrick Moran (1830-1911), born in Australia of Irish parents, became Archbishop of Sydney in 1884 and was made Cardinal a year later. Author of several books, he wrote *Irish Saints in Great Britain* and *The Life of Blessed Oliver Plunkett*, 17th century Archbishop of Armagh falsely convicted and executed for high treason against the English government.

Murphy

GAELIC: Ó Murchadha

With some 55,000 Murphys out of a population of 4¼ million, this is the most common surname in Ireland. It belonged to several native septs which arose independently in different parts of the country. The greatest of these was the Murphy clan of Leinster with its seat in Co. Wexford. Another Murphy sept flourished in southwest Munster along the Cork-Kerry border. Minor septs of the name also existed in east Connacht and in the Ulster counties of Donegal, Tyrone and Armagh.

Marie Louis O'Murphy (1737-1814) the beautiful daughter of an Irish soldier who settled at Rouen, was an influential mistress of Louis XV and a model for the painter Boucher.

Charles F. Murphy (1858-1924) was the absolute boss of Tammany Hall from 1902 to 1924. The son of Irish immigrants, he was born in New York City and began his political career as a New York state assemblyman. He then served several years as dock commissioner before assuming the Tammany throne in 1902. His 22-year reign as boss was longer than that of any other of Tammany's absolute rulers. He was responsible for the election of three Democratic mayors of New York City during that period and the election of two New York governors. At the time of his death Tammany Hall was at the highest point of its prestige and power. Murphy worked behind the scenes, quietly and tactfully, but with much influence and effect. His success has been attributed to his "taciturn diplomacy". He was "silent, unspectacular, and extraordinarily tactful." In his later years Murphy discovered and encouraged many politicians who became his protégés and is said to have remained remarkably open to their ideas and suggestions for change.

Michael Charles Murphy (1861-1913), coach and pioneer athletic trainer in the United States, is famous for introducing the crouching start – the greatest contribution to the art of sprinting in modern times. Murphy, who set up a training camp for athletes near his home in Westboro, Massachusetts in the 1880's, is credited with having made many innovations of technique in training in nearly all fields of athletics. He was alternatively athletic trainer at Yale and the University of Pennsylvania and was coach of the United States Olympic teams in London in 1908 and in Stockholm in 1912.

Frank Murphy (1890-1949), lawyer, public official, and U.S. Supreme Court Justice, was one of the early keen supporters of the New Deal. Born in Harbor Beach, Michigan, he practiced and taught law in Detroit. As judge of the recorder's court in that city from 1923-1930 he introduced the practice of naming a psychiatrist and a sociologist to the sentencing board in each case. In 1930 he was elected mayor of Detroit and one of his first moves was to reduce city expenses and use the savings to help feed those made jobless by the closing of the auto factories. He was also one of the first advocates of federal relief, actively supporting the WPA set up in the early day's of the Roosevelt Administration. In 1933 he was appointed governor general of the Philippines by Roosevelt, a post which he held until 1936 when he was elected governor of Michigan on the Democratic ticket. In 1939 Roosevelt appointed him U.S. Attorney General, and the following year the President appointed him Justice of the Supreme Court, where he "soon earned a reputation as a friend of the working man and of minority groups of all kinds". The only Roman Catholic member of the Supreme Court, Murphy came out strongly many times in his court career in defense of civil and religious liberties.

Audie Murphy (b. 1924), the most decorated American soldier

Audie Murphy

209

of World War II, once said that bravery in battle is often the result of "anger, hunger, wet and cold, and wanting to be home". Born on a farm in Kingston, Texas, he enlisted in the infantry at the age of 18 and took part in thirty months of fighting in Tunisia, Sicily, Italy, France and Germany. After the war the actor James Cagney saw his picture on the cover of *Life* and brought him to Hollywood. His first picture was *Beyond Glory* (1948), followed by *The Red Badge of Courage* (1951), *Cimmaron Kid* (1952), *Duel at Silver Creek* (1952), *Drums Across the River* (1954), and *To Hell and Back* (1958).

Murray
GAELIC: Ó Muireadhaigh
COMMON VARIATIONS: Murry, O'Murry, MacMurry

Most of the Murrays in Ireland come from Ulster and most of these are of Scottish descent. There were, however, several native Irish septs called O Muireadhaigh whose name was anglicized Murray. The most important of these was a Ui Maine sept in the barony of Athlone (Co. Roscommon). The name MacMurray is very common in Co. Donegal after the MacMuireadhaigh sept which was situated there. Sometimes the Gaelic name Mac Giolla Mhuire becomes Murray in English as an abbreviation of MacIlmurray. The usual anglicized form of this name, however, is Gilmore.

Several leading Irish architects have been Murrays, including two 19th century William Murrays and their contemporary James Murray (1831-1897), who worked with Pugin in London and designed public buildings and churches in many English cities. He is also known as the author of *Modern Architecture* and *Gothic Buildings*.

Thomas Edward Murray (1860-1929), inventor and consulting engineer, is the hero of one of America's greatest success stories. A second-generation Irishman and carpenter's son, Murray had to leave school and go to work at the age of nine when his father died. He continued to go to night classes and in 1881, at the age of 21, he was made operating engineer of the Albany Waterworks pumping plant. Here he caught the attention of Anthony M. Brady, an Irish-American who had made his fortune in railroads and electric lighting companies in Albany and Brooklyn, and in 1887 Brady hired him to take charge of the power station of the Albany Municipal Gas Co. From then on, under Brady's wing, Murrays rise was rapid. In 1895 he moved to New York City to consolidate the Brady properties in Manhattan and in 1900 was made vice-president and general manager of New York Edison Co. Under his direction many of the great power stations which supply New York City with electricity were built. Besides designing power plants and acting as a consultant for power companies, Murray also patented some 1,100 inventions, second to only Thomas Edison in number. These ranged from electrical switches to copper radiators for heating, from pulverized fuel equipment to automatic welding. He also invented a water-screen filter to reduce the amount of smoke and soot emitted by the Edison

Company's big smokestacks. Thomas Edison's invention of the incandescent bulb "may have been more spectacular and showy", says one of Murray's grandchildren. "But Grandpa Murray virtually invented everything *but* the light bulb—the circuits, switches, dynamos, and power systems that got the electricity to the bulb." The Murray family became one of the foremost Irish families in America and the eight Murray children "had the three prerequisites that are still needed for acceptance in society in New York: money, good looks, and good humor, which rank in importance in that order." The most distinguished of his children was Thomas E. Murray, Jr., himself an inventor and member of President Truman's five-man Atomic Energy Commission.

At the other end of the American social spectrum, Philip Murray was one of America's most prominent labor leaders. For many years he was president of the United Steel workers of America and later became president of the Congress of Industrial Organizations.

MacNamara

GAELIC: Mac Conmara

The homeland of the MacNamaras is Co. Clare. They were one of the most important septs of the ancient Dalcassian tribe of Thomond, second only to the O'Briens in power and importance. They served as hereditary marshals to the O'Briens and had the honor of inaugurating their chief who was often a king. At first the MacNamara sept was confined to a small territory in north Munster, but by the end of the 11th century they had become lods of Clancullen and their dominion had spread to include what is now much of East Clare. In time the sept divided, forming a West Clancullen and an East Clancullen branch. A long train of MacNamaras parade through the history of Co. Clare, and the family also produced several colorful figures whose fame and notoriety spread beyond the boundaries of their homeland.

Donough MacNamara (1715-1810), better known by the Gaelic form of his name—Donnchadh Ruadh MacConmara—is one of the best known Gaelic poets. Educated in Rome for the priesthood, he was expelled for wildness and returned to Ireland where he tried and failed several times as a schoolmaster and at various other jobs. He emigrated to Newfoundland for a while and also traveled on the Continent, but he always returned to Ireland. His finest poem, *Bán Chnoic Eireann Óigh—The Fair Hills of Ireland Eachtra Giolla and Amárain – The Adventures of a Luckless Fellow* – is a detailed portrayal of an emigrant voyage. He also wrote satires, humorous verse and a great *Song of Repentance Fellow"*—is a detailed portrayal of an emigrant voyage. He also wrote satires, humorous verse and a great Song of Repentance and is ranked among the best Irish poets of the 18th century.

Henry (Pantaleon) "Count" MacNamara (1743-1790) was the last of the long and distinguished line of MacNamaras in the French service. His grandfather John was one of the eight members of his family who went to France after the Jacobite War in Ireland and became officers in Clare's regiment, or Clare's Dragoons, in the Irish Brigade there. Henry was born in Rochefort in 1743. After joining the French navy he took part in many engagements against the English and Dutch navies. He received rapid promotion

Robert MacNamara

and ultimately reached the rank of Vice-Admiral. In 1782 he was created a Count by Louis XVI. An aristocrat and supporter of the Ancient Regime, he was hanged for his royalist sympathies in 1790.

James MacNamara (1768-1826) was a rear-admiral in the British navy and saw a great deal of service up until the Peace of Amiens in 1802. He was the center of much attention in London in 1803 when he killed a man in a duel over a dogfight. He was arrested and tried for murder. For his defense he called several naval officers, including Nelson and Hood, to witness to his being "an honorable, good-humored, pleasant, lively companion, exactly the reverse of a quarrelsome man". In light of the testimony he was acquitted.

Robert S. MacNamara (b. 1916), business executive, Secretary of Defense under Presidents Kennedy and Johnson, President of the World Bank, gained his business and management experience as a Ford Motor Co. executive in the years after World War II. He was one of a group of ten "Whiz Kids" hired by Ford to iron out production problems, cut costs, and increase efficiency. Gifted with a remarkable memory, he reportedly knew of every expenditure in the company. His rise was rapid and in 1960 he was named President of Ford Motor Co., the first person outside the family to hold the post. He resigned the following year to become Secretary of Defense under President Kennedy. During his seven years in Washington he wrested the control of the Pentagon from military men and did much to make the Defense Department more efficient and more economical. Because of his broad background and keen mind he was a favorite adviser to both Kennedy and Johnson, and was chief adviser on the Vietnam War. In 1967 he resigned as Secretary of Defense to become President of the International Bank for Reconstruction and Development – The World Bank.

O'Neill

GAELIC: Ó Neill

This is among the twelve most numerous Irish surnames and it is one of the very few which is spelled the same in English and in Irish. Although there are several septs by this name in Ireland, it was the O'Neill's of Ulster who played the greatest role in Irish history. The first man of this sept to bear the surname was Domhnall O'Neill, whose grandfather Niall, King of Ireland, was killed in a battle with the Danes in 919 A.D.

The O'Neills were the chief family of the Cinel-Eoghain ("Descendants of Eoghan") whose territory was called Tir-Eoghain (Eoghan's country), now known by its anglicized name, Tyrone. In ancient times this territory included not only the present-day county of Tyrone, but also most of Co. Derry and part of Co. Donegal. The name Eoghain derives from Eoghan, or Owen, the fifth son of Niall of the Nine Hostages (another Niall from the one mentioned above), an ancient King of Ireland and a remote ancestor of the O'Neills. This Niall is famous as the kidnapper of St. Patrick, whom he took to Ireland as a slave about the year 405 A.D. It was he who gave the name of "Scotia Minor" to Scotland when Ireland was still known as Scotia Major. From this early time until the end of the 17th century when Ulster ceased to be the leading Gaelic province of Ireland, the O'Neills figure prominently among the great men of Irish history.

The 16th and 17th centuries produced the most famous O'Neills in Irish history, men who stood out in Ireland's continuous struggle to cast off British rule. They include Con Bacach O'Neill (1484-1559), the first Earl of Tyrone; Shane O'Neill (1520-1567); Hugh O'Neill (1540-1616), second Earl of Tyrone; Owen Roe O'Neill (1590-1649); Sir Phelim O'Neill (1604-1653); and Hugh O'Neill (d. 1660). After the Battle of the Boyne in 1690 many O'Neills fled to the Continent and were to be found among the outstanding officers of the Irish Brigades in the French army.

Daniel O'Neill, born in 1612, was probably the first Irishman to hold cabinet rank in Britain. As a boy he served as a page in the Court of Charles I. But because he later took part in the 1641 Rebellion, his property in Ireland was confiscated and he was imprisoned in the Tower of London. He managed, however, to escape to France, and when Cromwell died and Charles II came to the throne, O'Neill was restored to favor. He returned to England where he was given an estate and the important position of Postmaster General. He soon became wealthy and built Belsize House as his London residence. He died in London on October 24, 1664, at the age of 52.

The American author Edward Duffield O'Neill was born in Philadelphia on August 9, 1823. A Reformed Episcopal clergyman, he wrote *Threads of Maryland Colonial History* (1867); *History of the Virginia Company of London* (1869); and *The English Colonization of America During the Seventeenth Century* (1871). He died on September 26, 1893.

Eoin MacNeill, a founder member of the Gaelic League, was born in Co. Antrim in 1867. He was professor of Early and Medieval Irish History at University College, Dublin, and also president of the Royal Irish Academy. He was a Minister in the first Dail (Irish Parliament). His book, *Phases of Irish History*, "is one of the most learned and penetrating summaries of Irish history from earliest times to the Recovery after the Norman Invasion." He died in 1954.

James O'Neill, father of the American playwright Eugene O'Neill, is said to have been born in the townland of Grennan, near Thomastown, Co. Limerick, in 1847. After marrying Ella Quinlan, he emigrated to the United States in 1850 a few years after the great Irish potato famine. There he became a leading actor and won fame playing the title role in the *Count of Monte Cristo*. He died in 1920.

The son of James O'Neill, Eugene O'Neill, is the most famous O'Neill of modern times. He was born on October 16, 1888 and his first stage success, at the age of 27, was *Bound East for Cardiff*. He directed the play himself and also played the role of the Mate. Subsequent works include *Anna Christie, Marco Millions, Mourning Becomes Electra, The Iceman Cometh,* and *A Long Day's Journey Into the Night*. This last play, although written in 1940, was not performed until 1956, three years after the playwright's death. The play depicts the relationships in O'Neill's family and shows the forces which at the same time held it together and drove it apart. O'Neill's daughter Oonagh O'Neill, married the famous silent film star Charlie Chaplin.

There is an interesting legend surrounding the famous Red Hand symbol of the O'Neill Coat of Arms. As the story goes, two chieftains were racing their boats in a bid to claim the fertile land of Ulster, for they had agreed that whomever touched shore first would claim ownership. One of them, seeing that he was about to be beaten, cut off his right hand and flung it ashore ahead of his rival. His claim to be the first to touch the shore was upheld and he was proclaimed Prince of Ulster. The Red Hand is now the symbol for the Province of Ulster and its nine counties and it is also incorporated into the coats of arms of several other septs who pledged their allegiance to the O'Neills.

Power

GAELIC: de Paor
NORMAN: Povre

This was originally one of the foreign names like Burke and Roche which were introduced into Ireland at the time of the Anglo-Norman invasion, but it has become one of the most common names in the country. Ironically, it is derived from the old French word *povre*, meaning poor. The Norman Powers settled in Co. Waterford in the 12th century and it is there and in the adjacent counties where the name is still most prevalent today. The Powers claim that their forebears included members of both English and French Royalty.

Power has been made a well-known name particularly by a family of Irish and American actors who took Tyrone Power for their stage name. The first W. Tyrone, born Thomas Powell (1797-1841) in Co. Waterford, was the most famous Irish comic character actor in London in the 1820's and 30's. He wrote several farces and comedies and in 1836 published his *Impressions of America* after his first visit to the United States. He died coming back from his fourth trip to America in 1841 when the ship he was sailing on sank.

The second Tyrone Power to appear on the stage was the first Tyrone's grandson. Born in London in 1869, he was sent to Florida as a boy to learn the citrus fruit business. But when he was seventeen he started acting and in the 1890's was appearing with Augustin Daly's repertory company in New York. Unlike his grandfather he favored serious roles and played them in the grand, oratorical style. Shortly before his death in 1931 he went to Hollywood to begin a new career in the movies.

Tyrone Power III (1914-1958), son of the above, began his acting career in 1931 with a Shakespeare repetory company in Chicago. After starring in *Romeo and Juliet* and *Saint Joan* in New York in 1935 and 1936 he was signed by Twentieth Century Fox for a seven year contract. In Hollywood he established himself immediately, starring in *Lloyds of London*, 1936. In the next six years he made some twenty films, including *Alexander's Ragtime Band* and *Blood and Sand*. After World War II he appeared in several colorful but not very demanding Hollywood roles, and in 1950 he returned to the stage in London, starring in *Mister Roberts*. His last complete pictures were *The Sun Also Rises* (1957) and *Witness for the Prosecution* (1958). He died of a heart attack in 1958 in Spain while on location for the filming of *Solomon and Sheba*.

W. Tyrone Power

Plunkett

GAELIC: Pluincéid
NORMAN: Blanchet

This name has been associated with the Dublin-Meath-Louth area since the time of the Anglo-Norman invasion when it was first introduced into Ireland. It has become an exclusively Irish surname and is one of the most distinguished names in Irish history. Plunketts have been prominent in Ireland in all periods since the Middle Ages and several branches of the family have been granted peerages.

One of the most outstanding members of the family was Blessed Oliver Plunket (1625-1681), Archbishop of Dublin, famous for his defiance of the English and for continuing to live and work in hiding in his diocese at a time when Catholics were hunted men. His persecutors finally caught him in 1679 and took him to London where he was tried on trumped up charges of treason. He was found guilty and in 1681 was hanged, drawn and quartered. He was the first of the Irish martyrs to be beatified in 1920.

Thomas Plunkett, born in Meath 1716, joined the Austrian army and fought in the Seven Years War. He rose to rank of General and was eventually appointed governor of Antwerp.

William Conyngham Plunket (1764-1854), Lord Chancellor of Ireland from 1830 until his retirement in 1841, started out as a lawyer in Dublin and soon became active in Irish and English politics. As an M.P. he was a staunch supporter of Catholic emanciption. In 1822 he was attorney general for Ireland and in 1827 was appointed chief justice of the common pleas in Ireland.

Sir Horace Curzon Plunkett (1854-1932), agricultural reformer and member of the British Parliament, founded the agricultural cooperative movement in Ireland. Much of his first hand knowledge of farming came from ten years spent on a farm in Wyoming after he graduated from Oxford. As an M.P. he was unionist strongly opposed to separation of Ireland from Great Britain and in 1919 he organized the Irish Dominion League to keep Ireland within the British Commonwealth. After the partition, however, he accepted a seat in the Senate of the Irish Free State from 1922-1923.

Edward Drax Plunkett, 18th Baron of Dunsany (1878-1957) was born in County Meath. He became a leading figure in the world of literature both as an exponent and as a patron. His own work has been compared with that of Tolkien and his titles include *The Gods of Pegana* and the *Glittering Gate*. As a patron he gave active encouragement to young Irish authors and poets.

Joseph Mary Plunkett (1887-1916) journalist, revolutionary poet, and one of the signers of the Republican Proclamation in 1916, was executed for his part in the Easter Rising of 1916. In 1913 he was a prominent member of the Irish Volunteers and took on the responsibility for drawing up the military plans for a rising. In 1914 he was associated with Edward Martyn and Thomas MacDonagh in founding the Irish Theater in Dublin. His *Complete Poems* were published after his death. His father George Noble Plunkett (b.1851), created a Papal County by Pope Leo XIII, and was for several years Director of the Science and Arts Museum in Dublin.

Oliver Plunkett

O'Quinn

GAELIC: O'Cuinn, O Coinne
COMMON VARIATIONS: Quin, Quinn, Quinney

With some 17,000 Quinns in Ireland today this is the 20th most common surname in the country. They are descended from five distinct septs. The most notable of these were the Dalcassian sept of Thomond whose territory was in the barony of Inchiquin in Co. Clare, and the sept in Ulster where the name has long been associated with the Glens of Antrim. There was also an important sept in Co. Longford related to the O'Ferralls of Annaly. Another sept originated in Tyrone where Quinn is now the most common name in the county.

Walter Quin (1575-1634), Dublin-born poet, was tutor and life-long associate of Charles I. His son James (1621-1659) is said to have charmed Cromwell with "his fine singing voice" and thus moved the Lord Protector to have him reinstated at Oxford after he had been expelled as a royalist.

James Quin (1693-1766), actor who shared the stage with Garrick, was born in London of Irish parents. He was soon taken to Dublin and made his first appearance on the stage there in 1714 at the Smock Alley Theater. The next year he began performing along side Garrick in the Drury Lane Theater in London. He was even considered by Horace Walpole to be superior to Garrick. A contemporary account describes him as having "many of the requisites of a good actor—an expressive countenance, speaking eyes, a clear and melodious voice, a retentive memory, a majestic figure; and he was an enthusiastic admirer of Shakespeare." He also had "the misfortune to kill two fellow-actors"—one in a duel in 1717, and another in a quarrel over the correct pronunciation of the name "Cato" in 1718. Moreover, Quin was known as "a coarse but capital story-teller" and for that reason was a much sought-after dinner guest.

Thomas Edward Quinn (1868-1929), sculptor and painter, was born in Philadelphia "of Irish ancestry and in humble circumstances." He was commissioned to do many public statues and monuments, including one of Edwin Booth as Hamlet and another of Henry Clay which was given to the Venezuelan government in exchange for a statue of the South American liberator Simon Bolivar. Several of his works are in New York, among them busts of James McNeill Whistler and Dr. Oliver Wendell Holmes at New York University.

O'Reilly

GAELIC: Ó Raghailligh
COMMON VARIATIONS: Reilly

O'Reilly ranks among the twelve most common names in Ireland. It comes from the name of a celebrated 10th century clan chief, Raighallach, which is said to be derived from the combination of

"Raigh", meaning arm, and "allach", meaning strong or powerful. This is indeed fitting, because for many centuries the O'Reillys were the most powerful sept in Breffny. In the 10th century the territory of Breffny was divided into two principalities – Breffny O'Rourke or West Breffny, and Breffny O'Reilly or East Breffny. (The Irish word Breffny means "hilly country".) In 1584, during the reign of Queen Elizabeth, Breffny O'Reilly was turned into a county and was called Cavan after its chief town. In ancient times this was the seat of the O'Reillys whose principal residence was on Tullymongan Hill on the outskirts of the town.

Their reputation for being an exceptionally tough, tenacious, and often violent sept goes back to earliest times. After the English, their biggest enemy appears to have been their neighbors to the west, the O'Rourkes of Leitrim, an equally fierce and pugnacious lot.

The illustrious and almost legendary 17th century figure "Miles the Slasher" typifies the fierce O'Reilly tradition. He distinguished himself as a commander in the ill-fated rebellion against the English to regain lost territory in the 1640's. Miles, who was High Sheriff of Co. Cavan before the insurrection broke out in 1641, later had to flee Ireland. He went to Spain and eventually ended up in France where he died about 1660 and was buried in the Irish monastery at Chalons-sur-Marne.

Another Miles O'Reilly made a name for himself some two centuries later writing about the Civil War in America. Miles O'Reilly was actually the pseudonym of Charles Graham Halpine (1829-1868). He was born near Oldcastle, Co. Meath in 1829 and went to America where he eventually worked for the *New York Times*. In 1861 he joined the Union forces, accepting a commission in Col. Michael Corcoran's 69th regiment. He became a colonel and later a brigadier general. His humorous poems and letters to the press won him tremendous popularity, but his fame rests mainly on "Sambo's Right to be Killed", said to be one of the most influential pieces in overcoming the objections of Union troops to letting Negroes join the army. Halpine died on August 3, 1868, at the age of 39.

John Boyle O'Reilly (1844-1890) also made a name for himself as a journalist and writer in America. Because of his activities in the revolutionary movement against England he was arrested in 1866, convicted, and sent to the convict settlement in Bunbury, Australia. In 1869 he managed to escape on an American whaler. He settled in Boston where he worked as a journalist and became editor and part owner of the *Pilot*, one of the most influential Irish-American newspapers in the United States. He continued to support the Irish revolutionary movement from America and he came to occupy a distinguished place in the literary society of Boston. His poetical works include *Songs from the Southern Seas* (1873); *Songs, Legends and Ballads* (1878); *The Statues in the Block, and other Poems* (1881); and *In Bohemia* (1886). He also edited *The Poetry and Songs of Ireland* (New York 1889). As a novelist O'Reilly will be remembered as the author of *Moondyne*, a story of convict life in Australia which was published in 1880 and ran through twelve editions.

The Irish revolutionary writer Thomas Devin Reilly (1824-1854) escaped from Ireland to New York in 1848 after charges were brought against him for authoring a scathing article which appeared in the United Irishman. For two years he edited the *New York*

Democratic Review and afterwards the *Washington Union*. He died suddenly in Washington on March 6, 1854, and was buried in Mount Olivet Cemetary.

The lexicographer Edward O'Reilly (d. 1829) published in 1817 one of the first Irish-English dictionaries. He also compiled a chronological account of nearly 400 Irish writers which appeared in 1820. His dictionary came too early to contain the phrase "the life of Reilly". The expression is said to have first appeared in a ballad composed about the time of the Crimean War (1854) by a Co. Westmeath doctor named William Nedley.

Today the spirit of the O'Reilleys is admirably represented by Tony O'Reilly, red-headed rugby hero and international entrepreneur.

O'Rourke

GAELIC: Ó Ruairc

COMMON VARIATIONS: Rourke, Rooke

The O'Rourkes come from that part of Ireland which they shared and fought over with the O'Reillys. This was the ancient territory of Breffny. In the 10th century this land was divided between the two septs into Breffny O'Rourke or West Breffni, and Breffni O'Reilly or East Breffny. In 1565 Breffny O'Rourke was made into Co. Letrim by the British Lord Deputy and named after the tiny village of Leitrim.

As with many Irish septs the golden age for the O'Rourke's was the period before the Norman Invasion. After that followed centuries of subjugation and resurgence. Whenever the fighting with the English was at a lull, however, the rivalry with the O'Reillys could always be rekindled.

After Cromwell's incursions in 1649 many of the O'Rourkes were deprived of their land and they fled to the Continent. Here they found places in the armies and several of them rose in rank to become leading officers. Their descendants were among the important families in Russia and Poland. Joseph O'Rourke, a prince in the Russian aristocracy, was General-in-Chief of the Russian Empire in 1700. Count Patrick O'Rourke held a distinguished position in the Russian army in the mid 19th century. Two O'Rourkes, both named Owen, were Counts in the service of Queen Marie Therese of Austria between 1750 and 1780.

Apart from those O'Rourkes who distinguished themselves in continental armies and other forms of foreign service, there have been many other notable Irishmen of that name. The earliest is Tiernan O'Rourke, Prince of Breffny, who was killed in battle in 1172. He is best known because of the events that followed the carrying off of his wife Dervorgilla by Dermot MacMorrogh. This eventually led to the situation which gave the English their first opportunity to invade Ireland.

Despite this blight on their record the O'Rourke's continued to play a strong part in resisting the English. There is the story of Brian O'Rourke, inaugurated Chief of the Name in 1564, who was accused of inciting various people to rebellion and of having "scornfully dragged the queen's picture att za horse-taile and disgracefully cut the same in pieces; had given the Spaniards

Robert Ruark

entertainment". He defied his captors to the last and came to his end, still without knowing a word of English, on the scaffold in London.

Three hundred years later, on a different kind of stage and under more propitious circumstances, Edmond O'Rourke (1814-1879) made his career as a successful actor known by his stage name Edmond Falconer. He was joint manager of Drury Lane Theater from 1862 to 1866 and after that he opened His Majesty's Theater in the Haymarket. He wrote plays—among them *Peep o' Day, Eileen Og,* and *Heart for Heart*—and also poetry. He spent three years in America from 1862 to 1865.

A marble monument in New Orleans, La. commemorates Margaret Gaffney, the daughter of William and Mary (nee O'Rourke) Gaffney. She was born in 1813 and emigrated with her parents to Baltimore in 1818. Only four years later her family died of yellow fever and Margaret was forced to find work as a poorly-paid servant girl. When she was 22 she married and moved to New Orleans with her husband. But he and the little boy of their marriage died a year later and from then on Margaret decided to dedicate her life to helping relieve human suffering. She contributed the profits from the successful dairy she had established to this end. When she died in 1882 her funeral was one of the largest New Orleans has ever seen. A "Margaret" club still exists in that city to help orphans. Her statue stands in Margaret Square.

Constance Rourke was born in Cleveland, Ohio in 1885 and graduated fron Vassar. She is best known as a writer of histories and biographies. Her works include *Trumpets of Jubilee* (1927), which deals with such figures as Beechers and P. T. Barnum; *Troupers of the Gold Coast* (1928), an account of Lotta Crabtree, Lola Montez and other actresses; *American Humor* (1931); *Davy Crockett* (1934); *Audubon* (1936); *Charles Sheeler* (1938); and *The Roots of American Culture* (1942). She died in 1941.

Garland Roark is a U.S. author of adventure stories. He was born in Groesbeck, Texas in 1904. His books include *Wake of the Red Witch* (1946) which was made into a film in 1948; *Fair Wind to Java* (1948), a film version of which appeared in 1953; *Rainbow in the Royals* (1950); *Star in the Rigging* (1954); *Outlawed Banner* (1956); *The Lady and the Deep Blue Sea* (1958); *Should the Wind Be Fair* (1960). He also wrote under the pen name George Garland.

Robert Ruark, an American, is the author of *Uhuru* and *Something of Value.*

Ryan

GAELIC: O'Maoilriain, O Riain

There are nearly 28,000 persons by the name of Ryan living in Ireland, making it one of the ten most common names in the country. The majority of Ryans come from the counties of Limerick and Tipperary where the traditional territory of the sept was located. Then known as O Maoilriain, or O'Mulryan, they settled in this area in the 14th century and afterwards became very powerful. But in spite of their numbers, they did not produce any really outstanding individuals in Irish history, with the exception of the popular romantic figure, Edmond O'Ryan

(1680-1724), known as Eamonn a 'chnuic, or Ned of the Hills—Gaelic poet, gentleman, soldier and repparee. It was in America that the Ryans distinguished themselves. The first Ryan came to America around 1690 and there have been Ryans on American soil longer than almost any other Irish-American family.

Abram Joseph Ryan (1838-1886) was the "Poet of the Confederacy." Born on the American side of the Atlantic of parents who emigrated from Clonmel to Norfolk, Virginia, sometime between 1828 and 1838, he became a priest and in 1862 joined the Confederate service as a free-lance chaplain. His wartime and post-war poems—"In Memory of My Brother," "The Conquered Banner," "Sword of Robert E. Lee," "March of the Deathless Dead"—were known all through the South. After the war he made frequent lecture tours through the United States and into Mexico and Canada, often to raise funds for Southern orphans and widows. His poems were collected and published in 1879 as *Father Ryan's Poems* and went through several editions. He also wrote a book of devotions, *A Crown for Our Queen,* published in 1882. Described as pensive, sad, and unwordly, Ryan died at a Franciscan monastery in Louisville and was buried in Mobile.

A later Father Ryan was Patrick John Ryan (1831-1911), Archbishop of Philadelphia. Born in Thurles, Ireland, he emigrated to America in 1852 where he completed his theological training in St. Louis and was ordained in 1853. He became one of the greatest preachers in the Church and one of the leading orators in the country and was referred to as Chrysotom of the West.

Yet another Father Ryan, Stephen Vincent Ryan (1825-1896) became Bishop of Buffalo in 1868.

Edward George Ryan (1810-1880) was one of Wisconsin's most colorful lawyers and outstanding judges. Born in Co. Meath, he came to the United States in 1830 where he completed his law studies in New York. Afterwards he went west to practice, first to Chicago, then on to Wisconsin. After a colorful and energetic career as a lawyer he was appointed Chief Justice of the state by Governor Taylor in 1874. Because of his quick and sometimes violent temper some thought he might not be fit for the post. According to a contemporary, "his passion burned, when lighted, like a flaming volcano, stoking him with a fearful violence, and belching the hot lava of his wrath on everything and everybody which stood in opposition." But this trait did not mar his work as a judge and he wrote opinions for many landmark cases in the state of Wisconsin.

Thomas Fortune Ryan (1851-1928) was one of the wealthiest men Wall Street has ever known. It was his money and "charm" which established the Ryans as one of the First Irish Families in America. Legend has it that Ryan, born on a small farm in Lovington, Virginia, of "southern Irish stock", was "left orphaned and penniless at 12" and at 17 made his way to Baltimore where he "walked the streets for days" until he was hired as an errand boy by a dry-goods commission merchant named John S. Barry. Ryan fell in love with Barry's daughter, Ida, married her and in 1872 at the age of 21 he and his bride went to New York where he got a job as a clerk in a brokerage house. He soon met the transit entrepreneur William C. Whitney who was so impressed by the young Ryan that he eventually made him his partner. According to Whitney, Ryan was "the most adroit, suave, and noiseless man that American finance has ever known", and he prophesied in

1901 that Ryan would become one of the wealthiest men in the country. By 1905, with interests including railroad networks, public utilities, life insurance companies, and tobacco companies Ryan was worth $50,000,000. His operations later extended to coal, coke, oil, lead, typewriters, and diamond, gold and copper mines in the Belgium Congo which he had been requested by King Leopold to reorganize.

Ryan built a huge mansion on Fifth Avenue. Part of it was an area covering nearly a third of a block devoted almost entirely to statuary, and nearly as much space was given over to his private chapel. His imposing presence, said Bernard Baruch, was combined with "the softest, slowest, gentlest Southern voice you ever hear. When he wanted to be particularly impressive, he would whisper. But he was lightning in action and the most resourceful man I ever knew intimately in Wall Street. Nothing ever seemed to take him by surprise." When he died in 1928 Ryan's fortune was estimated at over $200,000,000.

Roche

GAELIC: de Róiste
NORMAN: Roche

Though not a native Irish surname, Roche, like Burke, Butler, Barry, Walsh and other names which came to Ireland at the time of the Anglo-Norman invasion, became one of the most common names in the country, especially in Munster and Wexford where the first Roches settled. The name is particularly associated with Co. Cork because of the powerful Roche family which settled near Fermoy in that county. Their territory was long known as Roche's Country. In southern Ireland the name has been perpetuated in sixteen places called Rochestown.

Sir Boyle Roche (1743-1807), conservative M.P. for various pocket boroughs in Ireland, stood out in the House of Commons for his wit and so-called "bulls" – quips and ultimatums delivered in the true Irish oratorical style. Speaking for the union of England and Ireland he once said, "Gentlemen may tither and tither and tither, and may think it a bad measure . . . but when the day of jedgment comes, then honourable gentlemen will be satisfied at this most excellent Union. Sir, there are no Levitical degrees between nations, and on this occasion I can see neither sin or shame in marrying our own sister." Roche served as an officer in the British army during the American civil war. His brother, popularly known as "Tiger Roche", was a noted quick-tempered quick-fisted character in Dublin.

James Roche, colonel in the Williamite army in the late 17th century, swam to fame at the siege of Londonderry in 1869. He swam from the fleet to the besieged city carrying dispatches and was attacked and wounded on his return. Henceforth known as "The Swimmer", he was rewarded for his action by William III, who granted him the toll collections of all the ferries of Ireland.

James Jeffrey Roche (1847-1908), journalist and poet, went to the United States as a child and eventually became the American consul to Switzerland. For most of his life he wrote for the Boston *Pilot*, taking over the editor's chair in 1890. He also wrote three

221

volumes of verse, an adventure novel called *The Story of the Filibusters*, and a biography of John Boyle O'Reilly whom he succeeded as editor of the *Pilot*. Roche was appointed consul to Switzerland in 1908 but died shortly after assuming his post.

O'Scanlan

GAELIC: Ó Scannláin

COMMON VARIATIONS: Scanlan, Scannell

There were several distinct septs of this name, the most important of which was found in the Cork-Kerry-Limerick region of west Munster where Scanlans are still numerous. Another sept was situated in north Connacht and their descendants are now found for the most part in Co. Clare. The name also appears further north in Co. Sligo, but as a rule it is used as a synonym for Scannell in that area. At one time there were Scanlans scattered about Ulster, but they have died out almost completely by now.

Lawrence Scanlan (1843-1915), Bishop of Salt Lake City, Utah, was a remarkable prairie priest who worked in close harmony with the Mormons in their home territory. Born in Co. Tipperary, he was trained at the missionary seminary of All Hallows in Dublin. In 1868 he was adopted by Archbishop Joseph Aleman of San Francisco and brought out west. For five years he served variously as curate of St. Patrick's Church and St. Mary's Cathedral in San Francisco and as pastor in mining camps in California and Nevada. "A stalwart, militant man of over six feet in height and 200 pounds, he was especially well-suited for arduous visitations on horseback through wild mountainous country." From California he was transferred to Utah, where, in 1891, he became bishop of the newly created sept of Salt Lake City. In his first years there the Mormon elders frequently loaned him the use of their tabernacles. But finally he had his own cathedral, St. Mary Magdalen, in whose crypt he was buried when he died in 1915.

In 19th-century America three Irish Scanlons made their name as writers of some note. Two were brothers, John and Michael, the latter being the better-known of the pair as author of *Jackets Green* and *The Fenian Men*. William J. Scanlan (1855-1898) was a writer of songs as well as actor and singer.

O'Shea

GAELIC: O'Seaghdha

COMMON VARIATIONS: Shea, Shee

The home territory of this sept was in Co. Kerry where its chiefs were Lords or Iveragh. Although their power declined from the 12th century onwards, their numbers remained strong and it is in this part of Ireland where most of the 12,000 O'Sheas in the country today are found. In the 13th century a branch of the O'Sheas migrated to Kilkenny, where they became the leading family of the so-called "Ten Tribes of Kilkenny", and some of them also settled in Tipperary.

William Shea

Sir Willian Shee (1804-1868), M.P. for Kilkenny, was the first Catholic judge in Ireland since Jacobite defeat of 1690.

Sir Martin Archer Shee (1769-1850), Dublin-born painter, was president of the Royal Academy in London from 1830 until his death in 1850. A fashionable portrait painter, "honours were showered upon hime to which Catholics in England were little accustomed."

Michael Vincent O'Shea (1866-1932), American educator, was professor of education at the University of Wisconsin from 1897 until his death in 1932. He lectured widely on education and related topics in the U.S. and Great Britain and was editor of the World Book and the World Book Encyclopedia. He was also the author of several books, including *Social Development and Education* (1909) and *Newer Ways with Children* (1929).

In the entertainment world O'Sheas have made lasting contributions. "Two ton" Tessie O'Shea in the movies of the fifties is a prominent example.

William Shea, N.Y. lawyer, sportsman and political leader, was the driving force behind the construction of the "Shea" stadium in New York which became the home of the New York Mets and the Jets.

O'Sullivan

GAELIC: Ó Súileabháin

COMMON VARIATIONS: Sullivan

This is the third most common surname in Ireland, after Murphy and Kelly, and it is far and away the leading name in Munster where the ancient homeland of the sept was located. Today nearly 80% of the O'Sullivans are concentrated in the counties of Cork and Kerry, while the remainder are found chiefly in Co. Limerick or in Dublin.

The first O'Sullivans were descendants of Eoghan (Owen) Mór, father of the famous Oilioll Olum, the third-century King of Munster. They settled originally in south Tipperary but they were forced westward by the Anglo-Norman invasion and it was in the region of southwest Munster that they rose to prominence. Along with the O'Callaghans, the MacCarthys and the O'Keeffes, they became one of the leading families of the Munster Eoghanacht, as the descendants of Eoghan were called before the introduction of surnames. As the family grew in size and importance several sub-septs were formed, the most important of which were O'Sullivan Mór and O'Sullivan Beare.

The O'Sullivans are rarely mentioned in the Irish Annals before the 15th century, but by the 16th century the family was beginning to produce some remarkable individuals.

One of the outstanding O'Sullivans at this time was Donall O'Sullivan Beare (1560-1618), chief of the sept in the district of Beare, Co. Cork. He is particularly famous for his stand against the English at the seige of Dunboy Castle in 1602. But in the end Dunboy fell to the English and Donall undertook a long hazardous march to Ulster where he arrived with only 35 of the 1,000 men he started out with. Failing to receive a government pardon when James I ascended to the throne, he sailed for Spain. He died in

Madrid in 1618, killed by an Anglo-Irish refugee.

Donall's nephew Philip O'Sullivan Beare (1590-1660) is remembered for the valuable account of the Elizabethan wars with the Irish which he compiled and recorded from tales told to him by his father and his uncle in *Historiae Catholicae Iberniae Compendium.*

Owen Roe O'Sullivan (1748-1784) was a lively Gaelic poet, in Irish called Eoghan Ruadh, or Red-haired O'Sullivan. Born in Slieve Luachra, he made a living as an itinerant potato-digger and, for a time, as a teacher, while he wrote "witty and wicked" verses. His passion for the "frail sex," it is said, proved the undoing of him. He wrote many songs, satires on the Irish volunteers, and poems denouncing the English.

Arthur Seymour Sullivan (1842-1900), the musical half of the Gilbert and Sullivan duo, was born in London in 1842, the son of an Irish musician who was bandmaster at the Royal Military College at Sandhurst. Sullivan began his musical career as organist at St. Michael's, Chester Sq., London, and he was also organist at Covent Garden Opera House. His first collaboration with librettist W. S. Gilbert was on a short operetta, *Thespis,* in 1871, but this met with little success. They teamed up again four years later and won instant popularity this time with *Trial by Jury* which ran for more than a year. Then followed a series of hits in quick succession. *The Sorcerer* in 1877, *HMS Pinafore* in 1878, *The Pirates of Penzance* in 1880, and *Patience* in 1881. *Iolanthe, Princess Ida, The Mikado, Ruddigore, The Yeomen of the Guard,* and *The Gondolier* all appeared between 1882 and 1889 in the newly-built Savoy Theatre. Their operettas became a kind of national institution. Sullivan also wrote more serious and ambitious compositions, as well as composing many hymn tunes, including "Onward Christian Soldiers". He died in London on November 22, 1900, and was buried in St. Paul's Cathedral.

John Sullivan (1740-1795), born at Somersworth, New Hampshire of Irish parents, was a general in the Revolutionary War and first governor of New Hampshire. It has been said of him that "he seems to have inherited an antipathy for England which led him to the patriot side in the American Revolution". He led several campaigns against the British. After the war he was active in the government of his home state and was elected governor in 1786, 1787, and 1789. From 1789 until his death in 1795 he was U.S. district judge of New Hampshire.

John Lawrence Sullivan (1858-1918), the "Boston Strong Boy", is said to have inherited his fighting instinct from his father, a fiery, compactly-built laborer from Tralee, Ireland, while his mother, a "kindly giantess weighing 180 pounds", gave him his looks, his physique, and his good nature. Sullivan began his boxing career at the age of 19 in 1877 in a Boston theater where his first punch knocked his opponent into the orchestra. In 1880 he defeated the American champion Paddy Ryan and overnight became a popular idol. For the next ten years he dominated the American prize fighting ring. In 1889 he won the last bare-knuckle contest fought in America, taking the decision over Jake Kilrain after 75 rounds under a glaring July sun. Three years later, on September 7, 1892, his boxing career came to an end in the 21st round of a bout with the quick, clever, hard-hitting James Corbett.

Louis Henri Sullivan (1856-1924), pioneer in modern architecture, was born in Boston in 1856 of an Irish father and a

Maureen O'Sullivan

French-German mother. His greatest work was done during his partnership with Dankmar Adler from 1881-1895, when the firm Adler & Sullivan designed many of America's first steel-frame office buildings and skyscrapers. From 1887 to 1892 Sullivan had as his assistant Frank Lloyd Wright, who became one of Sullivan's most ardent disciples and always referred to him as "the Master". Sullivan also wrote a great deal about architecture and his philosophy of architectural design, based on the principle that "form follows function", was highly influential. Maureen O'Sullivan, born of Irish parents, was one of the new wave of Hollywood actresses who rocketed to fame in the years immediately following the Second World War.

O'Tracy

GAELIC: Ó Treasaigh

COMMON VARIATIONS: Tracey, Tracy

The Tracys are descended from three septs which arose independently in different parts of Ireland. In Southwest Galway they were an offshoot of the O'Maddens and, though they were dispersed as a sept at an early date, scattered families of the name are still found there today. The Tracys of Co. Leix were Lords of Slievemargy until they also were dispersed by successive invasions. The third and smallest sept, related to the O'Donovans, was situated in west Cork.

Nathaniel Tracy (1751-1796), merchant, philanthropist, American patriot, son of an Irish immigrant, was one of the leading financiers of the American Revolution. He contributed nearly $170,000 in cash as well as food and clothing to the government and between 1775 and 1783 his fleet of privateers and merchant ships captured ammunition and supplies intended for the British army. At the height of his affluence Tracy is said to have owned so many houses along the East Coast that he could travel from Newburyport to Philadelphia and sleep under his own roof every night along the way. His homes included the brick mansion in Newburyport, now the public library, and the Vassall House in Cambridge, now known as the Craigie or Longfellow House. He was elected to the Massachusetts State Senate in 1793 and was a charter member of the American Academy of Arts and Sciences.

Benjamin Franklin Tracy (1830-1915), Secretary of the Navy under President Harrison, (1889-93), initiated a program for building up a powerful navy and during his four years in office five battleships and destroyers were either completed or authorized. Trained as a lawyer, he had been appointed district attorney for the eastern district of New York by President Johnson in 1866 and while in the cabinet he was responsible for several interpretations of international law.

Spencer Tracy (1900-1967), one of Hollywood's top box-office draws for over thirty years, is best known for his portrayals of "rugged men pitted against great odds" in such films as *Bad Day at Black Rock* (1955) and *The Old Man and the Sea* (1958). He is the only actor ever to win two consecutive Academy Awards, in 1937 and 38, for his roles as the Portuguese fisherman in *Captains Courageous* and as Father Flanagan in *Boys' Town*. Noted for his

Spencer Tracy

restrained performances and quiet authority, he was dubbed "the Prince of the Underplayers" by Hollywood. His long time acting partner and close personal friend Katherine Hepburn said of him: "Spence is like an old oak tree . . . he belongs to an era when men were men."

O'Toole

GAELIC: Ó Tuathail
COMMON VARIATIONS: Toal

This is one of the great septs of Leinster, noted especially for their tough and long-lasting resistance against the English. Originally of Co. Kildare, they were forced to move to Co. Wicklow at the time of the Anglo-Norman invasion and there they managed to hold their own against the English up to the end of the 17th century when all of Ireland finally came under their domination. Today most of the O'Tooles in Ireland are found in Dublin and the adjacent county of Wicklow, though a fair number also live in counties Galway and Mayo where a branch of the family settled during the 18th century.

Of the many O'Tooles who stood out in the struggle with the English, one of the earliest was Saint Lawrence O'Toole (1132-1182), Archbishop of Dublin, who actually bore arms against the Anglo-Norman invaders and urged his people to join in united resistance against them. Later, in the 18th century, several O'Tooles fought as officers in the Irish Brigades on the Continent in the wars against the English. Laurence O'Toole (b.1722) of Co. Wexford, joined the Irish Brigade in France and had eight sons, all of whom served in the French army. The oldest of these, Col. John O'Toole (d.1823), was created a Count and is the ancestor of the present·Count O'Toole of Limoges.

Adam Duff O'Toole (d.1327) waged his personal campaign against the church.and religion and as a result was burned alive in Dublin for "advocating blasphemous doctrines." Holinshed refers to him under the year 1327 as "A gentleman of the familie of the O'Toolies in Leinster, named Adam Duffe, possessed by some wicked spirit of error, [who] denied obstinately the incarnation of our Saviour, the trinitie of the persons of the unity of the Godhead, and the resurrection of the flesh; as for the holie Scripture he said it was fable; the Virgin Mary he affirmed to be a woman of dissolute life, and the apostolike see erroneous. For such assertions he was burnt in Hogging [College] green, beside Dublin."

Peter Seamus O'Toole (b. 1934), the firey stage and screen actor, was born in Leeds, England of Irish parents. He is noted especially for his portrayal of Lawrence in the 1960 film *Lawrence of Arabia* and of Hamlet in the 1963 production which inaugurated Britain's National Theatre Co. He worked for a while as a not too successful reporter for the *Yorkshire Evening News* then studied at the Royal Academy of Dramatic Art from 1955-1958. He then spent a year with the Bristol Old Vic Theatre Co. playing some 73 different roles – which he has called the best repertory theater company in England. In 1959 he first drew the attention and praise of London drama critics in the role of Charlie Bamforth, the

Peter O'Toole

tough but compassionate Cockney hero of Willis Hall's antiwar play *The Long and the Short and the Tall*. Since then he has appeared in a number of plays and films including *Lord Jim, Lion in Winter, Goodbye Mr. Chips*, and *Under Milkwood*.

Walsh

GAELIC: Breathnach

This name simply means Welshman (in Irish: Breathnach) and came into being at the time of the Anglo-Norman invasion when Welsh invaders settled in many different parts of Ireland. As a result the name is not uniquely associated with just one or two prominent ancestors as is the case with other Anglo-Norman names in Ireland such as Burke, Fitzgerald, Roche, etc. Nevertheless, a first Walsh has been singled out. He is said to have been Hayden Brenach, alias Walsh, son of "Philip the Welshman" who was among the 1172 invaders. Most of the Walshes of southeast Ireland—Cork, Waterford, Wexford and Kilkenny—are descendants of this family. Descendants of other families are very prevalent in Mayo and Galway. After Murphy, Kelly and Sullivan, Walsh is the fourth most common name in Ireland. Sometimes the Gaelic form of the name (Breathnach) is re-anglicized to Brannagh, Brannick, etc.

Philip Walsh (1666-1708), shipbuilder and privateer, was the founder of a notable branch of the Irish Walshes in France. His father was commander of the ship which brought James II to France after his defeat at the Battle of the Boyne. Philip had four sons whose descendants have been very numerous and active in France up to the present day.

Several Walshes rose to prominence as bishops. One of the earliest was Nicholas Walsh (d.1585), Bishop of Ossory. He was the first to introduce Irish type into Ireland and "to cause the Church service to be printed in them, which proved an instrument of conversion to many of the ignorant sort of Papists in those days". He also produced part of the New Testament in Irish translation.

John Walsh (1830-1898), Archbishop of Toronto, went to Canada from Ireland in 1852. By 1876 he had seen to the establishment of 28 churches, 17 presbyteries, a college and an orphanage. He was appointed Archbishop in 1889.

Blanche Walsh (1873-1915), the famous actress of Irish ancestry, was born in New York's Lower East Side in 1873. Her father was a well-to-do saloon keeper and Tammany Hall politician known as "Fatty" Walsh. She made her stage debut in 1889 at the age of 16, appearing as Olivia in *Twelfth Night* at the Fifth Avenue Theater in New York. Her greatest success was in the role of the unfortunate servant girl, Maslova, in a dramatization of Tolstoy's novel *Ressurrection*.

Thomas James Walsh (1859-1933), Senator from Montana, was the chief investigator of the evidence which exposed the Teapot Dome Scandal of the Harding administration. The case involved the leasing of naval oil reserves in Wyoming and California to private oil companies. In 1933 Walsh was selected by President Roosevelt to be Attorney-General, but he died, at the age of 73, before the inauguration.

TRACING YOUR IRISH ANCESTORS

Ancestor hunting can be either an earnest pursuit or a leisurely pastime. It can be a demanding and frustrating occupation or just an excuse to go somewhere you haven't been before. It may be inspired by a wish to fill out the family pedigree or discover a link with some famous or infamous character of the past. Or it may just be casually nudged along by a desire to find out where your great-great grandfather came from, what kind of work he did, how he lived, what his community was like then and what it is like today. But whatever scale the search takes on, whether massive or humble, the basic methods of the pursuit will be the same, only more or less intensive. The following pages give some general guidelines and suggestions on how to trace your Irish ancestors and relatives through various sources.

It must be stated at the outset that the search for Irish ancestors is fraught with many difficulties because of the scarcity of records both private and public. Today this seems an ironic quirk of history when one considers that the early Gaelic septs were so conscious of keeping track of their past and present that they retained hereditary chronoclers and poets to monitor and transmit their family history. But in a land where much of the tradition was oral, where the inhabitants were continually being ravaged by invaders, where there was no permanent form of central government, and where powerful families were often feuding with one another many of the early records of the Irish people were lost or destroyed. Further destruction of records came during the wars with the English in the 16th and 17th centuries. The destruction of the Record Tower in Dublin Castle in 1710 further depleted the already scant primary source materials. And to top it all, when in modern times the Irish had finally gathered their genealogical records together in one place – the Public Record Office in the Four Courts Building – that building was seized during the Irish "troubles" of 1922 and the records were deliberately destroyed. Lost were the census records, most of the parish registers which had been collected there, and many Irish wills. Fortunately there are ways of working around these losses so that all hopes of establishing a link with the past in Ireland don't have to be abandoned. But the chances of filling in a complete pedigree are very slim, unless you happen to be on the track of a specially well-known or upper-class family.

Another problem which makes Irish ancestor hunting difficult is the circumstances under which most Irish emigrants left their homeland to settle in other English-speaking countries – the United States, Canada, Australia and England.

OVERLEAF: *The GPO in Dublin which together with the Records Office was fired by the Sinn Fein during the 1916 uprising. This was perhaps the most depressing action in Irish history for the genealogist.*

231

232

The conditions of poverty, the distances involved, emigration on such a mass scale weren't conducive to keeping up family ties and traditions. Compulsory emigration due to poverty rose sharply after 1800. Weak home industry was overwhelmed by competition from English factories and thousands of Irishmen left to seek a fresh livelihood in the New World. Then came the great potato famine of the 1840's. Within a decade, the population of Ireland was cut from eight million to four million by starvation and emigration. Families were split up and contacts between relatives broke down. In the haste and desperation in which hundreds of thousands of people left Ireland in the decade from 1845 to 1855 scarcely a single record was kept at ports of embarkation such as Queenstown, Dublin, Galway, Derry, and Belfast. Therefore the most common obstacle for people of Irish stock in search of their Irish heritage is identifying their original emigrant ancestor. With the knowledge of who that ancestor was and what part of Ireland he came from at least you have a foothold in the Old Country. Without him you are lost and it will be impossible for you to carry on your search in Ireland. So to begin with we will focus on the task of tracing your ancestors and relatives in America back to the original emigrant ancestor. After the gap across the Atlantic has been bridged we can then turn to the sources of genealogical material available in Ireland.

Personal records such as old letters, diaries, gravestones, and the family Bible should not be overlooked in trying to gather specific details on your ancestors. But as pointed out above, because of the nature of the mass Irish emigration in the last century, these sources will not exist in most cases. As a result the average inquirer in America will have to turn to such public records as passenger lists compiled for customs and immigration entry forms, census returns, military records and the like to try to identify his original Irish-American ancestor. These records are housed in the National Archives in Washington D.C. and can be consulted in person. Alternatively, letters seeking information about an ancestor, providing they supply enough detail, can prove fruitful.

Passenger lists of incoming ships were compiled for customs and immigration purposes at Atlantic and Gulf Ports and in most cases date from 1820. Those compiled at Philadelphia go back to 1800. The early lists, up to about mid-century, normally give only the name, age, sex, occupation and country of origin of the passenger in question. Later lists however, in addition to this information, usually include the actual birthplace and last place of residence.

The staff of the National Archives require quite a bit of detail before they can check their records for an inquirer. The basic information they need in addition to the name of the passenger and the port of entry is the name of the ship and approximate date of its arrival, or the name of the port of embarkation and the exact date of arrival. With this information the Archives staff can consult such indexes as it has to the customs and immigration passenger lists. A fuller search of the lists themselves requires either more preliminary details from the inquirer or a visit by him to go through the lists personally. The *Morton Allan Directory of European Passenger Steamship Arrivals* lists by year, steamship company, and exact date the names of ships arriving at New York between 1890 and 1930 and other ports from 1904 to 1925. This may provide you with sufficient detail to direct an inquiry to Washington.

Another likely source of genealogical data is census returns. A census of the American population has been taken every decade since 1790. The 1790-1840 returns give the names of heads of households only and the number of persons in each house. The returns from 1850 onwards, however, record the name, age and place of birth of all free persons in the household, and additional information is included in each succeeding census. The Archives staff will search for a specific name in any of its census indexes. They will make a very limited search for a specific name in a given year's returns if it is accompanied by the state, county, city or town in which the person lived. However, if the search is too extensive for the staff to undertake, microfilm copies of the relevant returns can be purchased from the Archives.

Military service records are also kept in the National Archives. Enlistment registers and service records of volunteers are admittedly not the most likely places to find much in the way of personal detail, not even place of birth, but occasionally they do supply helpful information about a person's background.

The land records in the Archives sometimes provide valuable genealogical information in the form of supporting documents which show an immigrants country of birth and sometimes the date and port of arrival. These records go back to 1800 and include homestead applications and donation land entry files pertaining to public land states. Hence they do not apply to the original thirteen states. Obviously an inquiry demands some prior knowledge of the location of the land and date of claim.

If you do not plan to make use of the National

RIGHT: *A typical emmigrant passenger list of 1849.*

Peggy Kennedy 17
Ellen " 3
Kennedy 33
Daniel Kennedy 18
Michael " 17
Pat " 12
Ann " 15
Bridget " 9
Catherine " 9
Mary Ann " 6
Abegail Killalea 27
Biddy " 25
Catherine " 20
Ellen " 17
Catherine Killalea 45
Ann " 20
Catherine " 7
Margaret " 15
Bridget Egan 51
John " 18
Michael " 10
Pat " 14
Michael Glynn 55
Julia " 53
Michael " 21
Pat " 16
Timothy " 8
Bridget " 26
Margaret " 19
Mary " 24
Peggy " 23
Leonard
Peter Grady or Gready 31
Mary " 27
Thomas " ½
Catherine8 " 2
Thomas Grady or Gready 41
Catherine " 36
John " 14
Michael " 3 mths.
Pat " 6
Thomas " 2
Ann " 11
Bridget " 4
John Guinnessy 27
Hanora " 25
John " 2
Thomas " 3 mths.
Pat " 55
Mary " 51
James " 20
Malachy " 16
Pat " 13
Ann " 14
Catherine Guinnessy 3
Catherine Hanbury,
Hambury or Hamberry 36
Michael Hart 36
Pat " 2
Mary " 8
Catherine Hart 32
James " 23
John " 1
Michael " 17
Thomas " 16
Catherine " 14
Catherine Kelly 21
Ellen Rafferty 24
Catherine " 15
Mary " 20
Bridget White 36
John " 6
Pat " 16
Bridget " 8
Margaret " 10
Mary " 16
Bridget White 39
Ann " 14
Catherine " 6
Mary " 15
Sally " 19
Michael White 21
Margaret " 22
Thomas White 26
Honor
or Harriet White 28
Michael " 6
Bridget " 3
Margaret " 7
John Looby, Luby
or Lubey 15

Margaret or
Mary Lynskey 61
Mary " 20
Thomas McLoughlin 37
Ellen " 35
Bridget " 4
Catherine " 1
Anthony Manahan or
Monaghan 20
Pat Mannion 38
Peggy " 40
John " 17
Malachy " 10
Pat " 13
Thomas " 8
Mary " 5

List of Passengers from
Cork via Liverpool to
New York on board
COLUMBUS, 7 September,
1849.

John Casey 56
Michael Casey 13
Bab or Barbara Casey 19
Johanna " 18
Rosean " 16
David Connell 45
Margaret " 35
Dan " 15
Jerry " 10
John " 13
Pat " 3
Eileen " ½
Johanna " 8
Margaret " 9
Mary " 5
Patrick Connell 50
Ellen " 44
Dan " 16
John " 13
Philip " 19
Johanna " 4
Judy " 15
Margaret " 7
Mary " 22
John Cremin 28
Kitty " 25
Timothy " 3 mths.
Daniel Daly 50
Margaret Daly 50
John " 26
Bessy " 25
Judy " 20
Margaret " 19
Denis (Daniel) Danihy 40
Johanna " 40
Con " 15
Dan " 17
Denis " 7
Matt " 5
Michael " 13
Mary " 19
Mary " 13
Denis (Matt) Danihy 60
Johanna " 50
Daniel " 19
Denis " 7
John " 17
Matt " 21
Michael " 11
Tade " 3
Bridget " 15
Eileen " 10
Mary " 23
Tim Danihy 40
Mary " 42
Con " 3
Dan " 13
Michael " 8
Tade " 5
Nelly " 10
Daniel Fenigan 55
Johanna " 48
Johanna " 20
Judy " 7
Kitty " 10
Mary " 22
John Foley or Fowley 52
Eileen " 50

Dan Foley or Fowley 18
John " " 21
Pat " " 16
Eileen " " 28
Johanna" " 11
Julea " " 8
Mary " " 24
John Galvin 32
Margaret Galvin 30
Patrick " 2
Tade " 4
Biddy " 6
Tade " 30
Margaret Keeffe -or
O'Keeffe 50
Eugene " 17
Jeane " 13
Johanna " 21
Nano " 23
Daniel Kelleher 69
Dan " 29
Kitty " 26
Tade " 2
Kitty " 3
Mary " 21
John " 36
Connor or Daniel Leary 55
Ellen Leary 50
Jerry " 11
John " 18
Eileen " 16
Johanna " 20
Mary " 13
Peggy " 5
Matthew Leary 50
Mary " 45
Dan " 6
Darby " 18
John " 16
Matt " 1
Pat " 13
Johanna " 4
Judy " 20
Denis McAuliffe 28
Michael " 22
Robert " 17
Johanna " 24
Margaret McCarthy 22
John Sullivan 35
Ellen " 30
John " ½
Mary " 25

List of passengers from
Galway to New York on
ship BARK CARACTACUS
4 May, 1849

James Morgan, labourer 24
James Lawless, do. 50
Rose Lawless, spinster 41
John Keely, labourer 33
Judy Murphy, spinster 40
Biddy Murphy, do. 21
Peter Higgins, labourer 30
Martin King, do. 21
Honor Fury, spinster 25
Michael Morris, carpenter
Thomas Murphy, labourer 19
Margaret Cahill, child 14
Honor " do. 11
Patrick Tynan, mason 41
Peter Scully, labourer 19
John Tracey, do. 21
Thomas Donoghue, do. 18
Thomas Killen, do. 20
Dudley Ridge, do. 21
Sabina Dolan, spinster 17
John Burke, child 5
Mary Kelly, spinster 18
Catherine Kelly, do. 16
Judy Burke, spinster 30
John Cunniff, labourer 45
John Fagan, " 25
Biddy Connors, spinster 19
Conor Brodie, labourer 27
John Burke, do. 27
James Nolan, labourer 22
James Shaughnessy, 18

List of passengers from
Belfast to New York on
ship Emma Pearl, 4, May,
1849

Andrew McClelland, labourer 60
Sarah " do. 55
Margaret " spinster 27
Richard " labourer 23
Mary McKnight, spinster 60
William McKnight, 22
Elizabeth " 21
Mary " infant
Thomas Clegg, labourer 35
Sarah " 21
David " infant
Thomas Boyd 28
Margaret Boyd 26
John Rogan 24
Rose Rogan 25
Patrick Bannon 56
Mary " 40
Cecily " 19
James " 17
Mary " 9
Betty " 7
Anne " 3
Catherine " 10 months
Daniel Comb 21
John McComb 26
John Moreland 29
Eliza " 29
Thomas " infant
William Bryen 25
Catherine Bryen 25
Margaret " 3
Eliza " infant
Francy Wallace 26
John Fox 26
Bernard Lally 24
Bridget " 24
Henry Hollan, labourer 40
Eliza " 35
Sarah " 12
Rachel Hogg, spinster 17
John Donaghy 38
William Donaghy 3
John " infant
Daniel McDonald 21
Bernard McNally 20
Biddy Canavan 16
William Boyle 20
James Hamilton 20
Nancy McDonald 20
Isabella Anderson 34
Robert " 14
Rebecca " 7
William " 5
John Donley 24
Jane " 22
Thomas Maguire 25
Mary Maguire 17

LIST of passengers from NEWRY,
Ireland, to New York on Ship
JAMES 10 May, 1849

Michael Vallely, labourer 30
Margaret " wife 28
James McKeon, labourer 20
Sally McKenna, servant 20
Margaret O'Neill do. 23
Susan " do. 19
John Hanvey, labourer 18
Pat " do. 15
Bridget Hanvey, servant 11
Jane McNally, do. 19
Hugh McGeogh, labourer 21
Jane McCartin, servant 19
Bridget Quin, " 17
Mary Fanning, " 23
Mary McGrory, " 18
William Dongan, shoemaker 30
Jane " wife 25
Anne McDermott, servant 24
Roger White, labourer 20

ABOVE: *Emmigrants leaving from Cork for the New World.*

Archives it is helpful to have the *Guide to Genealogical Records in the National Archives* which is available from the Superintendent of Documents, U.S. Government Printing Office, Washington D.C. 20402.

A search in the National Archives is the most likely bet to turn up information on your original emigrant ancestor. But genealogical documents also exist at state and local levels which may also prove helpful, or even indispensable. Many of these are now kept in state archive offices or in offices of historical societies located in state capitals, while others, often poorly looked after, remain in the hands of town clerks or local libraries. On the whole the most useful state and local records are registrations of births, marriages and deaths kept by church and civil authorities. The office of the county recorder or state archivist can supply information in civil registrations. Church records are more elusive, and

besides it is not always easy to find out which church in an area your ancestor belonged to. A helpful reference work in this area is E. Kay Kirkham's *Survey of American Church Records* which deals in several volumes with both major and minor denominations in some detail.

Other state and local records which sometimes contain important genealogical material are local land records, cemetery records or burials, mortality schedules, state military records, tax assessment lists, pension records of veterans, voting

OVERLEAF: *The departure of Irish emmigrants during 1881.*

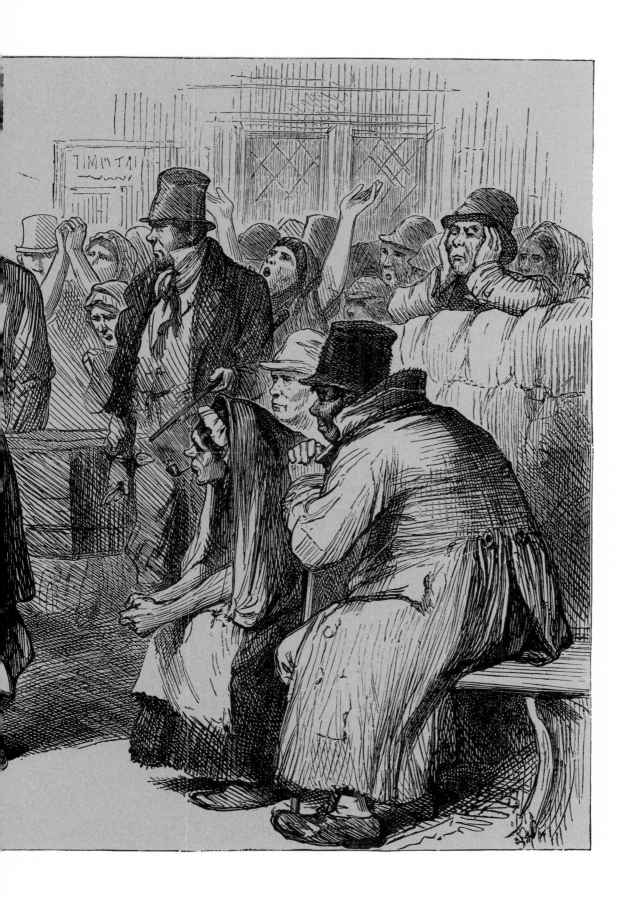

lists, directories, newspapers and church minutes.

Another valuable source of genealogical information and advice in America is the Genealogical Society in Salt Lake City run by the Mormon Church. The Society is an outgrowth of the very active Mormon interest in their forbears. Today it has become a sort of genealogical headquarters in the United States. The Society has pedigree sheets on thousands of families which may be consulted and copies of them are sent out on request. They also operate a pedigree referral service that can provide the name and address of anyone who has worked or is working on your family line. Moreover, the Society's library of books and microfilms of genealogical records is one of the best in the world. They have also published a number of reference books and guides to genealogical research. *Search and Research* by Noel C. Stevenson (Salt Lake City 1959), for instance, contains addresses of libraries and societies throughout the United States with genealogical collections.

Other helpful reference works for locating already existing genealogies are *American and English Genealogies in the Library of Congress*, a micro-card index compiled by C. K. and L. C. Jones (1954). An earlier version was published as a printed catalogue (2nd ed. 1919). The *American Genealogical-Biographical Index* edited by Fremont Rider in some 90 volumes is a guide to genealogical material on over 12 million Americans.

Once you have found your Irish ancestor who emigrated to America and know the name of the town or village he came from you are ready to direct your search to Irish sources. The first step is to determine the exact location of the place of origin in Ireland. This may not be so straightforward as you think if the name of the place you are looking for exists in five or six different counties, an event which is not at all unlikely. But assuming that you know the county in which the town is located or that there is only one town or village with that name, then you can look up the town in *The Alphabetical Index to the Townlands and Towns of Ireland*, a copy of which any good library should have. The *Index* gives the size of the town in acres and also the county, barony, parish and poor law union in which it is located. It also gives the number of the Ordnance Survey map on which a listed townland or town can be found. These maps are available from the Government Publications Sales Office, G.P.O. Arcade, Dublin at £1 per sheet. If the place you are looking for is so obscure or forgotten that it isn't listed in the *Index* then you might be able to locate it through the Place Names Commission, Phoenix Park, Dublin.

A useful aspect of the *Alphabetical Index* is the inclusion of parishes in which the towns are located. For then you can turn to Samuel Lewis' *A Topographical Dictionary of Ireland* which gives brief descriptions of Irish parishes. A typical entry runs as follows:

"Killavinoge or Clonmore—a parish, in the union of Roscrea, barony of Ikerrin, county of Tipperary, and province of Munster, 4 miles (N.E.) from Templemore, on the road from that place to Rathdowney; containing 3557 inhabitants. It comprises 8160 statue acres, including a considerable quantity of bog; and contains the residence of Dromard. It is a rectory and vicarage, in the diocese of Cashel, forming part of the union of Templemore; the tithe rentchare is £227/18/6, and there is a glebe of 36 acres. In the Roman Catholic divisions the parish forms part of the district of Templemore, and contains a chapel."

At this point you may be sufficiently satisfied just to know what part of Ireland your ancestors came from and a little bit of what it was like where they came from. If you want to find out more, the next step, short of a visit to Ireland itself, is to write a letter to a provincial newspaper covering the area in which your ancestor lived asking for family connections. A list of Irish provincial newspapers is published in *Handbook on Irish Genealogy*. If there is anyone in a town or village – you might even have distant relatives – who knows anything about your family, they are usually more than willing to be of help.

The destruction of many valuable genealogical documents in the Public Record Office Fire of 1922 means that the search for genealogical information in Ireland is inevitably going to be in many scattered sources, many of them containing only secondary materials. The result is bound to be far from complete. But it is possible with the records available to have a pretty fair go at tracking down a few of your ancestors. You might even be able to go quite a ways in filling out your family pedigree.

In the absence of census records which were destroyed in the fire of 1922 one of the most valuable sources for tracing families living in Ireland around the middle of the last century are the great property valuations which were made to determine the amount of tax to be paid by each "tenant" or property owner for the support

RIGHT: *Gravestones are an important source of genealogical information.*

OVERLEAF: *The gravestone of one Patrick Flanagan.*
The inscription gives precise genealogical information of the type essential if one is to establish links with the past.

OF your Charity
Pray for the Soul of
RICHARD CONNELL
who died 7ᵗʰ Nov 1857.
May he rest in peace
Amen

Murder Memorial. West Meath

IRISH EMIGRANTS LEAVING HOME.—THE PRIEST'S BLESSING.

THE DEPOPULATION OF IRELAND.

THE Census Returns, when published, will enable us to ascertain, in some degree, the extent of the combined ravages of famine and pestilence, in the first place, and of despair and emigration, in the second, in the depopulation of Ireland. But even these returns, authentic as they will be, cannot be complete; or the emigration that has gone on since the census was taken, and which still continues, will compel the statist to make large deductions from the amount which the census will yield, if he wish to ascertain the real number of the Irish people. The annals of the modern world offer no such record as that presented in the history of Ireland, since the memorable and deplorable years of the potato famine, and of the pestilence that followed in its track. The splendid emigrant ships that ply between Liverpool and New York, and which have sufficed in previous years to carry to the shores of America an Irish emigration, amounting on the average to 250,000 souls per annum, have, during the present spring, been found insufficient to transport to the States the increasing swarms of Irish who have resolved to try in the New World to gain the independence which has been denied them in the old.

"Emigration," says a letter dated a few days back, "is proceeding to an extent altogether unprecedented; but much less, in proportion, from Ulster than the other provinces. From most of the southern counties, the small farmers are hastening in vast numbers; and even in Leinster the mania for emigration prevails far and wide. The remittances from America are far greater in amount than in any previous year, and considerable sums are paid by the banks and private commercial establishments, from day to day, on orders from the United States. From some districts in Ulster, numbers of the smaller tenantry are taking their departure. From one of the principal estates in Monaghan near one thousand persons of the cottier class are about to be sent to Canada at the expense of the landlord, who, it is stated, has made arrangements for providing them with a comfortable passage, and some small allowance of money to each family after reaching the port of their destination."

The number of emigrant vessels proceeding to America direct from Irish ports is quite unprecedented, and is one of the most extraordinary circumstances of the time. Within eight days, the following eleven vessels, carrying 1568 passengers, sailed from the single port of Cork:—The *Dominique*, for Quebec, 150 passengers; the *Don*, for New York, 160; the *Lockwoods*, for New York, 280; the *Marchioness of Bute*, for Quebec, 120; the *Sara*, for Boston, 104; the *Solway*, New York, 196; the *Try Again*, for Quebec, 130; the *Favourite*, for Boston, 120; the *Clarinda*, for New York, 100; the *Swift*, for Boston, 120; the *Field Marshal Radetzsky*, for New York, 88 passengers. In addition to those vessels, the *Hotspur* went down the Cork river, on Tuesday, with 100 paupers on board, from the Kenmare Union-house.

of the poor within his Poor Law Union. The most important valuation was Sir Richard Griffith's *Primary Valuation of Tenements 1848-1864*. This Valuation, which forms the basis of the present day taxing system in Ireland, was printed by the government and runs to over two hundred volumes. Obviously anything approaching a complete set is only contained in the major libraries such as the National Library of Ireland and in the Public Record Office and Genealogical Office in Dublin. The *Valuation* gives the name of each occupier or tenant, the name of the townland or city in which he lived, a brief description of his holding or holdings and the size, and of course the valuation assessment of the property. The "tenements" for the purposes of the Valuation included any kind of property from moory pasture and bog land to houses and gardens and offices. Unfortunately the Valuation covers a relatively short span of time, but it can certainly be helpful for tracing families with any kind of holdings in Ireland between 1848 and 1864.

For persons born in Ireland after this period vital statistics may be obtained from the records of births, marriages and deaths. These have been kept since 1864. The records are housed in the Registrar-General's Office, Custom House, Dublin.

As the search for genealogical material extends back into the first half of the 19th century and prior to that period documents become more and more scarce. But it is worthwhile to try to locate any old family wills because of the accurate and detailed information they provide on family relationships. Although most of the Irish wills were destroyed in the Four Courts fire of 1922, several will abstracts were compiled from the originals before they were lost. The most important collections of these abstracts are in the Genealogical Office. Printed indexes are available for some of these collections. *A Guide to Copies of Irish Wills* by Wallace Clare, on hand in any well-stocked Irish Library, is an index to wills contained in learned journals, family histories and rare manuscripts.

Wills do often contain a wealth of information but not always of a kind that can be useful to a pedigree hunter. Here is an example of an extraordinary will made in Ireland in 1674:

"I, John Langley, born at Wincanton, in Somersetshire, and settled in Ireland in the year 1651, now in my right mind and wits, do make my will in my own hand-writing. I do leave all my house, goods, and farm of Black Kettle of 253 acres to my son, commonly called

But what is most remarkable is, that, while this **enormous emigration is** ng on, leading to a fear in some parts of the country that sufficient people l not be left to cultivate the land, the owners or mortgagees of Irish estates tinue to evict their tenantry with as much virulence as ever. The *Galway adicator* states :—" There were 195 ejectments entered—13 at the suit of the stees of A. H. Lynch, one of Mathew S. Coneys, and 181 were brought by the w Life Insurance Company ; and of 183 entries of civil bills, 87 were at the t of the insurance company. With the exception of three or four, the eject- nts were all undefended. They were disposed of at the rate of one each nute ; so that, taking an average of five souls to each family ejected, we will ve 300 per hour, and in the entire 905 human beings cast upon poor-house ief."

The same journal estimates the total evictions in Connemara during the present son at upwards of 4000. In Limerick and Kerry the same system is carried ; the evicted remaining in the union workhouse until remittances arrive from eir friends in America, when they shake from their feet the dust of their tive land, and rejoin their friends and relations across the Atlantic.

The following letter from our Correspondent in Cork— accompanying a series Sketches, which we have engraved for our present Number—gives the latest ormation upon this interesting subject :—

(From our Correspondent at Cork.)

"The constant appearance of the heading 'Emigration from Ireland,' and the

LEFT : *The Priest blesses emmigrants as they leave their homes during 1851.*

245

stubborn Jack, to him and his heirs for ever, provided he marries a Protestant, but not Alice Kendrick, who called my "Oliver's whelp". My new buckskin breeches and my silver tobacco stopper with J.L. on the top I give to Richard Richards, my comrade, who helped me off at the storming of Clonmell when I was shot through the leg. My said son John shall keep my body above ground six days and six nights after I am dead; and Grace Kendrick shall lay me out, who shall have for so doing Five Shillings. My body shall be put upon the oak table in the brown room, and fifty Irish men shall be invited to my wake, and every one shall have two quarts of the best acqua vitae, and each one skein, dish and knife before him: and when the liquor is out, nail up the coffin and commit me to the earth whence I came. This is my will, witness my hand this 3d of March 1674."

John Langley

Before turning to a fuller description of records and record repositories in Ireland it must be stressed that there is much to be said for actual "field work" in that part of the country where your ancestors came from. Many family gravestones in the local cemetery are virtual genealogical tablets in themselves, often marking the births and deaths in a family for four generations. Memorials to the dead abound in Ireland, ranging from simple iron crosses to elaborate monumental tombs. In fact, there is even an Association for the Preservation of the Memorials of the Dead in Ireland`which, over the years, has published in its journal thousands of inscriptions from gravestones throughout the country.

Because the practice of keeping parish registers didn't become generally established in Ireland until about 1800 gravestone inscriptions are often the only means of tracing earlier generations of Irish families.

In addition to the main centers of genealogical information in Ireland already mentioned – The Public Record Office, The Genealogical Office, The Office of the Registrar-General and the National Library and Archives – there are several other smaller record repositories and archives containing much genealogical material.

The Registry of Deeds in Dublin houses records of deeds, leases, business transactions, marriage licences and wills dating back to 1708.

The records of the State Paper Office unsuspectingly include records relating to convicts and criminals such as convict reference books, criminal index books, registers of convicts to be transported, registers of convicts sentenced to penal servitude, the 1798 Rebellion papers,

proceedings of the Dublin Society of United Irishmen, Fenian and Land League records, and papers of the evicted tenants commission.

If your ancestor was more studious than rebellious then you might find him listed in the register of Trinity College, Dublin, which is the oldest institution of higher learning in Ireland. Registers of the College have been published from the year of its foundation in 1593 up to about 1860. The *Alumni Dublinenses* contain particulars on some 35,000 students.

There is also a considerable amount of genealogical material which has been collected in Northern Ireland and is of particular interest to persons whose ancestors came from the six northeastern counties of the island. Most of this material is housed in the Public Record Office of Northern Ireland located in the Law Courts Building in Belfast. The office has an excellent card index to its collections of pedigrees, family notes, wills, land records, deeds, leases, marriage settlements etc. It also has microfilm copies of Church of Ireland and Presbyterian parish registers for the Six Counties – Armagh, Antrim, Down, Derry, Tyrone and Fermanagh.

Also located in the Law Courts Building is the Ulster-Scot Historical Foundation. This is the genealogical division of the Public Record Office set up to help persons of Ulster ancestry find out details about their ancestors in Northern Ireland. The foundation gives advice on genealogical matters free of charge and will undertake more extensive research on a fee-paying basis.

The Registrar-General of Northern Ireland has records of births, marriages and deaths in Ulster but these have only been kept since 1921. His office in Belfast also has the census returns for 1931 and 1951.

Besides state records the other important source of official genealogical material in Ireland is the churches. Since it was well into the 19th century before civil authorities began to keep records, parish books are often the only source of genealogical material before that time. The earliest church registers date from about 1750, though even the keeping of registers didn't come into common practice until about 1800. Most of the parish books from Catholic churches have been microfilmed by the National Library of Ireland. Unfortunately the Protestant registers were dealt a severe blow in the Public Record Office Fire of 1922 when more than half of them were destroyed. Most of the remaining books have been microfilmed by the Registrar-General's Office and the Public Record Office.

In the event that your Irish ancestors belonged to one of the smaller religious denominations chances are good that some record of them exists. For although Ireland probably suggests the Catholic Church and the Church of Ireland to most people, nevertheless the Presbyterians have always had a very strong following in the country ever since the first Presbyterian minister settled in County Antrim in 1613. As might be expected from this first settlement, their stronghold has always been in Ulster. The Presbyterian Historical Society in Belfast has an impressive list of baptismal and marriage registers going back to the 18th century. The Society's records also contain copies of the Religious Census of 1766 for many Ulster parishes, lists of Protestant householders for counties Antrim, Derry and Donegal in 1740, and a census of Presbyterians taken in 1775. The Religious Census of 1766 was instituted by the Irish House of Lords. It listed by parish the heads of households as either Catholic or Protestant for purposes of tithe assessment. The original census lists were lost in the fire of 1922.

The Presbyterian Historical Society also has records of other church documents such as Certificates of Transference which may contain useful genealogical information. These certificates were made out for members leaving a district to show that they were free of church censure. For a fee the Society will prepare a report on your family's ancestors.

Quakers or the Society of Friends have been established in Ireland since the middle of the 17th century. Because of the great value placed by the Society on the preservation of records of all kinds Irish Quakers are one of the most well-documented segments of the Irish population. Their records make it possible to identify an entire family group through several generations. Records relating to the provinces of Munster, Leinster and Connaught are housed in the Friends Meeting House in Dublin. These contain many 17th and 18th century wills, letters, journals, diaries and a large file of manuscript pedigrees. Records relating to the province of Ulster are preserved in the Friends Meeting House, Lisburn, Co. Antrim. A full account of Quaker records in Ireland is given in *Guide to Irish Quaker Records* by Olive C. Goodbody which can be purchased through the Government Publications Sales Office, G.P.O. Arcade, Dublin.

It goes without saying that persons descended from upper class families stand a far better chance of filling in their pedigrees than those coming from the poorer classes. Hundreds of manuscripts and printed books containing heraldic arms and pedigrees of numerous Gaelic, Norman and Anglo-Irish families are kept in the Genealogical Office in Dublin Castle. This is the office of the Chief Herald of Ireland who has charge of the records of the former Ulster Office and Office of Arms. There is also much useful information along these lines in such books as *Walford's County Families*, the *Dublin Register* and various editions of *Burke's Landed Gentry*, notable the 1898, 1904, 1912 and 1958 editions which deal specifically with Irish Landed Gentry.

A useful periodical for those interested in Irish ancestry is *The Irish Genealogist*, journal of the Irish Genealogical Research Society which has its office at The Irish Club, 82 Eaton Square, London S.W.1. The Society actively promoted and encourages the study of Irish genealogy and is always ready to welcome new members.

Another periodical specializing in interesting background material is the *Irish Ancestor*. This lavishly illustrated magazine is published twice yearly. Inquiries regarding subscription rates or other information should be addressed to Pirton House, Dundrum, Dublin 14.

A concise, informative and handy guide to Irish genealogical work is *Handbook on Irish Genealogy* (Heraldic Artists Ltd., 2nd ed. 1973). It has descriptions of the various records, record repositories and archives of genealogical material in Ireland including the addresses and times of opening of the different offices, societies and institutions. It also contains examples of such documents as passenger lists, public record office files, printed pedigrees, land valuation lists etc. as well as an atlas of the counties of Ireland. It also devotes a section to tracing your Irish ancestors in America, Canada, Australia and England.

Two small books which provide concise information and advice on ancestor hunting in general are *Your Family Tree* by David Iredal (Shire Publications, Tring, Herts, 1970) and *Trace Your Ancestors* (London 1966) by L. G. Pine.

BIBLIOGRAPHY

BAGWELL, Richard: *Ireland under the Tudors*, London, 1890
Ireland under the Stuarts, London, 1916

BARY, Alfred de: *De l'origine des Barry de Irlande*, Guebwiller 1900

BARRY, James Grene: *The Bourkes of Clanwilliam*

BOYLE, E. M.: *Genealogical memoranda relating to the family of Boyle*, Londonderry 1903

O'BRIEN, Donough: *History of the O'Briens from Brian Boroimhe – AD 1000 to 1945*, London 1949

O'BRIEN, Maire and Conor Cruise: *A concise history of Ireland*, London 1972

BURKE, J. B.: *A genealogical and heraldic list of the landed of Ireland*, London 1912

BUTLER, W.: A *Genealogical memoranda of the Butler family*, Sibsagor, Assam, 1845

O'BYRNE: *Historical reminiscences of the O'Byrnes, O'Tooles and O'Kavanaghs and other Irish chieftains*, London 1943

O'CALLAGHAN, J. C.: *History of the Irish Brigades in the service of France*, Dublin 1854

O'CARROLL, E.: *Pedigree of the O'Carroll family*, Dublin 1883

MACCARTHY, D.: *A historical pedigree of the MacCarthys*, Exeter 1880

MACCARTHY, Samuel, T.: *The MacCarthys of Munster*, Dundalk, 1922

CHUBB, Basil: *The government and politics of Ireland*, London 1970

CLARE, Rev W.: *A simple guide to Irish genealogy*, London 1937

O'CONNOR, Roderic: *Historical and genealogical memoirs of the O'Connors, Kings of Connaught*, Dublin 1861

CRONNELLY, R. F.: *Irish Family History*, Dublin 1864-65

MACCURTAIN, Margaret (editor): *A History of Ireland* (3 vols) Dublin 1969

CURTAYNE, Alice: *The Irish Story*, Dublin 1962

CURTIS, Edmund: *A history of Ireland*, London 1936
A history of medieval Ireland: 1068-1513, London 1938

O'CUIV, Brian (editor): *Seven centuries of Irish learning, 1000-1700*, Dublin 1961

DALY, E. E.: *History of the Dalys*, New York 1937

MACDERMOT, Frank: *Theobald Wolfe Tone*, London 1939

DEVELIN, J. C.: *The O'Develins of Tyrone: The story of an Irish sept*, 1938

GREAVES, C. D.: *The life and times of James Connolly*, London 1916

GREHAN, Ida: *Irish family names*, London 1973

GWYNN, Stephen: *The history of Ireland*, 1923

HARRISON, Henry: *Surnames of the United Kingdom*, London 1912

O'HART, John: *Irish pedigrees*, Dublin 1887

O'HEGARTY, T. F.: *A history of Ireland under the Union*, London 1952

HERALDIC ARTISTS: *A genealogical history of the Milesian families of Ireland*, Dublin 1968
Handbook of Irish genealogy, Dublin 1973

HULL, Eleanor: *A history of Ireland* (two vols), 1926-1931

KENNEDY, F. M. E.: *A family of Kennedy of Clogher and Londonderry*, Taunton 1938

LYNCH, E. C.: *Lynch record, containing biographical sketches of men of the name Lynch, 16th century to 20th century,* New York 1925

MACLYSAGHT, Edward: *Irish life in the seventeenth century,* Cork 1950
Irish families, Dublin 1957
More Irish families, Dublin 1960
The surnames of Ireland, Dublin 1969

MACNAMARA, N.: *The story of an Irish sept,* London 1896

PINE, L. G.: *Trace your ancestors,* London 1966

POWELL, T. G. E.: *The Celts,* London 1963

RAFTERY, Joseph: *Prehistoric Ireland,* London 1951

O'RAHILLY, T. F.: *Early Irish history and mythology,* Dublin 1946

SCHRIER, Arnold: *Ireland and the American emigration, 1850-1900,* Minneapolis, 1958

SULLIVAN, T. D.: *Bantry, Berehaven and the O'Sullivan sept,* Dublin 1908

TREDAL, David: *Your family tree,* Herts 1970

O'TOOLE, P. L.: *History of the clan O'Toole and other Leinster septs,* Dublin 1890

WALL, Maureen: *The penal laws, 1691-1760,* Dundalk, 1961

WOODHAM-SMITH, Cecil: *The great hunger,* London 1962